Lecture Notes
in Business Information Pr

T0238718

Series Editors

Wil van der Aalst
Eindhoven Technical University, The Netherlands

John Mylopoulos
University of Trento, Italy

Michael Rosemann
Queensland University of Technology, Brisbane, Qld, Australia

Michael J. Shaw
University of Illinois, Urbana-Champaign, IL, USA

Clemens Szyperski
Microsoft Research, Redmond, WA, USA

Brian Fitzgerald   Kieran Conboy
Ken Power   Ricardo Valerdi
Lorraine Morgan   Klaas-Jan Stol (Eds.)

Lean Enterprise Software and Systems

4th International Conference, LESS 2013
Galway, Ireland, December 1-4, 2013
Proceedings

 Springer

Volume Editors

Brian Fitzgerald
University of Limerick, Ireland
E-mail: bf@ul.ie

Kieran Conboy
National University of Ireland, Galway, Ireland
E-mail: kieran.conboy@nuigalway.ie

Ken Power
Cisco Systems, Galway, Ireland
E-mail: kepower@cisco.com

Ricardo Valerdi
The University of Arizona, Tucson, AZ, USA
E-mail: rvalerdi@sie.arizona.edu

Lorraine Morgan
National University Ireland, Galway, Ireland
E-mail: lorraine.morgan@nuigalway.ie

Klaas-Jan Stol
University of Limerick, Ireland
E-mail: klaas-jan.stol@lero.ie

ISSN 1865-1348   e-ISSN 1865-1356
ISBN 978-3-642-44929-1   e-ISBN 978-3-642-44930-7
DOI 10.1007/978-3-642-44930-7
Springer Heidelberg New York Dordrecht London

Library of Congress Control Number: 2013951883

Typesetting: Camera-ready by author, data conversion by Scientific Publishing Services, Chennai, India

Printed on acid-free paper

Springer is part of Springer Science+Business Media (www.springer.com)

Preface

The Lean Enterprise Software and Systems (LESS) conference was the first scientific conference dedicated to advancing the "lean enterprise software and systems" body of knowledge. It fostered interactions between practitioners and researchers by joining the lean product development and agile software development communities. Now the conference has been established as a conference series and has expanded to become a conference that stretches across disciplines to look at issues such as beyond budgeting. The LESS 2013 conference now welcomes this broad, multidisciplinary community to Galway, Ireland, during December 1–4 to continue this tradition and expand the conference agenda to incorporate emerging research areas such as portfolio management, open innovation, and general enterprise transformation.

The 2013 LESS conference had a number of submission formats to cater for diverse academic and industry research activity. Industry submissions attracted several leading consultants and practitioners from large companies. All of the full and short paper proposals (irrespective of whether they were academic or industry based) were reviewed by at least two Program Committee members. All talk proposals were reviewed by track chairs. Track chairs were fully empowered to design their tracks. The LESS conferences will continue to build upon this value of trust and empowerment of communities to develop novel, engaging avenues. The selected papers represent a diverse range of experiences, studies, and theoretical angles. The selected talks represent some of the most eminent speakers from their respective communities. LESS 2013 was organized in four tracks: (1) lean software development, (2) quality and performance, (3) case studies, and (4) emerging developments. The conference also hosted a range of other engaging avenues including tutorials, workshops, panels, open spaces, lightning talks, and social networking programs.

LESS offers several avenues for knowledge exchange to create a highly collaborative environment. Each year, we aim to bring novelty to a program that fosters collaboration, letting new ideas thrive during and after the conference. This year we achieved this through a number of distinctive initiatives.

To increase the dissemination of the work post-conference, we will publish selected, substantially revised research in a special issue of the *Journal of Enterprise Transformation* (JET). JET is designed to provide a forum for original articles on trends, new findings, and ongoing research (both theory and application) related to enterprise transformation and brings together interdisciplinary research across areas such as management, industrial and systems engineering, information systems, organizational behavior, political science, and economics.

We would like to extend our deep gratitude to all those who contributed to the organization of the LESS 2013 event. The authors, the sponsors, the chairs, the reviewers, and all the volunteers: without their help this event would have not been possible. Furthermore, we thank the lean, agile, and beyond budgeting communities, whose integral role made this conference an exciting platform for sharing and presenting innovative research.

We hope that you enjoy the proceedings of the LESS 2013 conference.

December 2013

Brian Fitzgerald
Kieran Conboy
Ken Power
Ricardo Valerdi
Lorraine Morgan
Klaas-Jan Stol

Conference Organization

Executive Organizing Committee

General Chair

Brian Fitzgerald   University of Limerick, Ireland

Program Chairs

Kieran Conboy   National University of Ireland Galway, Ireland
Ken Power   Cisco Systems, Inc., Ireland
Ricardo Valerdi   University of Arizona, USA

Organizing Chairs

Lorraine Morgan   Lero, National University of Ireland, Galway
Klaas-Jan Stol   Lero, University of Limerick, Ireland

Track Chairs

Pekka Abrahamsson   Free University of Bozen-Bolzano, Italy
Bjarte Bogsnes   Statoil, Norway
Peter Bunce   Beyond Budgeting Institute, UK
Robert Cloutier   Stevens Institute of Technology, USA
Vasco Duarte   Avira Operations GmBH, Germany
Martin Höst   Lund University, Sweden
Sten Minör   Sigrun, Sweden
Orla O'Dwyer   Lero, National University of Ireland, Galway
Johanna Rothman   Rothman Consulting Group, USA
J.K. Srinivasan   Massachusetts Institute of Technology, USA

Doctoral Symposium Chairs

Xiaofeng Wang   Free University of Bozen-Bolzano, Italy
Patrick Stacey   Lancaster University, UK
Juan Garbajosa   Polytechnic University of Madrid, Spain

Program Committee

Mary Bone   Stevens Institute of Technology, USA
Peter Bunce   BBRT, UK
Oisín Cawley   Lero, University of Limerick, Ireland
Cecil Eng Huang Chua   University of Auckland, New Zealand
Torgeir Dingsøyr   Norwegian University of Science and
         Technology, Norway

Meghann Drury	Fordham University, USA
Vasco Duarte	Avira Operations GmBH, Germany
Fabian Fagerholm	University of Helsinki, Finland
Markus Feyh	Blekinge Institute of Technology, Sweden
Daniel Graziotin	Free University of Bozen-Bolzano, Italy
Patrik Johnson	University of Helsinki, Finland
Raija Kuusela	VTT Technical Research Centre, Finland
Petri Kuttunen	University of Helsinki, Finland
Andrey Maglyas	Lappeenranta University of Technology, Finland
Alanah Mitchell	Appalachian State University, USA
Jürgen Münch	University of Helsinki, Finland
Jaana Nyfjord	Swedsoft, Sweden
Kai Petersen	Blekinge Institute of Technology, Sweden
Stacie Petter	University of Nebraska, USA
Björn Regnell	Lund University, Sweden
Alexander-Derek Rein	Technical University of Munich, Germany
Juha Rikkilä	Free University of Bozen, Bolzano, Italy
Christoph Rosenkranz	Goethe University, Germany
Barbara Russo	Free University of Bozen-Bolzano, Italy
Klaas-Jan Stol	Lero, University of Limerick, Ireland
Roger Sweetman	National University of Ireland Galway, Ireland
Richard Turner	Stevens Institute of Technology, USA
Xiaofeng Wang	Free University of Bozen-Bolzano, Italy

Conference Sponsors

Lean Development of Muscular Software
(Keynote)

David Lorge Parnas

President, Middle Road Software, Inc.
Professor Emeritus, University of Limerick, Ireland
Professor Emeritus, McMaster University, Canada

Lean management concepts evolved in a manufacturing environment. When manufacturing cars, cameras or computers, a lean organization devotes most of its energy to producing product for customers. Everything else can be viewed as waste and waste should be minimized.

When lean concepts are applied to software development, it is natural to view the code as the product and to treat anything else as waste. However, software development is design, not manufacturing. Further, the code is only one of the products that are needed. The code that is delivered is not even a permanent product. It is frequently updated. The real product is a continuously upgraded service.

This talk discusses some implications of the basic lean principles when applied to software development. It argues that preparing and using design documents that are precise and complete is an implementation of Lean principles that will reduce waste and result in a more successful product. It then illustrates such documents and outlines how they can be produced and used.

About David Lorge Parnas

Dr. David Lorge Parnas has been studying industrial software development since 1969. Many of his papers have been found to have lasting value. For example, a paper written 25 years ago, based on a study of avionics software, was recently awarded a SIGSOFT IMPACT award.

Dr. Parnas has won more than 20 awards for his contributions. In 2007, Parnas was proud to share the IEEE Computer Society's one-time sixtieth anniversary award with computer pioneer Professor Maurice Wilkes of Cambridge University.

He received his B.S., M.S. and Ph.D. in Electrical Engineering from Carnegie Mellon University. and honorary doctorates from the ETH in Zurich (Switzerland), the Catholic University of Louvain (Belgium), the University of Italian Switzerland (Lugano), and the Technische Universität Wien (Austria). He is licensed as a Professional Engineer in Ontario.

Dr Parnas is a Fellow of the Royal Society of Canada (RSC), the Association for Computing Machinery (ACM), the Canadian Academy of Engineering (CAE), the Gesellschaft fü r Informatik (GI) in Germany and the IEEE. He is a Member of the Royal Irish Academy.

He is the author of more than 275 papers and reports. Many have been repeatedly republished and are considered classics. A collection of his papers can be found in:

Hoffman, D.M., Weiss, D.M. (eds.), *"Software Fundamentals: Collected Papers by David L. Parnas"*, Addison-Wesley, 2001, 664 pgs., ISBN 0-201-70369-6.

Dr. Parnas is Professor Emeritus at McMaster University in Hamilton Canada, and at the University of Limerick Ireland and also an Honorary Professor at Ji Lin University in China. He is President of Middle Road Software in Ottawa, Ontario.

LESS 2013 Doctoral Symposium

Xiaofeng Wang[1], Patrick Stacey[2], and Juan Garbajosa[3]

[1]Free University of Bozen/Bolzano, Bolzano, Italy
xiaofeng.Wang@unibz.it
[2]Lancaster University, Lancaster, UK
patrick.stacey@lancaster.ac.uk
[3]Polytechnic University of Madrid, Madrid, Spain
jgs@eui.upm.es

The LESS 2013 Doctoral Symposium provided doctoral students with an opportunity to present their research work in a relaxed and supportive environment, receive feedback and suggestions from experienced senior researchers as well as fellow PhD students. It is also a good occasion to discuss concerns about their research plan, supervision, publication venues, future job market and other issues that may concern them. The doctoral symposium also provided a good opportunity to network with peers and future colleagues.

Doctoral students engaged in research on Lean and Agile development and related areas were encouraged to submit their research proposals to the symposium. Proposals included the description of the research problem and its significance, a brief review of related literature and how the proposed research fits in the exisiting research, description of proposed research methodology, results achieved so far and future plan.

Eligible candidates were those who already defined the research questions and theoretical basis, developed research methodologies and started their empirical work. Meanwhile, at the time of the symposium they were expected to have at least 6 to 12 months work remaining before expected completion.

Based on these requirements we accepted five research proposals which covered a variety of topics include agile and lean thinking for safety-critical software development, cloud strategy and organizational agility, collaborative prioritization of requirements for multi-requestor-systems, measuring strategic alignment in portfolios of complex dynamic IT projects, and development of a new model for managing complex software development with a high degree of uncertainty.

The doctoral symposium was run in an interactive manner with an agile structure. The goal was to provide a better learning experience for the students, and also help them to engage with other conference attendees to provide constructive feedback on their research. In addition to the three academic committee members, other researchers and practitioners were welcome to join the symposium and provide feedback to the research presented at the symposium.

Table of Contents

Lean Software Development

Quality and Performance

Case Studies

Emerging Developments

The Early Stage Software Startup Development Model: A Framework for Operationalizing Lean Principles in Software Startups

Jan Bosch[1], Helena Holmström Olsson[2], Jens Björk[1], and Jens Ljungblad[1]

[1] Department of Computer Science and Engineering
Chalmers University of Technology
Gothenburg, Sweden
jan.bosch@chalmers.se, {jensbj,jenslj}@student.chalmers.se
[2] Department of Computer Science
Malmö University, Sweden
helena.holmstrom.olsson@mah.se

Abstract. Software startups are more popular than ever and growing in numbers. They operate under conditions of extreme uncertainty and face many challenges. Often, agile development practices and lean principles are suggested as ways to increase the odds of succeeding as a startup, as they both advocate close customer collaboration and short feedback cycles focusing on delivering direct customer value. However, based on an interview study we see that despite guidance and support in terms of well-known and documented development methods, practitioners find it difficult to implement and apply these in practice. To explore this further, and to propose operational support for software startup companies, this study aims at investigating (1) what are the typical challenges when finding a product idea worth scaling, and (2) what solution would serve to address these challenges. To this end, we propose the 'Early Stage Software Startup Development Model' (ESSSDM). The model extends already existing lean principles, but offers novel support for practitioners for investigating multiple product ideas in parallel, for determining when to move forward with a product idea, and for deciding when to abandon a product idea. The model was evaluated in a software startup project, as well as with industry professionals within the software startup domain.

Keywords: Software startup companies, agile software development, lean principles, process support.

1   Introduction

New software companies are started every day, and emerging technologies such as smartphones, cloud infrastructure platforms and enhanced web development tools have made it even quicker and easier to get started. The many success stories surrounding software startups, such as for example Facebook, Twitter and Instagram, contribute to their popularity and allure. However, contrary to what media portrays,

B. Fitzgerald et al. (Eds.): LESS 2013, LNBIP 167, pp. 1–15, 2013.

far from all software startup companies succeed [1], [2]. If looking at new product ideas, over 98% fail [1]. This has led researchers, e.g. [3], [4], [5] and [6], to try and identify what factors contribute to software startups succeeding. In recent years, several authors [1], [7], [8], [9], [10] have embraced lean thinking and customer focused development as the way forward.

In order to understand the many challenges that software startups face, we need to understand what constitutes a software startup. According to Ries [8] a startup is a human institution designed to deliver a new product or service under conditions of extreme uncertainty. Most often, startups have limited resources in terms of people and funding, and are run on very tight schedules. In addition to that, they are commonly exploratory in nature, lacking clear requirements, customers and even business models. With this in mind, being efficient and systematic is of high importance; efficient in terms of minimizing the develop effort while maximizing value gained, and systematic in terms of continuously validating if what you develop generate customer value. During the early 2000's, lean development principles [3], [4], [11], [12] gained popularity in the startup community. Especially, lean principles emphasizing continuous learning based on customer validation of functionality, experimentation with customers to test hypotheses and assumptions, and short feedback cycles to avoid efforts on activities that do not generate customer value, have attracted significant attention from practitioners. However, while lean principles have permeated the software development industry for a while now, research on how to apply these principles in practice, and especially in the context of startups, is scarce. In related research, we see that while well-established companies might succeed in implementing selected parts of agile and lean principles, they experience difficulties with maintaining these throughout the development cycle [13], and this becomes even more difficult in the context of a software startup. To explore this further, and to propose a decision-making model as support for software startup companies operating in highly uncertain contexts, this study aims at investigating the following research questions:

- What are the typical challenges when finding a product idea worth scaling?
- What solution would serve to address these challenges?

Based on the Design Science Research (DSR) framework [14] we iteratively explored our research questions based on qualitative interviews with practitioners in nine startup companies, in order to capture the challenges they experienced in relation to balancing multiple product ideas, deciding on when to move forward with an idea, and how to know when to abandon and exit a product idea. In parallel with this, and as a natural following on the insights we acquired in the interviews, we started formulating hypotheses as the basis for development of a solution to their problems. As a result of our study, we propose the Early Stage Software Startup Development Model (ESSSDM). The model extends lean principles by offering more operational process support and hence, better decision-making support, for startup companies. The model is evaluated in a startup setting and based on the results from this evaluation we see that it is found useful for addressing the challenges experienced by the practitioners involved.

The contribution of this paper is twofold. First, we present a validated process model that manages a portfolio of ideas, whereas existing approaches typically focus on only one idea. Second, the model we propose provides a detailed approach for managing ideas, i.e. it offers operational guidance in terms of stage gates and exit criteria that have so far been difficult to find in existing methods and supporting frameworks.

The paper is structured as follows. First, we outline agile and lean principles as the two most influential approaches in software startups. Second, we describe our research approach based on design science research involving a qualitative interview study at nine software startup companies in Sweden. We present our interview findings, followed by a section in which we introduce the Early Stage Software Startup Development Model (ESSSDM) as a solution to the challenges revealed in the interviews. Finally, we present the evaluation process of the model and the conclusions of the study.

2 Background

2.1 Agile Software Development

During the last decade agile methods have dramatically changed the way software development is performed. Unlike traditional development methods characterized by sequential phases and heavy upfront planning, agile methods deal with unpredictability and change by relying on people and close customer collaboration rather than formalized processes [15]. Agile methods are characterized by short development cycles, collaborative decision-making, rapid feedback loops, and continuous integration of code changes into the product baseline. Thus, agile methods operate on the principle of "just enough method" and seek to avoid cumbersome and time-consuming processes that add little value to the customer [16].

Today, many different agile methods are in use [11]. During the last decade, XP and Scrum have become well established in small-scale, as well as large-scale software development. While XP is basically a collection of well-known software engineering practices taken to the extreme, Scrum is a simple, low-overhead process for managing software development [17]. The two methods are highly compatible in that XP provides engineering techniques and Scrum essentially works as a wrapper for such techniques. Although agile methods differ in details and techniques, overall agile principles such as 'flexibility', 'working code' and 'customer collaboration' lie at the heart of all of them. As highlighted in this paper, agile methods have become increasingly common in software startups due to their flexible, lightweight and adaptive nature with a strong focus on close customer collaboration throughout the development process.

2.2 Lean Principles

In emphasizing customer collaboration, short feedback loops and flexibility, agile software development methods can be seen as one way to operationalize some of the values that permeate lean principles. These principles originate from lean manufacturing, i.e. a production practice that considers the expenditure of resources for any goal other than the creation of value for the end customer to be wasteful, and thus a target for elimination. Working from the perspective of the customer who consumes a product or service, "value" is defined as any action or process that a customer would be willing to pay for. Essentially, the lean concept is centered on preserving value with less work. The philosophy focuses on getting the right things to the right place at the right time in the right quantity, to achieve perfect work flow, while minimizing waste and being flexible and adaptable to change [18]. In aiming to make work simple to understand, do and manage, the lean concept is characterized by four rules: (1) all work shall be highly specified in terms of content, sequence, timing, and outcome, (2) every customer-supplier connection must be direct, (3) the pathway for every product and service must be simple, and (4) any improvement must be made in a systematic and scientific way at the lowest possible level in the organization.

2.3   The Lean Startup

While agile development processes are primarily solution focused and answers 'how' to build products fast, they do not answer 'what' products to build. That is, they are mainly applied in situations where the problem is fairly well understood but the solution is not. In a startup context, however, neither the problem nor the solution is well understood. Therefore, a software developer working in a startup context, needs to be focused not only on the technical solution itself, but also on overall business strategies and needs, e.g. an associated business model, targeted marketing efforts, and the establishment of customer relationship models. Recently, the solution focused thinking that characterizes agile practices has gained increasing attention due to Eric Ries [8] and the 'Lean Startup' movement. In his book, Ries notices that because of this solution focused thinking a lot of software startups are failing, including his own. Instead of actively evaluating what customers value, most startups spend time and money developing products that people are not interested in. While projects are delivered on time and on budget, nobody wants the product. Ries [8] underscores the importance of understanding the problem before developing the solution. In his work, Ries is heavily influenced by the 'Customer Development Model' that was outlined by Blank in 2005 [7]. In this model, customers are considered from the very start. It is a structured process for testing business model assumptions (or hypotheses) about markets, customers, channels and pricing etc. The model consists of four steps, i.e. customer discovery, customer validation, customer creation and company building. While the first two steps are about capturing the vision and break it down into testable business model assumptions, the last two steps concern building demand for the product, start scaling the business and transition from a startup to a fully fledged company executing the validated business model.

A central concept within the Lean Startup is 'The Pivot', a term used when a startup company changes direction based on what they have learned about customers. Ries [8] claims that having "pivoted" is the most frequently occurring commonality among successful startups, i.e. successful startups seldom end up doing what they initially set out to do, and they change direction based on efficient collection of customer data. By reducing the time between pivots, it is possible to increase the odds of success before running out of money. Another central concept is the 'Build-Measure-Learn' (BML) loop, which is described as the concept of validated learning [8]. In this loop, ideas are turned into products, data is gathered by measuring how the product is actually used by its customers, and ideas for product improvement and innovation are based on what is learned by analyzing the data collected from customers. In this way, focus is always on delivering customer value, and the risk of being too solution-oriented is minimized.

2.4 Lean in Practice

While the Lean Startup presents many interesting concepts and ideas, it can be difficult to understand how to apply them in practice. Hence, several authors have tried to clarify this, and there are a number of handbooks and guidelines to support the practical implementation of lean principles in software startups. One of the more influential ones is 'Running Lean' in which Maurya [10] outlines a process based on the principles in Blank's work on customer centered development [7], and Ries work on lean startups [8]. As such, Running Lean provides a process for applying Lean Startup principles when developing a software business. The process is divided into three distinct steps:

- *Document the initial plan.* This is done by capturing and focusing on the entire business model, not only the product/solution. The "solution box" should be kept small to keep solution-oriented developers from spending too much time there. The goal is to capture the vision of the business.
- *Identify the most risky parts of the plan.* After having documented the initial plan, risks are assessed and prioritized. The risks that are considered highest should be dealt with first. Three types of risks are identified, i.e. product risks, customer risks, and market risks.
- *Systematically test the plan.* With an initial plan in place, and with risks prioritized, the rest of the process focuses on systematically testing and iterating the plan using methods such as Ries' BML loop [8].

3 Research Method

This paper is based on a study conducted between the authors and Chalmers School of Entrepreneurship (CSE), in Gothenburg, Sweden. Two of the authors, together with master students from CSE, co-founded a startup that was run in an incubator setting, i.e. an advanced entrepreneurial education combined with real business incubation. This paper presents the results of the research conducted during an eight-months period (fall 2012 – spring 2013). In our study, the following research questions were investigated:

- What are the challenges in terms of finding a product idea worth scaling in early stage software startups?
- What solution would serve to mitigate the identified challenges?

The study was performed using Design Science Research (DSR) [14]. DSR differs from other research approaches in that it focuses on learning through design, i.e. the design and development of artifacts. DSR is conducted iteratively, with lessons learned from earlier phases feeding back into later ones. DSR consists of five phases: (1) problem or problem area awareness resulting in an initial research proposal; (2) first approach to solving the problem; (3) realization in the form of an artifact; (4) evaluation of the artifact according to defined criteria; (5) stop iterating and reach conclusions. DSR allows for moving back and forth between phases in an iterative fashion, iterating until the evaluation criteria are met. For the purpose of this study, DSR was deemed a good fit due to the context of our research. With the authors taking part in the forming of a startup, and with the design of an artifact aimed at mitigating typical challenges, DSR seemed as an interesting and relevant approach. Furthermore, the close proximity to a real-world startup meant that the artifact could be rapidly iterated and evaluated, an opportunity which is advocated in DSR.

3.1   Research Process

In applying DSR, the following activities were undertaken in each of the five phases:

(1) Problem awareness: In the first phase, research questions were formulated and a literature review focusing on agile and lean development practices was conducted. The research questions were defined as: (1) What are the typical challenges in terms of finding a product idea worth scaling in early stage software startups, and (2) What solution would serve to mitigate the identified challenges? After having our research questions formulated and our literature review completed, semi-structured interviews with practitioners in nine startup companies in Sweden were conducted. The purpose of these interviews was to get an in-depth understanding of how software startups typically work in the early stages, what challenges they face, and if any best practices could be observed. When selecting interviewees, we used criteria such as (1) they should work at a software startup company with at least one product on the market, (2) they should be the CTO or similar of the company, and (3) they should have worked at the company from its start. All interview sessions were about 60 minutes long, and two sessions per interviewee were conducted with two of the authors present. The first session was exploratory in nature and took a broad perspective. The second session aimed at exploring further what was said in the first session, and to move beyond the initial understanding. An interview guide with template questions served as a guideline. However, the structure of the interviews was flexible so that discussions could go in new and interesting directions. All interviews were recorded and transcribed.

(2) Problem solution: As a result of phase one in which the literature review and the qualitative interviews contributed to a deep understanding of the problem area, an initial research proposal was formulated. Our initial problem solution was to design a

process model that would address the challenges as pointed out in literature and in our interviews and hence, provide effective operational support for managing software startups and increase their odds of success.

(3) Development of artifact: In the third phase, and in response to the challenges that were identified in literature and in our interviews, we developed the Early Stage Startup Software Development Model (ESSSDM). The model extends existing lean startup principles by incorporating knowledge gained in previous research as well as recent challenges experienced by practitioners participating in our interview study.

(4) Evaluation of artifact: In the forth phase, the ESSSDM model was evaluated as part of a startup project at the School of Entrepreneurship at Chalmers University of Technology in Gothenburg, Sweden. In this evaluation, criteria such as perceived usefulness, multiple product portfolio support, support for pursuing or abandon a product idea, and techniques for validation were used. During this evaluation, revisits to the problem solution phase were frequent, and we were aware that revisions of our initial problem solution were most likely to happen. In addition, the model was evaluated by a subset of the interviewees in four of the nine companies involved in the study.

(5) Conclusion: As a result of our evaluation, we revised and improved the Early Stage Software Startup Development Model (ESSSDM) to include clear guidance on multiple product ideas, on when to move product ideas forward, on when to abandon an idea, and finally, what techniques to use for validating product ideas.

4   Interview Findings

Nine founders, CTOs and early employees of software startups in the Gothenburg region in Sweden were interviewed. The interviews focused on the following topics:

- How did the initial product idea emerge?
- Does the initial product idea differ from the current product?
- How are product ideas validated?
- What business and software development practices are used?
- What are the challenges faced in early software startup?

Based on our interviews, we see that all of the companies use agile practices when developing their software, and seem to have a good understanding of how to apply them in practice. However, lean development principles were unfamiliar to most of the interviewees, and those who did know them found them difficult to implement in practice. Overall, very few worked with continuously validating product concepts with customers to try to identify problems before building a full solution. One explanation for this might be that some companies started from existing solutions, thereby reducing the need for extensive problem validation. Companies that did not copy existing solutions, but instead tried to innovate, put more effort into understanding the problem. Their current products are the result of having pivoted multiple times. However, our interviews do not show on any systematic approach or method for knowing when to pivot.

Based on the interviews, no obvious best practices for building a successful startup could be derived. All companies understand how to build software efficiently using agile methods, but few work with lean startup practices such as the Customer Development Model [7], or validated learning [8]. Our interviewees confirmes that it is very difficult to know how to work in a straightforward manner in early stage startups, and that operational process support, i.e. decision-making support, is limited. Based on our interviews, we identify a number of key areas where operational process support is needed:

- Existing processes and theories do not adequately support working on, or investigating, *multiple product ideas in parallel.*
- Existing processes and theories provide insufficient validation criteria for *moving product ideas forward.*
- Existing processes and theories lack clear guidance on when to *abandon a product idea.*
- Existing processes and theories provide insufficient suggestions of what *techniques to use during validation of product ideas.*

5   The Early Stage Software Startup Development Model

In response to the challenges mentioned by our interviewees, and as summarized in the key areas above, we developed the Early Stage Software Startup Development Model (ESSSDM). The model extends existing Lean Startup principles [8], [9], [10], [19], incorporates the results from our interviewees with entrepreneurs within the software startup domain, and builds on the author's previous experience from working with software startups. Figure 1 presents an overview of ESSSDM.

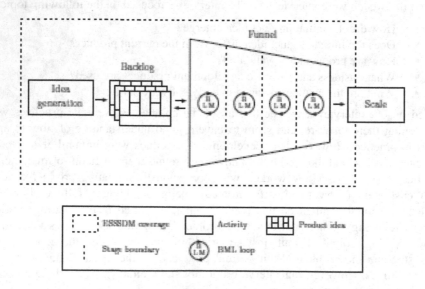

Fig. 1. The Early Stage Software Startup Development Model (ESSSDM)

The model supports multiple product ideas being investigated in parallel, it defines a step-by-step process with clear exit criteria, and it presents guidance concerning the techniques and practices to employ during the different stages. The purpose of the ESSSDM model is to find one product idea worth scaling. There are three parts to the process, i.e. (1) idea generation, (2) a prioritized ideas backlog, and (3) a funnel through which ideas are systematically validated using the Build-Measure-Learn (BML) loop [8].

5.1   Step 1: Idea Generation

We consider idea generation to be part of the startup process. Typically, it occurs prior to incorporation, but sometimes an existing company wants to expand their product portfolio, and thus needs to come up with new ideas. There are a number of techniques to generate and extract ideas:

- *Exploratory interviews:* One way to extract problems from potential customers is to go out and talk with them. It is recommended to investigate one customer segment at a time, so that the team stays focused and dig deep within each segment. The purpose is to understand how potential customers run their businesses, and what problems they experience.
- *Follow-me-homes:* One way to discover problems is to ask potential customers for permission to spend a day at their office in order to see their work habits in action. This is useful in order to extract tacit knowledge. However, the practice is very time consuming, and it can be hard to convince people to participate if there is no prior relationship. During follow-me-homes, monotonic work, complex workflows, communications paths, information load and time consuming tasks are useful items for observation.
- *SCAMPER:* This is a brainstorming technique used to systematically generate new ideas by modifying existing product concepts [20]. Each letter in the acronym represents a different way of thinking in terms of modification, (i.e. Substitute, Combine, Adapt, Magnify/modify, Put to other use, Eliminate and Rearrange/reverse).

5.2   Step 2: The Backlog

All ideas for potential products are put in a prioritized backlog. In similar with user stories within an agile product backlog, all product ideas in the backlog have to be written in a comparable format. If this is not done, the task of prioritization becomes increasingly complex. Being able to compare and prioritize among ideas is crucial when working on multiple ideas in parallel. After having documented ideas in a comparable format, they need to be prioritized. The following criteria are useful when prioritizing among product ideas:

- *How much do customers care about the problem?* The problem should be significant in order for a solution to generate interest and revenue.
- *How much does the team care about the problem?* A software startup will require an enormous investment in terms of effort and time. All involved need to be personally devoted to the task.

- *How large is the market potential?* If relevant, it is worth considering if the idea can be bootstrapped or if it will need investments.
- *How much domain knowledge exists within the team?* A skilled team with domain expertise reduces uncertainty regarding the problem and saves valuable time during the problem/solution validation stages.
- *Has the team experienced the problem themselves?* Known as "scratching your own itch" [21], and reduces uncertainty regarding the problem and saves valuable time during the problem/solution validation stage.
- *Are customers easy to reach?* To get going, the team needs good access to potential customers. The easier access they have to people experiencing the problem, the easier it is to get rapid feedback.

5.3   Step 3: The Funnel

Ideas from the backlog are fed into a 'funnel' where they undergo systematic validation using the Build-Measure-Learn (BML) loop. Multiple ideas can exist in the funnel at the same time, and be investigated and validated in parallel. The funnel is divided into four stages, and each stage has its own set of risks and exit criteria. Ideas move through the funnel stages as a result of a validated learning process in which data needed to mitigate risks and fulfill exit criteria are provided. The four stages are (1) Validate problem, (2) Validate solution, (3) Validate Minimum Viable Product (MVP) small-scale, and (4) Validate Minimum Viable Product (MVP) large-scale (see sections 5.3.1 – 5.3.4 below for details on each stage).

There are several reasons why investigating multiple ideas in parallel is worthwhile during the early stages of a startup: (1) The increased ability to stay objective. Growing attached to one particular idea too early can be damaging [14] [30]. In the early stages, an open mind and a willingness to change direction are advantageous traits. (2) Having a pipeline of ideas means there is always something to work on when other ideas are on hold, e.g. waiting for experiments to run, or interview session dates to be set. It is also useful when neither pivoting nor persevering is an attractive option, i.e. when a risk becomes blocking. (3) Most startups investigate and prioritize multiple ideas prior to picking one around which the company is formed.

When working on multiple ideas in parallel, it is important to enforce a limit on how many ideas can be worked on simultaneously. This number becomes smaller during the later stages of the funnel. During stages one and two, we found three ideas in a team of five to be efficient. During stage three and onwards, it often becomes a matter of available resources, and the size of the MVP. A simple approach for dealing with ideas in different stages of the funnel is to assign points to each idea, and then limit the amount of points each team member can work on in parallel.

The process that each individual idea goes through while in the funnel can be described as a feedback loop comprising risk prioritization, followed by validated learning using the BML technique [8] [10]. At the end of each BML iteration, a decision is taken whether to move the idea forward, pivot, persevere, or put it on hold in favor of another idea. If an idea is not ready to move to the next stage, a decision need to be taken about whether to pivot, persevere or put the idea on hold. Pivoting is a significant strategic change, while still remembering what has been learned about customers so far [8]. Persevering means staying on the course, doing minor adjustments, and hoping for better results in time. The third option, to put on hold, is introduced as part of the concept of multiple ideas in parallel. If a risk becomes so severe that neither pivoting nor persevering is an attractive option, the risk becomes blocking and the product is put on hold until such time when the risk can be dealt with. In the meantime, a new idea is picked from the backlog and moved into the funnel to begin the process of validation.

5.3.1 Funnel Stage 1: Validate Problem

The purpose of the first stage of the funnel is to investigate and validate the underlying problem(s) that customers want to have solved. It specifically tries to answer (1) What is the problem? (2) Who has the problem? (3) Is the problem big enough to make a business out of?

Exit criteria for this stage are when a majority of customers (potential customers) indicate that they (a) want the problem solved, (b) are willing to pay for a solution, and (c) are willing to participate in solution testing.

5.3.2 Funnel Stage 2: Validate Solution

The purpose of the second stage of the funnel is to define a solution that solves the problem(s) that customers want to have solved. This stage specifically tries to answer (1) What features are needed for the Minimum Viable Product (MVP)? (2) Who is the early adopter? (3) How much is the solution worth to customers?

Exit criteria for this stage are when a majority of customers (potential customers) indicate that they (a) believe that the solution solves the identified problem, (b) are willing to test the MVP, and (c) are willing to pay for the MVP (verbal commitment).

5.3.3 Funnel Stage 3: Validate MVP Small-Scale

The purpose of the third stage of the funnel is to build an Minimum Viable Product and test it on a small set of early adopters. It specifically tries to answer (1) Does the MVP solve the problem(s) that customers want to have solved? (2) How to access early adopters? (3) Are customers willing to pay for the MVP?

Exit criteria for this stage are when a majority of customers (potential customers) indicate that they (a) customers understand the Unique Value Proposition (UVP), and (b) customers accept the pricing model.

5.3.4 Funnel Stage 4: Validate MVP Large-Scale

The purpose of the fourth stage of the funnel is to further validate the MVP on a larger group of early adopters. This stage specifically tries to answer (1) Has the MVP reached product/market fit? (2) Is there a viable path to early adopters? (3) Is the business model suitable for the product?

Exit criteria for this stage are when the MVP (a) has passed relevant tests such as the Sean Ellis Test [22], (b) develops inbound channels that repeatedly delivers early adopters into the conversion funnel, and (c) produces a Customer Lifetime Value (CLV) > User Acquisition Cost (UAC).

Once an idea has moved through all four stages of the funnel it is considered validated and ready for commercial scaling. At this point, the objective of the Early Stage Software Startup Development Model (ESSSDM) has been fulfilled.

6   Evaluation

The Early Stage Software Startup Development Model (ESSSDM) was evaluated as part of a startup project at the School of Entrepreneurship at Chalmers University of Technology in Sweden, and through interviews with industry professionals. Two of the authors, together with three master students from Chalmers School of Entrepreneurship, co-founded a startup that was run in an incubator setting for eight months. The team was provided with initial funding and office space, and experienced industry professionals, business advisors and legal experts were also made available. The purpose of the startup was to find a promising product in the small business segment. In accordance with the Design Science Research framework, the following design goals were defined for evaluating the model (see below). For each design goal the evaluation sought for consensus from both the project team and from the industry professionals that were interviewed.

1) The process must support working on, or investigating, multiple product ideas in parallel.
2) The process must provide clear guidance on when to abandon a product idea.
3) The process must provide clear guidance on when to move product ideas forward through process stages.
4) The process must provide clear guidance on what techniques to use and when, while validating product ideas.

In the evaluation, consensus from the project team was derived by talking to each individual team member, while consensus from industry was derived by talking to a subset of all interviewees (representing four of the nine companies that were initially interviewed). They were asked to rate whether the design goal had been fulfilled, by choosing a number between 1 ("strongly disagree") and 5 ("strongly agree").

1) The model must support working on, or investigating, multiple product ideas in parallel
Consensus of project team: The project group consisted of five students: three business developers and two software engineers, working in an incubator setting. At the beginning of the project, no ideas existed. Doing exploratory interviews with potential prospects made the team both knowledgeable with how small businesses operate, and provided ideas on promising product concepts.

Overall, the team felt investigating multiple ideas in parallel was worth doing from a project perspective. Having a prioritized backlog was a good way to keep work focused, although there was some struggling before the team aligned in how to interpret the prioritization criteria. Having to document ideas in a comparable format made the prioritization process easier and forced the team to consider all aspects of the business model, not only the solution. A potential drawback of this was that vague ideas were not entered to the backlog due to difficulties in documenting them.

The workload was distributed so that the three business developers were responsible for one idea each, while the software engineers worked on all three ideas at once. When it came to building the MVP for the most promising idea, all other ideas were put on hold. Working in this way allowed for good momentum; there was always something in the pipeline for the team to work on. Sharing of assets between ideas happened frequently. HTML-mockups could often be put together using code, libraries and frameworks used on previous mockups. The team felt that reusing assets mitigated switching cost that comes when working on multiple ideas in parallel.

Consensus of industry professionals: Mean value: 4.4. Lowest value: 3.5. Consensus reached.

2) The model must provide clear guidance on when to abandon a product idea

Consensus of project team: The process gave clear guidance on when to abandon a product idea. The team constantly evaluated whether exit criteria had been reached or not. When experiments began to reach diminishing returns, and there was no clear path towards fulfilling the criteria, the team took a decision: pivot, persevere or abandon. If there was no obvious way to pivot, the team usually opted to abandon the idea in favor of another idea from the backlog. This way-of-working was well supported by the ESSSDM.

Consensus of industry professionals: Lack of data.

3) The model must provide clear guidance on when to move product ideas forward through process stages

Consensus of project team: The team appreciated having exit criteria as guidance on when to move forward with an idea. Having such clear goals enabled the team to keep a good momentum and allowed each team member to work independently. Also, it made it easier for the team to not miss anything critical during the validation process, something that is otherwise common in a chaotic startup setting. The stages were felt to be appropriate, even though the clearest separation was perhaps between stage two and three; one and two could probably be rolled into a single stage. Stage four was never reached. The exit criteria themselves were generally clear and unambiguous. The biggest problem was deciding on how many people to talk to, and how to gauge their reactions and feedback.

Consensus of industry professionals: Mean value: 4.6. Lowest value: 4. Consensus reached, but with some reservations, e.g. exit criteria are not to be blindly trusted but used as guide together with common sense.

4) The model must provide clear guidance on what techniques to use when validating product ideas

Consensus of project team: The definition of a relevant technique in this context is that (1) the outcome is valuable learning: it mitigates important risks and supports stage exit criteria, (2) the time it takes to execute is kept to a minimum. The team felt that in general, the techniques provided by the process were relevant; there was a clear connection between techniques, risks and exit criteria. Although, future versions of the process might benefit from more detailed instructions, taking additional consideration to context, i.e. what has been done, what is about to be done etc. *Consensus of industry professionals:* Lack of data.

Concluding, the Early Stage Software Startup Development Model (ESSSDM) addresses the challenges identified in the problem awareness and problem statement phase of software startups. As a result of an evaluation made with team members in a startup setting (students), as well as with industry professionals in the startup domain, we see that the model provides operational support for implementing lean principles in both planning and in execution stages of a software startup.

7   Conclusions

Software startups are more popular than ever and growing in numbers. They operate under conditions of extreme uncertainty, and face a number of challenges. In this paper, we identify these challenges by conducting a literature study on agile and lean development, and by conducting an in-depth interview study with industry professionals within the software startup domain. The result shows that few practitioners apply Lean Startup methods because these are found too vague and imprecise to implement in practice, i.e. they provide limited operational support. In response to this, we propose the 'Early Stage Software Startup Development Model' (ESSSDM) addressing the challenges identified in literature, as well as by professionals. The evaluation of the model shows that:

- ESSSDM supports working on, or investigating, multiple product ideas in parallel, as part of an idea portfolio.
- ESSSDM provides clear guidance on when to move product ideas for- ward through process stages.
- ESSSDM provides clear guidance provides clear guidance on when to abandon a product idea
- ESSSDM provides clear guidance on what techniques to use when validating product ideas.

To conclude, ESSSDM provides operational support for early stage software startups. Novel parts include (1) having a backlog with product ideas written in a comparable format, (2) a list of backlog prioritization criteria, (3) the concept of validating ideas through a funnel, and (4) the introduction of abandoning ideas as an alternative to pivot or preserve.

References

[1] Mullins, J., Komisar, R.: Getting to Plan B: Breaking Through to a Better Business Model. Harvard Business Review Press (2009)
[2] Crowne, M.: Why Software Product Startups Fail and What to Do About It. In: Proceedings of the IEEE International Engineering Management Conference, Cambridge, UK, August 18-20 (2002)

[3] Baron, J., Hannan, M.: Organizational Blueprints for Success in High-Tech Start-Ups: Lessons from the Stanford Project on Emerging Companies. California Management Review 44(3), 8–36 (2002)

[4] Brinckmann, J., Grichnik, D., Kapsa, D.: Should Entrepreneurs Plan Or Just Storm the Castle? A meta-analysis on contextual factors impacting the business planning performance relationship in small firms. Journal of Business Venturing 25(1), 24–40 (2010)

[5] Kakati, M.: Success Criteria in High-Tech New Ventures. Technovation 23(5), 447–457 (2003)

[6] Watson, K., Scott, S., Wilson, N.: Small Business Start-Ups: Success Factors and Support Implications. International Journal of Entrepreneurial Behaviour & Research 4(3), 217–238 (1998)

[7] Blank, S.: The Four Steps to the Epiphany: Successful Strategies for Products that Win, 3rd edn., Cafepress.com. (2005)

[8] Ries, E.: The Lean Startup: How Constant Innovation Creates Radically Successful Businesses. Penguin Group, London (2011)

[9] Furr, N., Ahlstrom, P.: Nail It Then Scale It: The Entrepreneur's Guide to Creating and Managing Breakthrough Innovation. NISI Institute (2011)

[10] Maurya, A.: Running Lean: Iterate from Plan A to a Plan That Works, 2nd edn. O'Reilly Media (2012)

[11] Adlin, T., Pruitt, J.: The Essential Persona Lifecycle - Your Guide to Building and Using Personas. Morgan Kaufmann Publishers, Burlington (2010)

[12] Campbell, D.: Software as a Service: spend and payment solution. Summit: Canada's Magazine on Public Sector Purchasing (May 25, 2010), http://www.summitconnects.com

[13] Holmström Olsson, H., Bosch, J.: Post-Deployment Data Collection in Software-Intensive Embedded Products. In: Herzwurm, G., Margaria, T. (eds.) ICSOB 2013. LNBIP, vol. 150, pp. 79–89. Springer, Heidelberg (2013)

[14] Vaishnavi, V., Kuechler, W.: Design Science Research in Information Systems (May 25, 2004), http://www.desrist.org/design-research-in-informationsystems

[15] Cockburn, A.: Agile Software Development. Addison-Wesley, Boston (2002)

[16] Larman, C.: Agile and Iterative Development: A Manager's Guide. Addison-Wesley (2004)

[17] Schwaber, K., Beedle, M.: Agile Software Development with Scrum. Prentice-Hall, Upper Saddle River (2002)

[18] Poppendieck, M., Poppendieck, T.: Lean Software Development: An Agile Toolkit. Addison-Wesley Professional (2003)

[19] Blank, S.: The Startup Owner's Manual: The Step-by-Step Guide for Building a Great Company. K&S Ranch, Inc. (2012)

[20] Serrat, O.: The SCAMPER Technique. Knowledge Solutions (February 2009)

[21] Fried, J., Hansson, D.H., Linderman, M.: Getting Real: The smarter, faster, easier way to build a successful web application. 37signals, Chicago (2009)

[22] Ellis, S.: The Startup Pyramid. Startup Marketing, http://www.startupmarketing.com/the-startup-pyramid/ (May 25, 2013)

Lean Software Development – What Exactly Are We Talking About?

Oisín Cawley[1], Xiaofeng Wang[2], and Ita Richardson[1]

[1] Lero-The Irish Software Engineering Research Centre
University of Limerick, Ireland
[2] Free University of Bozen/Bolzano, Dominikanerplatz 3, I-39100
Bozen/Bolzano, Italy
{Oisin.Cawley,Ita.Richardson}@lero.ie, Xiaofeng.Wang@unibz.it

Abstract. As the Software Engineering landscape continues to evolve and new paradigms are introduced, there can be a tendency for both industry and academia to enthusiastically embrace new approaches and march forward under whatever banner conventional wisdom has decided to adopt. One such banner is Lean Software Development, a paradigm that continues to see a growth in interest driven by the need for cost reductions within industry. The term lean attracts the attention of business, but precisely how it applies within software development is still being debated. In addition, its relationship to the better understood agile methodologies is also a topic for debate. Having been drawn into this research area ourselves, we present here a review of Lean Software Development and try to distil out for the reader some understanding of this somewhat undefined topic. We conclude with some thoughts on where this subject might go to from here.

Keywords: Software Engineering, Software Development, Lean, Agile.

1 Introduction

We are living in a period of history which is witnessing a drive for cost reductions and efficiencies across almost every business segment in almost every developed country. Traditionally businesses have been able to find efficiencies and cost reductions through automation and organisational restructuring of the more routine and repeatable processes. However, many businesses are now looking at higher skilled functions, such as Information Technology, including Software Development, and asking how such functions might play their part in finding more cost effective ways to operate.

The manufacturing world in particular benefited greatly from the Japanese concepts, and indeed philosophy, which grew out of the Toyota Production System of the 1940s. With evidence of huge productivity gains, the declarative term of "Lean Manufacturing" wasn't coined until 1990 [1]. Driven by a need to become and remain competitive in business, the term 'Lean' is now being applied to functions outside of the manufacturing context.

B. Fitzgerald et al. (Eds.): LESS 2013, LNBIP 167, pp. 16–31, 2013.

Only recently has the term Lean Software Development started to become a household name within the Software Engineering vernacular. It is quite common for businesses to have a lean ethos and run lean campaigns to improve processes and reduce costs [2]. However, we should be careful not to assume that by prefixing any activity with the word 'lean', it should automatically generate more cost effective processes and instil employees with a new sense of direction. This, naturally, does not follow and we need to be clear what we actually mean when we refer to something as being lean. We therefore suggest that although Lean Software Development has piqued the interest of many within industry and academia, it lacks a formalised description which fuels the confusion which has grown up around it [3], [4], [5]. This paper aims to begin a process of definition by presenting a view of the origins and subsequent contributions that have been made to LSD as we know it to date.

To this end the remainder of the paper is organized as follows: Section 2 is a retrospective on the origin and fundamentals of Lean. Section 3 is focused on the application of Lean within a software development context. Specific Lean principles pertinent to software development are reviewed. It is followed by a discussion of the relation of Lean Software Development and agile methods, which is a frequently debated topic where Lean practices are concerned. Then our interpretation of Lean Software Development in the light of the agile and lean debate is presented in Section 5. The paper ends with a conclusion section in which the contributions of the paper are highlighted and future research directions proposed.

2   Lean Fundamentals

2.1   The Origin of Lean

The origins and taxonomy of Lean are generally attributed to the now well studied Toyota Production System (TPS) developed in Japan around the 1940s [6]. The TPS is a form of what Womack et al. Coined 'Lean Manufacturing' [1]. It is an approach to manufacturing which revolutionised the automobile industry and allowed the Japanese become one of the dominant forces in the industry worldwide. Interestingly, some of the concepts were actually used prior to this by the Ford Automobile company [7]. The core principles underlying lean manufacturing, are not confined to manufacturing processes either but have been shown to be applicable in many other disciplines too [8].

One of the cornerstones of Toyota's success was their ability to produce high quality cars at the end of the production line with little or no need for rework. This was achieved by the early detection of defects and the immediate focus on eliminating the cause of the defect so that it would never happen again. This basic principle is of course transferable to many other domains/situations. In an interview, sportsman Brendan Cummins, one of the leading hurling[1] goalkeepers in Ireland, when asked what advice he would give to young players said:

---

[1] http://www.gaa.ie/about-the-gaa/our-games/hurling/

"Go home and practice until you eliminate the mistakes that led to the defeat. It's the only way to get better."

In a Software engineering context the parallel can be drawn with finding and eliminating defects in your code as quickly as possible and learning not to make those same mistakes again. [9] suggests that each bug found by a developer should lead to the following two questions:

— How could I have automatically detected this bug?
— How could I have prevented this bug?

However, lean is not only concerned with defect identification and eradication but equally concentrates on the surrounding processes, and getting work to 'flow' smoothly through the entire process. While this is easier to visualise in a manufacturing setting where product can be seen to flow down the assembly line [10], this can also be applied in a product development environment [11].

2.2   Lean Concepts

Lean is more a way of thinking about, or a mental approach taken, to a particular process or set of processes. Lean is about achieving more with less [12], or producing in one-third the time, at one-third the cost, and with one-third the defect rate [13]. The primary focus and guiding principle is the identification and elimination of process waste in order to focus on creating customer value [14], [15], [10], [16]. An important aspect is that value is determined by the customer not the producer, and so any cost incurred in the process needs to be in support of activities which add value to the customer (Fig. 1).

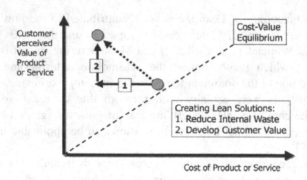

Fig. 1. Relationship between Value, Cost and Waste (Hines et al., 2004)

There are five main modern lean concepts [8]:

1. Value: It is defined by the customer and it is paramount to have a clear understanding of what that is;
2. Value Stream: A map that identifies every step in the process and categorises each step in terms of the value it adds;

3. Flow: It is important that the production process flows continuously;
4. Pull: Customer orders pull product, ensuring nothing is built before it is needed;
5. Perfection: You strive for perfection in your process by continuously identifying and removing waste.

However, a 6th concept is a recurring and important one:

6. Respect for People [17],[18] [19].

This is highlighted by [17] where they describe the key facets of the Toyota Production System. This last principle is very significant and a key component of Toyota's second basic concept: "To make full use of workers' capabilities". In addition, [20] see it as a key component in building what they call a 'lean enterprise', and it has also been incorporated into the International Council on Systems Engineering's model for Lean Enablers for Systems Engineering [18]:

"The "People" principle promotes the best human relations at work based on respect for people: trust, honesty, respect, empowerment, teamwork, stability, motivation, drive for excellence, and healthy hiring and promotion policies" [19].

Petersen and Wohlin summarise lean manufacturing under two important headings, the removal of waste and continuous flow [21]. It is instructive to take a brief look at both of these.

The Removal Of Waste
Lean thinking classifies work into 3 categories [8]:

— Value-adding activities
— Required non-value adding activities
— Non-value adding activities

By mapping out a work process using a value stream map, process steps which do not contribute to creating value can be identified, thus allowing for a concentrated effort on reducing or eliminating these steps. The concept of waste can therefore be quite broad but Taiichi Ohno – the founder of the Toyota production process - defined 7 types of waste [14], and an eighth has been added by [6]. These are:

— The waste of over-production
— The waste of time on hand (waiting)
— The waste of transportation
— The waste of over-processing or incorrect processing
— The waste of stock on hand (excess inventory)
— The waste of movement
— The waste of making defective products
— The waste of unused employee creativity

It is the identification of these different types of waste which make a lean approach so powerful, since it does not suggest that any particular part of the process should be targeted, but rather waste in any form and in any place should be sought out.

Continuous Flow

Within a manufacturing context the control of excess inventory is a constant focus for a number of reasons, such as storage and transportation costs, longer lead times, and the masking of quality problems [22], [6]. The reduction of inventory is given special attention in a lean context [1, 8]. The Toyota company's approach was in fact not to manage excess inventory but to seek to eliminate it [6]. Especially within the wider supply chain this becomes an increasingly difficult problem to manage [20].

Lean aims to achieve a smooth and continuous flow of inventory through the production process [23]. By linking together disjointed operations, thereby increasing teamwork and feedback, quality problems are identified earlier [6]. A consequence of this linking up is that it becomes possible to better schedule the generation and delivery of inventory to downstream processes in a just-in-time fashion [14], [6].

One technique used to achieve this smooth flow is termed Kanban. A Kanban system is:

> "A production control system for just-in-time production and making full use of workers' capabilities." [17].

The core objective of the Kanban system is to minimise the amount of Work-In-Progress (WIP), or inventory. This is achieved by inventory being "pulled" through the system as it is needed, as opposed to "pushing" it through. Only when a downstream process is ready and needs to do some more work does it pull inventory from an upstream process. The signalling between upstream and downstream processes is typically done via some sort of coloured card (the Kanban) which physically travels between processes [24]. The aim is to keep the process flowing at an even but continuous rate. This is achieved by controlling the number of Kanban cards which are in circulation within the process. Reducing the number of cards reduces the amount of inventory in circulation, and is therefore used to control WIP. The other important aspect of Kanban is that it includes a visual display of the entire process so everyone has visibility and can see if and where issues are starting to appear.

3   'Leaning' Software Development

An important question to ask is how do lean manufacturing practices - typically repeating identical tasks and producing the same product as output - relate to product development activities which always produce something different? Don Reinertsen, an expert in product development management, has applied lean manufacturing practices to product development [25] and details some significant differences he sees between the two [11]. Consequently he suggests that blindly trying to drive up efficiencies and drive down variability without considering the economic consequences is fundamentally wrong.

Looking specifically at lean from a Software Development perspective, Raman attempted to *"... see whether the basic Lean principles ... can be applied to software development"* [26]. He concluded, that with practices such as rapid prototyping, quality function deployment, continuous integration, object oriented and component-based development:

"The question whether Lean Software Development is Feasible can easily be answered with "yes" " [26].

Similarly, [23] suggest that:

"Results of lean product development are more interesting for software engineering than the pure manufacturing part as the success of software development highly depends on an integrative view".

They conclude that lean principles may be beneficial in a software development context but that:

"Further evaluation of lean principles is needed to understand how they affect the performance of the software process" [21].

3.1   Waste in Software Development

A common core focus of all lean software development proponents is delivering value by identifying and eliminating waste, but the interpretation of waste and how to address it can vary. For example, while [27] and [28] identify specific wastes which should be addressed immediately, [11] suggests that only when the proposed waste has been converted into economic terms does it become useful in deciding whether it is waste and what to do about it. Additionally [29] talks about addressing what he calls the waste of negative iterations. Referring to iterative design, he says a negative iteration is one which could be eliminated without any loss in value. Table 1 shows an interpretation of waste based on [6, 27, 28].

Table 1. Waste in Lean Software Development

Lean Manufacturing	Lean Software Development
Over-Production	Extra Features/Code
Time On Hand (waiting)	Delays
Transportation	Task Switching
Over-Processing or Incorrect Processing	Extra Processes
Stock On Hand (excess inventory)	Partially Done Work
Movement	Movement
Making Defective Products	Defects
Unused Employee Creativity	Unused Employee Creativity

3.2   Lean Software Development Principles

The core intent of lean can be summarised as follows:

"All we are doing is looking at the timeline from the moment a customer gives us an order to the point when we collect the cash. And we are reducing that timeline by removing the nonvalue-added wastes" [14].

By applying this approach through the application of lean principles [6] within the context of software development, we can see how many of the modern software development techniques support them. The contemporary understanding of lean software development is largely driven by practitioners writings [27], [30], [28] and [31], however the broad nature of lean means that lean software development has much in common with related domains such as lean product development [11] and lean systems engineering [19]. In [32] Robert Charette developed 12 principles of Lean Development:

1. Satisfying the customer is the highest priority
2. Always provide the best value for money
3. Success depends on active customer participation
4. Every LD project is a team effort
5. Everything is changeable
6. Domain, not point, solutions
7. Complete, don't construct
8. An 80 percent solution today, instead of 100 percent solution tomorrow
9. Minimalism is essential
10. Needs determine technology
11. Product growth is feature growth, not size growth
12. Never push LD beyond its limits

Table 2 lists some of the sets of lean principles proposed in the literature more specific to a software development context and well know within the agile community. While these sets differ slightly in the lean principles they advocate, they all share some core lean concepts such as waste elimination. Poppendieck and Poppendieck tell us that waste is anything which does not add value, Anderson tells us it is important to be able to visualise such process waste within the workflow, and Reinertsen agrees but suggests that we must weigh up the economic cost of eliminating a particular type of waste. Lean principles and practices continue to evolve but a synthesis of what we can call lean practices has been started by [5].

Table 2. Lean Principles Relevant to Software Development

Lean Software Development Principles (Poppendieck and Poppendieck, 2003)	The Principles of Product Development Flow (Reinertsen, 2009)	The Kanban Principles (Anderson, 2010)
• Eliminate waste • Build quality in • Create knowledge • Defer commitment • Deliver fast • Respect people • Optimise the whole	• Use an economic view • Manage queues • Exploit variability • Reduce batch size • Apply WIP (Work in Progress) constraints • Control flow under uncertainty • Use fast feedback • Decentralise control	• Visualize the workflow • Limit WIP • Manage Flow • Make Process Policies Explicit • Improve Collaboratively (using models & the scientific method)

4   Lean or Agile

We look now specifically at the confusion which has emerged about the differences/similarities between Lean Software Development and Agile Software Development. According to Robert Charette - originator of "Lean Development" [13] – LSD is a key component in building a change tolerant business [32]. The key difference he sees between lean and agile is that agile is a bottom up approach while lean is a top down approach.

The toolkit of lean SD practices developed by [27] contains many practices already well established within the agile community. This has both helped the agile community to embrace lean, but also added to the confusion as to what exactly the difference between lean and agile is. Consequently the boundary between lean SD and agile SD is something that is currently being debated [33], [34], [5]. [35] performed a comparison between lean concepts and generic agile practices, with specific focus on the Scrum methodology, drawing parallels between them, but concluding that lean thinking can help a company analyse its software development process irrespective of the development methodology in use. Petersen [4] performed a more detailed comparison between two development paradigms (lean and agile) and concludes that: "(1) Agile and lean agree on the goals they want to achieve; (2) Lean is agile in the sense that the principles of lean reflect the principles of agile, while lean is unique in stressing the end-to-end perspective more; (3) Lean has adopted many practices known in the agile context, while stressing the importance of using practices that are related to the end-to end flow". He also concludes that "agile uses practices that are not found in lean" but does not state the reciprocal i.e. that lean utilises practices not found in agile, as reported by [5].

Waste elimination, within a lean manufacturing perspective, means removing steps in your process that do not directly contribute to adding customer value. From a software development perspective, one interpretation of waste is the identification and elimination of defects in the software, and so effort is expended to ensure defects are found and removed as quickly as possible. Another interpretation is writing too much code such as developing features which were not requested (over production), something which [28] suggests that Behaviour Driven Development (BDD)[2] can help address. Similarly, if defects are allowed to propagate through the system and are identified late in the project, then a considerably larger effort is required to remove them than if they were caught early. This wasted effort may be eliminated by following a test-first approach such as the agile practice of test driven development (TDD) [36]. TDD proposes that even before any code is written, a test case is written for the code. Only when the test passes does the developer move on to the next coding task. This significantly reduces the possibility of defects going undetected.

---

[2] BDD aims to help focus development on the delivery of prioritised, verifiable business value by providing a common vocabulary that spans the divide between Business and Technology.

4.1   Agile and Lean Practices

Many agile practices have been mapped to form a toolset of lean SD practices by [37], [30] and a guide on implementation was written by [28]. Table 3 shows a cross section of these practices.

Table 3. Agile Practices within Lean Software Development

- Run software tests as soon as code is written
- Write code instead of more documentation or detailed planning
- Propose user interfaces and get feedback instead of more detailed requirements
- Test the top 3 tools instead of trying to pick the right one first time
- Develop in short iterations
- Features that are too big for 1 iteration need to be broken down
- The highest priority feature should be developed first
- High risk items should be addressed earlier rather than later
- Make progress visible
- Automate software builds and build tests
- Spanning (a portion of the application is built to completion which spans all modules and dependencies)
- Set-based development (multiple initial options developed in parallel)
- Object oriented design
- Component-based development
- Avoid extra features
- Fast feedback loops
- Empower the team through self-organisation
- Pull systems make the work self-directing
- Make work packages small to assist with work flow

Some lean practices however do not have any specific reference within agile practices. For example, in 1988, Harold Thimbleby published an article entitled "Delaying Commitment" [38], in which he advocates delaying software decisions as long as possible. Although this could be termed lazy evaluation, he argued that there is much benefit in keeping your options open and as flexible as possible to be able to quickly cater for any changes that crop up further along in the project. This later became one of the lean SD practices as described by [37]. Although the agile manifesto similarly values "Responding to change", the specific practice of delaying commitment has not been seen within the corresponding methodologies. Another example is the practice of Poka-Yoke [39], where processes are defined that make it impossible for mistakes to happen, and where that is not achievable, to design the processes in such a way that defects are easily detected and corrected. For clarification, Table 4 shows a compilation of practices which have been categorised as having only lean origins [5].

Table 4. Lean (only) Software Development Practices

- Jidoka (build quality in) [6]
- Poka-Yoke (Defect detection and prevention) [9]
- Kano analysis to link voice of the customer to requirements [40], [41]
- Quality Function Deployment [41]
- Value Stream Mapping [8], [6], [27], [42]
- Transparency [8]
- Make project status highly visible
- Visualise all work items
- Limit WIP (Work in Process), [43], [31]
- Workload levelling "Heijunka" [6], [40]
- Addressing bottlenecks [6], [44, 45], [40], [27]
- Deferring decision making [38], [27]
- Moving variability downstream [27]
- Reducing slack [22]
- Measure and manage [46]
- Employ Queuing Theory [25], [44, 45] but measure the right things [11]
- Employing Pull systems
- Kanban, Limitied WIP, CONWIP (Sugimori et al., 1977; Bradley, 2007; Kniberg and Skarin, 2010), [31]
- Batch control processing [47], [11]
- Value stream Kaikaku [8]
- Relentless reflection "Hansei" and continuous improvement "Kaizen" [6], [28], [48]
- Avoiding too much local optimisation [27]
- Hiding individual performance [27]
- Root cause analysis
- The 5 whys? [16]
- Promoting a 'safe' environment. Instil a "stop the line" mentality [27], [16]
- Developing appropriate incentives/rewards [49]
- Pragmatic governance (enable first, manage/control second) [49]

A more scientific approach is taken by [11] and [31], where focus is placed on measurements derived from areas such as queuing theory, variability and transaction cost analysis and using those measurements to shape and adjust the development processes.

4.2   Kanban

The most recent addition to the lean/agile methodology affray has been that of Kanban software development, and it takes its name from the Kanban scheduling system developed at Toyota [50], [51], [31] and explained in section 1.2 above.

The Kanban approach is applied within the software development domain by means of a Kanban board. Fig. 2 shows an example of a typical software Kanban board, reconstructed from photos of boards used at Yahoo [52].

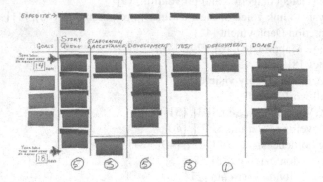

Fig. 2. A Kanban Board for Software Development [52]

Development tasks are written on sticky notes and move (or flow) [51] from left to right across the board. High level objectives are listed to the left, and the next column, similar to agile, is a queue of prioritised stories which progress through the various development stages as identified by the column headings.

Although the process shares similarities to agile approaches, such as a prioritised feature list, Kanban's primary concern is to limit work in progress (WIP). However, there is a second significant difference between it and agile methodologies. The concept of a time-boxed (fixed duration) iteration is no longer used. Instead, the Kanban board is used to set clearly visible limits to the number of tasks allowed in any of the columns. These limits are identified as circled numbers in Fig. 2. There is no fixed number for each WIP limit but by measuring the lead-time of individual tasks, the WIP limits and process itself can be optimised [53]. While an agile approach (agile kanban) would start a clean board for each iteration [50], kanban software development pursues the concept of continuous flow or what [50] refers to as "Sustaining Kanban".

The adoption of kanban SD can be difficult for those already familiar with an agile approach due to the lack of iterations. However, the inability of agile methodologies to easily scale up, is something that is pushing teams to look to alternatives. One emerging approach is to combine agile and kanban into some form of hybrid methodology. An example of such an approach is the methodology termed Scrumban [54], where the more structured and tightly coupled activities as defined by the SCRUM methodology are merged with the pull based workflow approach of kanban.

5   Lean Software Development – An Integrated View

Drawing upon the literature reviewed in the previous sections, we propose that LSD can be viewed as the merging of lean concepts with modern software development practices, such as those found in agile, and other general best practices for software development (Fig. 3). General best practices are those which are common to any disciplined SD approach, such as structured code, in-code commenting, object oriented, and source code control.

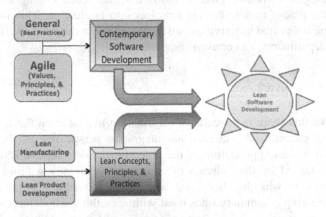

Fig. 3. Foundations of Lean Software Development

To position LSD in a broader context, since lean is a philosophy which can be applied at an organisational level, and agile is typically focused at a more practical level, agile methods can be seen as supportive practices of a lean software development philosophy as depicted in (Fig. 4).

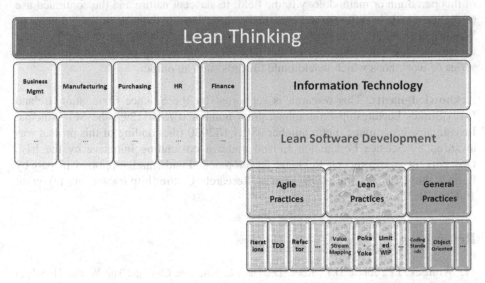

Fig. 4. The positioning of lean and agile SD practices within the organisation

In Fig. 4 we have positioned LSD within a wider umbrella of 'Lean Thinking' which spans the entire organisation. This is important to realise, since getting the entire value-stream working together towards a common goal in a continuously flowing fashion is the real aim of a 'Lean Enterprise' [8]. Trying to optimise one piece of the process, for example, writing the software code, may lead to sub-optimising the wider process [45]. [3] for example, when examining their internal processes leading to software delivery, found that the actual coding accounted for only 10% of the time it took to deliver a project into production. This indicates that 90% of the time is devoted to activities outside the actual coding and overflowing into other groups, departments, and or even companies.

6   Where to Now?

We have shown that there is a wealth of information available on the topic of Lean Software Development, and presented an integrative perspective of the topic. We hope the reader has an appreciation of the potential that we believe LSD holds for industry as evidenced by the volumes of contributions already within the domain. However, similar to what has happened with Agile SD adoption, once again the Software Engineering community finds itself with something which has evolved from industry and conventional wisdom. The academic world is struggling to pin down the phenomenon with any level of empirical foundation: *"Further evaluation of lean principles is needed to understand how they affect the performance of the software process"* [21].

Due to the subjective nature and qualitative aspects of being 'lean', we suggest that as a research community we need to try and bring some form of unified understanding of this paradigm or methodology to the field. Its nascent nature and the continued use of the term LSD in different contexts, makes it difficult to even begin such a process. We therefore refrain from proposing a possible framework to adopt or adapt in order to achieve this, but rather call on the Software Engineering community to begin a series of workshops which would build towards such an output.

Acknowledgments. This research is supported by the Science Foundation Ireland (SFI) Stokes Lectureship Programme, grant number 07/SK/I1299, the SFI Principal Investigator Programme, grant number 08/IN.1/I2030 (the funding of this project was awarded by Science Foundation Ireland under a co-funding initiative by the Irish Government and European Regional Development Fund), and supported in part by Lero - the Irish Software Engineering Research Centre (http://www.lero.ie) grant 10/CE/I1855.

References

1. Womack, J.P., Jones, D.T., Roos, D.: The Machine that Changed The World: How lean production revolutionized the global car wars, 352 p. Simon & Schuster Ltd. (1990)
2. Cawley, O., Richardson, I., Wang, X.: Medical Device Software Development - A Perspective from a Lean Manufacturing Plant. In: O'Connor, R.V., Rout, T., McCaffery, F., Dorling, A. (eds.) SPICE 2011. CCIS, vol. 155, pp. 84–96. Springer, Heidelberg (2011)

3. Parnell-Klabo, E.: Introducing Lean Principles with Agile Practices at a Fortune 500 Company. In: Proceedings of the Conference on AGILE 2006, pp. 232–242. IEEE Computer Society (2006)
4. Petersen, K.: Is Lean Agile and Agile Lean?: A Comparison between Two Software Development Paradigms. In: Modern Software Engineering Concepts and Practices: Advanced Approaches 2011, pp. 19–46. IGI Global (2011)
5. Wang, X., Conboy, K., Cawley, O.: "Leagile" software development: An experience report analysis of the application of lean approaches in agile software development. Journal of Systems and Software 85(6), 1287–1299 (2012)
6. Liker, J.: The Toyota Way. McGraw-Hill (2003)
7. LeanManufacturingConcepts. History of lean manufacturing (2008), http://www.leanmanufacturingconcepts.com/HistoryOfLeanManufacturing.htm (August 8, 2011)
8. Womack, J.P., Jones, D.T.: Lean Thinking: Banish Waste and Create Wealth in Your Corporation. Simon & Schuster (1996)
9. Robinson, H.: Using Poka-Yoke Techniques for Early Defect Detection. In: Sixth International Conference on Software Testing Analysis and Review (1997)
10. Cumbo, D., Kline, D.E., Bumgardner, M.S.: Benchmarking performance measurement and lean manufacturing in the rough mill. Forest Products 56(6), 25–30 (2006)
11. Reinertsen, D.G.: The Principles of Product Development Flow: Second Generation Lean Product Development. Celeritas Publishing (2009)
12. Christopher, M., Towill, D.R.: Supply chain migration from lean and functional to agile and customised. Supply Chain Management 5(4), 206–213 (2000)
13. Charette, R.: Challenging the Fundamental Notions of Software Development (2007)
14. Ohno, T.: Toyota Production System: Beyond Large-Scale Production, 152 p. Productivity Press (1988)
15. Hines, P., Holweg, M., Rich, N.: Learning to evolve: A review of contemporary lean thinking. International Journal of Operations & Production Management 24(10), 994–1011 (2004)
16. Womack, J.P., Jones, D.T., Roos, D.: The Machine that Changed The World: How lean production revolutionized the global car wars, 352 p. Simon & Schuster Ltd. (2007)
17. Sugimori, Y., et al.: Toyota production system and Kanban system Materialization of just-in-time and respect-for-human system. International Journal of Production Research 15(6), 553–564 (1977)
18. INCOSE. International Council on Systems Engineering (1990), http://www.incose.org (August 8, 2011)
19. Oppenheim, B.W., Murman, E.M., Secor, D.A.: Lean Enablers for Systems Engineering. Systems Engineering 14(1), 29–55 (2011)
20. Womack, J.P., Jones, D.T.: From Lean Production to the Lean Enterprise (cover story). Harvard Business Review 72(2), 93–103 (1994)
21. Petersen, K., Wohlin, C.: Measuring the flow in lean software development. Software: Practice and Experience 41(9), 975–996 (2011)
22. Middleton, P.: Lean Software Development: Two Case Studies. Software Quality Journal 9(4), 241–252 (2001)
23. Petersen, K., Wohlin, C.: Software process improvement through the Lean Measurement (SPI-LEAM) method. Journal of Systems and Software 83(7), 1275–1287 (2010)
24. Institute for Manufacturing. Kanbans (2011), http://www.ifm.eng.cam.ac.uk/dstools/process/kanban.html (August 8, 2011)

25. Reinertsen, D.: Managing the Design Factory: The Product Developer's Toolkit. The Free Press (1997)
26. Raman, S.: Lean software development: is it feasible? In: Proceedings of the 17th AIAA/IEEE/SAE Digital Avionics Systems Conference, DASC (1998)
27. Poppendieck, M., Poppendieck, T.: Lean Software Development: An Agile Toolkit. Addison-Wesley Professional (2003)
28. Hibbs, C., Jewett, S.C., Sullivan, M.: The Art of Lean Software Development. 128 p. O'Reilly Media (2009)
29. Ballard, G.: Positive vs negative iteration in design. In: The 8th Conference of the International Group for Lean Construction, Brighton, U.K. (2000)
30. Poppendieck, M., Poppendieck, T.: Implementing Lean Software Development from Concept to Cash. Addison-Wesley Professional (2006)
31. Anderson, D.J.: Kanban 2010. Blue Hole Press (2010)
32. Highsmith, J.: Agile Software Development Ecosystems. Addison Wesley (2002)
33. Fowler, M.: Agile VersusLean (2008), http://martinfowler.com/bliki/AgileVersusLean.html (August 11, 2011)
34. Wang, X.: The Combination of Agile and Lean in Software Development: An Experience Report Analysis. In: Agile 2011, Salt Lake City, Utah, USA (2011)
35. Consulting, ON.: Benefits of Lean and Agile Compared (2007), http://www.oakleigh.co.uk/page/3341/White-Papers/Whitepaper-Articles/Benefits-of-Lean-and-Agile-Compared (cited January 12, 2010)
36. Beck, K.: Test Driven Development: By Example, 240 p. Addison-Wesley Professional (2002)
37. Poppendieck, M., Poppendieck, T.: Lean Software Development: An Agile Toolkit. In: Cockburn, A., Highsmith, J. (eds.) Agile Software Development. Addison-Wesley Professional (2003)
38. Thimbleby, H.: Delaying commitment [programming strategy]. IEEE Software 5(3), 78–86 (1988)
39. Grout, J.R., Downs, B.T.: A Brief Tutorial on Mistake-proofing, Poka-Yoke, and ZQC (2012)
40. Middleton, P., Flaxel, A., Cookson, A.: Lean Software Management Case Study: Timberline Inc. In: Extreme Programming and Agile Processes in Software Engineering, pp. 1–9 (2005)
41. Raffo, D., et al.: Integrating Lean principles with value based software engineering. In: 2010 Proceedings of PICMET 2010: Technology Management for Global Economic Growth, PICMET (2010)
42. Mujtaba, S., Feldt, R., Petersen, K.: Waste and Lead Time Reduction in a Software Product Customization Process with Value Stream Maps. In: 2010 21st Australian Software Engineering Conference, ASWEC (2010)
43. Ladas, C.: Scrumban. Lean Software Engineering-Essays on the Continuous Delivery of High Quality Information Systems, vol. 2011. Modus Cooperandi Press (2009)
44. Goldratt, E.M.: The Goal: A Process of Ongoing Improvement. North River Press (1992)
45. Goldratt, E.M.: Critical Chain, 248 p. Gower, Aldershot (1997)
46. Anderson, D.J., Garber, R.: A Kanban System for Sustaining Engineering on Software Systems (2007)
47. Bradley, R.: Push to Pull: How Lean Concepts Improve a Data Migration. In: AGILE 2007 (2007)
48. Joyce, M., Schechter, B.: The Lean Enterprise—A Management Philosophy at Lockheed Martin. Defense Advanced Research Journal (August-November 2004)

49. Ambler, S.W., Kroll, P.: Best practices for lean development governance (2007), http://www.ibm.com/developerworks/rational/library/jun07/kro ll/(cited January 22, 2010)
50. Hiranabe, K.: Kanban Applied to Software Development: from Agile to Lean (2008), http://www.infoq.com/articles/hiranabe-lean-agile-kanban (cited January 12, 2010)
51. Birkeland, J.O.: From a timebox tangle to a more flexible flow. In: Sillitti, A., Martin, A., Wang, X., Whitworth, E. (eds.) XP 2010. LNBIP, vol. 48, pp. 325–334. Springer, Heidelberg (2010)
52. Patton, J.: Kanban Development Oversimplified (2009)
53. Kniberg, H., Skarin, M.: Kanban and Scrum-Making the most of both, InfoQ (2010)
54. Ladas, C.: Scrumban. Lean Software Engineering-Essays on the Continuous Delivery of High Quality Information Systems (2008), http://www.leansoftware engineering.com/ksse/scrum-ban/ (cited September 28, 2011)

Lean Software Development Measures and Indicators - A Systematic Mapping Study

Markus Feyh and Kai Petersen

School of Computing, Blekinge Institute of Technology, Karlskrona, Sweden
marfeyh@gmail.com, kai.petersen@bth.se

Abstract. Background: Lean Software Development (LSD) aims for improvement, yet this improvement requires measures to identify whether a difference has been achieved, and provide decision support for further improvement.
Objective: This study identifies measures and indicators proposed in literature on LSD, then structures them according to ISO/IEC 15939, allowing for comparability due to a use of a standard.
Method: Systematic mapping is the research methodology.
Result: The published literature on LSD measures has significantly increased since 2010. The two pre-dominant study types are evaluation research and experience reports. 22 base measures, 13 derived measures, and 14 indicators were identified.
Conclusion: Gaps exist with respect to LSD principles. In particular: *deferring commitment*, *respecting people* and *knowledge creation*. The principle of *delivering fast* is well supported.

Keywords: lean software development, measures, metrics, indicators, systematic mapping, ISO/IEC 15939, measurement information model.

1 Introduction

Lean software development (LSD) is an agile software development paradigm focusing on creating customer value and removing waste (everything that does not contribute to value creation for the customer) [1], and at the same time the end to end flow [2]. The common principles of Agile processes have been described in an agile manifesto (see [3]). As LSD is a fairly recent process [4] research has begun investigating the benefits it brings. Furthermore, many of these improvements are attributed to using measurements [5,6,7]. Many of the measurements found in LSD have been been adapted from its origin, i.e. lean product development [8].

In the field of LSD measurement, Poppendieck and Poppendieck [9] recommend to *"measure up"*, by focusing on measurements that optimize the whole process as a pose to sub-optimizing parts of it. This is echoed in research, when the flow of work or inventory through the value stream has been investigated [5]. Given the focus on the measurements to optimize the end-to-end flow, an understanding of what measurements are actually researched, presented or used in literature within the field is needed.

B. Fitzgerald et al. (Eds.): LESS 2013, LNBIP 167, pp. 32–47, 2013.

A need for a greater understanding of measurements in LSD literature has led to the research presented in this paper. In order to accomplish this, a systematic mapping study investigating measures in the context of LSD has been conducted. A systematic map aims at structuring an area of research, with the aim of discovering research gaps. As a means for structuring measures in LSD, ISO/IEC 15939 [10] has been used. The specific contributions of this mapping study are:

- Analysis of publication trends over time
- Identifying base measures, derived measures, and indicators from literature
- Analysis of research types and contributions
- An analysis of the relation between identified measures, indicators, and their support of lean principles and practices.

The paper is organized as follows. Section 2 presents related work on LSD and measurement. Section 3 describes the research method used. Section 4 shows the identified measures and indicators, followed by a discussion of the findings in Section 5. Section 6 concludes the paper.

2   Related Work

2.1   Lean Software Development (LSD)

The term *"lean"* has its origin in manufacturing where it was defined by Liker with four concepts [11]. The concepts were: philosophy, process, partnerships and problem solving. Later, fourteen principles were distilled from the four concepts by Womack et al. [12] in the context of manufacturing. The principles defined by Womack et al. [12] can be grouped into the following four sections:

- *Long-term philosophy:* Focusing on long-term value;
- *Right process will produce right results:* removal of waste and focus on value;
- *Value to organization by developing people:* human development, supporting the corporate identity and working as a team as well as with suppliers;
- *Solving root problems drives organizational learning:* continuous improvement based on consensus based decision making where multiple options are considered.

Next, Middleton [13] was one of the first researchers to publish on lean manufacturing principles in an industrial software development context. Middleton found that resource allocation, flow and lead time improved through the use of lean. In addition, the most well-known interpretation of lean, in software development, is provided by Poppendieck and Poppendieck [4], who based it on the lean manufacturing literature. They proposed lean as a way of shortening feedback loops that cause delays, defects and unneeded code. Based on their writing on LSD, Poppendeick and Poppendeick defined seven principles which are specifically focused on LSD [14] and were used in the systematic mapping:

- *Eliminate waste:* not building the wrong product or the product wrong; work done in a continuous flow;

- *Build in quality:* proofing the process for mistakes, using continuous integration, and zero tolerance of defects;
- *Create knowledge*: use the scientific method, paying attention to the small intricacies of the process;
- *Defer commitment:* make decisions that commit the organization until the last responsible moment;
- *Deliver fast:* use the queuing theory to manage the work-flow. Speed, quality and low cost goes hand in hand;
- *Respect people:* provide them with purpose, challenges and responsibility;
- *Optimize the whole:* purposefully think in sustainable ways that focuses on long term solutions. Focus on the whole and avoid sub optimization.

Lean was included in a systematic literature review of agile development [1] as a type of agile methodology. While similar in most principles to agile software development, LSD is different [2]. Lean differentiates itself through the principle, "see the whole" [4] and a low-dependency software architecture. Lean's differences are important, because by focusing on the whole, the sub-optimization of local processes can be avoided. It was found in a comparison between Kanban (a practice using pull strategies and limiting the work in process and SCRUM (an agile process) that Kanban was preferable since it did not artificially time box sprints and allocate resources [15]. In the comparison of Kanban and SCRUM [15], research indicated that productivity is higher when using Kanban.

2.2   ISO/IEC 15939 Measurement Information Model

Using the ISO/IEC 15939 measurement information model for measurement program planning it has been shown that it can lead to a five times faster process implementation [16].

The meta-model in Figure 1 presents a simplified version of ISO/IEC 15939 focusing on the relationships between information needs, indicators, derived measures, base measures, attributes, and entities.

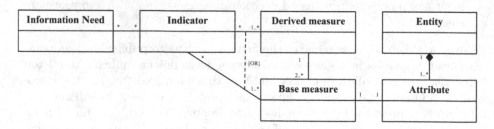

Fig. 1. Metamodel adapted from ISO/IEC 15939 measurement information model

Information needs provide *"insight necessary to manage objectives, goals, risks and problems"* [10]. The standard defines that indicators provide *"an estimate or evaluation of specified attributes derived from a model with respect to defined information needs"* [10], they fulfill the information need. Attributes are properties of entities that be quantified or qualified, and entities are either products, processes, projects or resources [10]. A measure is the variable value which the result of the measurement is assigned to, while derived measures combine base measures through measurement functions, i.e. rules of how to combine different base measures [10].

3 Research Methodology

The primary research methodology used in this paper was systematic mapping [17]. A systematic mapping study aims at structuring an area, and discovering research gaps and directions for future research. In contrast to systematic reviews, systematic mapping studies are broader in scope, and do not aim at aggregating evidence. The process consists of the following steps: (1) defining the research scope through research questions; (2) conducting the search; (3) selection of literature; (4) identification and structuring of the identified measures using content analysis and ISO/IEC 15939.

Our process resulted in a total of 27 literature sources. Table 1 provides an overview of the number of literature sources identified and selected in each step.

Table 1. Studies identified and selected

Selection step	Studies selected
Identified studies database search	472
Selection title and abstract (database)	21
Selection of studies after fulltext reading (database)	16
Identified studies backward snowballing	404
Selection title (snowballing)	73
Selection abstract (snowballing)	17
Selection of studies after fulltext reading (snowballing)	11
Final set of primary studies	27

Aim and Research Questions

The overall aim of this mapping study is to identify and structure the measures and indicators reported by literature on LSD. To fulfill this aim we ask the following research questions:

- RQ1: Which trends can be seen in terms of number of publications and publication forums over time?
- RQ2: How were measures evaluated in terms of research types (validation, evaluation, solution, philosophical, opinion, and experience, cf. [18] for definitions)?
- RQ3: Which measures and indicators have been proposed?

Furthermore, we link the measures to lean principles, which allows to reflect on why the information is collected (i.e. the information needs), however, given that studies reporting measures were not following the ISO model, they often did not report the information needs to be answered so this works provide the basis for these information needs.

Search Strategy: *Search string:* It is suggested [19] to formulate the search string considering the population, intervention, and outcome. The population was literature on LSD, i.e. books in relation to lean product development are excluded from the analysis. The intervention focused on measures used in LSD. This led to the following string: *TITLE-ABS-KEY(lean OR kanban) AND software AND (process OR project OR management OR development OR engineering) AND (measur* OR metric*)*. The search query was piloted and able to identify key papers known to us prior to the search.

Databases: We searched the following four electronic databases: Scopus, ACM Digital Library, IEEE Explore, Elsevier, and Springer Link. IEEE, Elsevier, and Springer cover the major journals in software engineering, as well as the major conferences in the field. Scopus is an index search engine which covers a wide range of publisher web-pages, and hence has been searched as well.

Backward snowball sampling: When searching for literature, Kitchenham and Charters [19] recommend using backwards snowball sampling in order find additional sources not discovered using the database queries. Moreover, it can be effective to identify relevant sources with less noise, i.e. irrelevant papers. The snowballing process consisted of a number of steps in order to find relevant papers. The first step consisted of collecting all references from the relevant literature found using search query and collecting all relevant titles which met the inclusion and exclusion criteria. Next, the abstract from the relevant titles from research papers were read using the inclusion and exclusion criteria. For books, the table of contents was examined in order to see if there were relevant sections.

Selection of Literature: By screening papers it allowed for the identification of relevant papers. The process refined research inclusion and exclusion based on the relevance to the posed research questions. As a result, the following inclusion and exclusion were applied:

Inclusion: The abstract explicitly mentions the software development process used as being lean or Kanban. Moreover, the paper must describe the use of measurements.

Exclusion: Abstracts that fall outside of the software engineering domain. Papers that discuss measurements only to compare methodologies. Also, papers that mention lean but do not make it their focus. Finally, papers that focus on describing measurements specifically for lean manufacturing will not be taken into consideration.

Data Extraction and Analysis: Content analysis [20] is based on well defined categories (here the ISO 15939 model) and focuses on counting occurrences of themes. The themes used as a basis for this research were: publication details, research paper methodology and measurement details. Publication details provided information about the (*i*) title, (*ii*) author, (*iii*) year of publication and (*iv*) which conference, book or journal it comes from. Next, the methodology used in the scientific papers was examined. This consisted of whether the article was empirical and what type of research was conducted. Both the publication details and methodology were straight forward to code.

The goal of codifying measurements was to place identified measurements in the context of the measurement meta-model (see Figure 1). The coding was done using the following seven steps: identify the name of the measurement and classify it initially as either a base measure, derived measure or indicator; extract a short description of the measurement; the most relevant information need for the measurement is identified; extract the lower level measurements, eg. derived measured and/or base measures; the attributes which are measured are identified; based on the attributes from the previous step, identify the relevant entities; repeat for each measurement identified in paper.

We reviewed the relevant literature using sticky notes for marking the relevant literature directly inside the identified articles, and extracting everything relevant to the measures, consisting of descriptions on the use of measures, the measures themselves and how they were used. This was done with inclusivity in mind since it was used as the basis for creating initial codes in the next step.

Validity Threats: Validity threats are important to discuss to judge the reliability of the results, the main threats relevant for this study are related to search and researcher bias.

Missing studies in the search: One threat to validity is missing important literature relevant for the research question. In order to reduce this threat we complemented database search with backward snowball sampling. This threat was further reduced as all studies known prior to the research were identified.

Researcher bias: Researcher bias is a threat during the selection of literature and the extraction and interpretation of results. The study selection was done by an individual researcher, which poses a threat. By being as inclusive as possible and not excluding any articles when in doubt at an early stage (reading abstract and title) the threat was reduced. In order to increase the reliability in interpretation, the results of measurement identification and specification using ISO 15939 were reviewed by the second author. The second author was also an author of a subset of included studies, which allowed for the verification of whether the interpretations were correct.

4   Results

The results are organized according to the research questions in Section 3.

4.1   RQ1: Publications over Time

To answer the first research question, the number of publications in different forums (journals, conferences, books) over time were analyzed. Figure 2 shows the number of publications for each year in the three forums. Only few scientific studies with a focus on measurement in LSD have been published before 2010. Only recently (2010 and onwards) has the number of publications increased

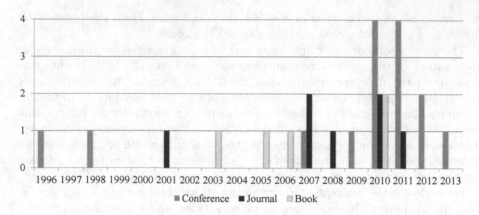

Fig. 2. Publication Trends over Time

significantly. After 2006 the number of journal publications increased visibly. This indicates an increased interest in measures related to LSD.

With respect to publication forums we found that 15 studies have been published in conferences, and 7 in journals. Furthermore, we identified 5 books reporting on measures in LSD. Two conferences attracted two papers each, namely *Digital Avionic Systems Conference* and the *Lean Enterprise Software and Systems Conference (LESS)*. All other journals and conferences in which the included studies have been published in occurred only once. Overall, no clear trend with preference for publication forums could be identified.

4.2 RQ2: Research Types

Wieringa et al. [18] distinguishes different research types, namely validation research (techniques are evaluated in lab experiments), evaluation research (techniques are implemented and evaluated in industry practice), solution proposal (a solution is proposed without evaluation), philosophical papers (taxonomies and conceptual frameworks), opinion papers (expressing personal opinion), and experience papers (experts report form their practical experience). According to the above types, we classified the primary studies included in our research.

Table 2 shows the research types, number of studies, and the references to the primary studies. It is visible that the majority is originating from expert experience. Also, a large portion of studies has been conducted using research methods in industry. Only few studies have been conducted in the lab, are pure solution proposals, or present opinions.

4.3 RQ3: Proposed Measures and Indicators

Base Measures (BM): We structure the identified base measures along the entities.

In relation to the entity *"Process/Project"* (see Table 3) we identified 12 base measures (BM1 to BM12). Overall, it is noteworthy that the majority of studies

Table 2. Research Types

Study type	Study Count	References
Validation	1	[21]
Evaluation	9	[22,23,24,25,13,26,27,6,5]
Solution	2	[28,29]
Philosophical	–	–
Opinion	4	[30,31,32,33]
Experience	11	[9,34,35,36,33,14,4,37,38,39,40]

are related to measuring time, i.e. the general duration to complete work (BM1), as well as more specifically in relation to value and non-value added time (BM3 and BM4).

Table 3. Base measures for the "Product" and "Process" entities

ID	Measure	Attribute	Study Count
BM1:	Duration in time units	Timestamps	12
BM2:	Value transition	Time of value transition	3
BM3:	Value added time	Time spent adding value	7
BM4:	Non-value added time	Time spent not adding value	5
BM5:	Number of work items	Work items	9
BM6:	Schedule slippage	Time delay in completion	2
BM7:	Failure load	Work items needing rework	4
BM8:	Financial costs	Costs	4
BM9:	Financial revenues	Revenues	2
BM10:	Bounce backs	Reworked items needing rework	2
BM11:	Fault slippage	Slip through defects	1
BM12:	Cost of investment	Investment costs	1

The base measures for the "Product" and "Process" entities can be shortly described as:

- Duration in time units (**BM1**): Measuring the time available and time spent as duration [23,37,28,39,13,41,26,29,27,33,14,4].
- Value transition (**BM2**): The number of work items moved between activities based associated with time stamp [24,39,26].
- Value added time (**BM3**): Time that is actually spent on adding value (also referred to as touch time or in process time) [24,5,14,4,33,34,39].
- Non-value added time (**BM4**): Non-value adding time as reported as delay time, transmission time, set-up time, and queue time [5,14,4,34,39].
- Number of work items (**BM5**): Amount of work items to be worked on (also referred to as work in process - WIP), e.g. requirements to be implemented, test cases to be run, or faults to be fixed [38,39,13,6,40,14,4,26,33].
- Schedule slippage (**BM6**): The duration by which work items exceed the original project plan (planned delivery date) [13,40].
- Failure load (**BM7**):Number of work items to be processed again as a result of defects caused by previous low quality work [24,39,33,22].

- Financial costs (**BM8**): Recurring and non-recurring costs, investment needed to realize a return on investment [14,4,34,26].
- Financial revenues (**BM9**): Revenues from making an investment [14,4].
- Bounce backs (**BM10**): The number of iterations needed to get a defect fixed after testing [4,24].
- Fault slippage (**BM11**): Number of defects slipping through a defect detection activity undetected [6].
- Cost of investment (**BM12**): The equipment and tools invested in [26].

For the entity *"Product"* we identified seven base measures (BM13 to BM19), shown in Table 4. From the measures it is clear that the size sof the defect backlog and work items is frequently presented.

Table 4. Base measures for the "Product" entity

ID Measure	Attribute	Study Count
BM13: No. of passed acceptance tests	Passed acceptance tests	1
BM14: No. of defects in the backlog	Defect backlog	4
BM15: Cohesion and coupling	Relatedness of source code	2
BM16: Code churn	Added, removed or edited language statements	1
BM17: Code coverage	Language statement test coverage	1
BM18: Lines of code	Language statements	1
BM19: Story points	Work item size	4

The base measures for the "Product" entity can be shortly described as:

- Number of passed acceptance tests (**BM13**): Counts the number of acceptance tests with test verdict "pass" [29].
- Number of defects in the backlog (**BM14**): Number of defects that have been reported, and not fixed yet [4,39,24,23].
- Cohesion and coupling (**BM15**): Object oriented measures to capture the internal code quality of a product [29,21].
- Code churn (**BM16**): Number of code statements that have been changed, removed, or added [28].
- Code coverage (**BM17**): Amount of code covered through tests [41].
- Lines of code (**BM18**): Measures size through counting the lines of code [29].
- Story points (**BM19**): Requirements based size measure counting story points [37,38,40,4].

For the entity *"Stakeholder"* we identified three base measures, shown in Table 5. Two measures are related to satisfaction, one focusing on the customer and the other on the employee. Both are perceived assessments through rating. The emotional seismograph, however, has not been explained in the paper [40]. Furthermore, the skill level is assessed, considering both required and available skills.

The base measures for the "Product" entity can be shortly described as:

Table 5. Base measures for "Stakeholder" entity

ID	Measure	Attribute	Study count
BM20: Perceived customer satisfaction	Customer satisfaction	4
BM21: Employee seismograph	Employee satisfaction	1
BM22: Perceived skill level	Skill level	1

- Perceived customer satisfaction (**BM20**): The customer rates satisfaction on a Likert scale with respect to the overall product or a feature [6,14].
- No information about how the emotion is captured is provided [40].
- Employee satisfaction (**BM21**): No information about how the emotion is captured is provided [40].
- Perceived skill level (**BM22:**): Rating the skill level of team members/teams, and skills needed for a task [13].

Overall, it is clearly visible that process related measures are emphasized in the lean literature. Among the process related measures, time (BM1, BM2, BM3, and BM4) and work in process (BM5) seem to be given a lot of emphasis.

Derived Measures (DM): Derived measures use measurement functions to combine base measures and other derived measures. Table 6 summarizes the derived measures and provides a description of how to combine measures using the mathematical function based on the availability of information provided in the studies.

Overall, thirteen derived measures have been identified (DM1 to DM13). Measuring efficiency is supported by multiple measures, indicating that it can be understood and determined in different ways. For example, one understanding is to relate value added time to the overall elapsed time, another understanding is to capture the throughput of what has been achieved in an elapsed amount of time. Speed is quantified by two measures, cycle time and lead time. Both are strongly related, and can be computed from each other (see Table 6).

Table 6. Derived measures

ID	Measure	Consisting of	Study Count
DM1:	Throughput	BM2, BM5	5
DM2:	Cycle time	BM1, BM2, BM5	9
DM3:	Lead time	BM1, BM2	9
DM4:	Capacity	BM3, BM4, BM5	7
DM5:	Profit and loss	BM8, BM9	4
DM6:	Inventory	BM2, BM5	7
DM7:	Time efficiency	BM2, BM3	3
DM8:	Value efficiency	BM1, BM9, BM12	1
DM9:	Net promoter score	BM20	1
DM10:	Initial quality	BM5, BM11	2
DM11:	Return on investment	BM8, BM9	2
DM12:	Design debt	BM16	1
DM13:	Rework rate	BM5	2

The identified derived measures can be shortly described as:

- Throughput (**DM1**): Number of work items completed in a specified period of time (also referred to as velocity), uses base measures BM5 (number of work items) in combination with when they were completed, BM2 [23,39,27,33,14].
- Cycle time (**DM2**): Duration of time per work item using the number of work items (BM5), duration in time units (BM1), value transition (BM2). It is computed as: *Cycle time = Lead-time (DM3)/Work in process (BM5)* [37,13,9,31,34,35,36,14,4].
- Lead time (**DM3**): Uses the duration in time units (BM1) and value transition (BM2). It captures the total elapsed time spent on the process, following the definition of **DM2** it can also be determined as *Lead time = Cycle time (DM2) * work in process (BM5)* [24,37,39,6,5,34,35,36,33].
- Capacity (**DM4**): The amount of work that can be completed (BM5) in a given time period, for example including (BM3) and (BM4) [27,6,40,34,14,33,4].
- Profit and loss (**DM5**): Compares revenue made (**BM9**) in relation to the the costs incurred to achieve the revenue (**BM8**) [33,14,4,30].
- Inventory (**DM6**): Uses the number of work items (BM5) as well as their value transitions (BM2) and is also known as the amount of work-in-process [26,6,34,36,27,39,24].
- Time effeciency (**DM7**): The percent of value added time (BM2) as a percent of the total time including the non-value added time (BM3) [14,4,34].
- Value effeciency (**DM8**): The effeciency caclulated from the investment (BM12) and the financial revenues (BM9) over the duration of time (BM1) [26].
- Net promoter score (**DM9**): Uses the perceived customer satisfaction (BM20) to calculate the net score based on their satisfaction [14].
- Initial quality (**DM10**): The fault slippage (BM11) as a percent of the number of work items (BM5) [33,34].
- Return on investment (**DM11**): Uses financial costs (BM8) and revenues (BM9) to calculate the projected return on investment [14,4].
- Design debt (**DM12**): Uses object oriented measures such as cohesion and coupling (BM16) [29].
- Rework rate (**DM13**): The number of work items with defects (BM5) [34,24].

Overall, the most prominently found in the literature were throughput (DM1), cycle time (DM2), lead time (DM3), capacity (DM4) and inventory (DM6). Of note is that the prominently identified derived measures consist of common base measures.

Indicators: Indicators provide the information needed in order to help answer information needs. Indicators are also often visualized graphically and used in organizational dashboards to support decision makers. We identified 13 indicators in the literature, shown in Table 7. The table also shows the measures it has been presented as consisting of in the *Consisting of* column. The number of studies where the indicator has actually been presented is shown in the *Study count* column. Interestingly, indicators have mainly focused on the visualization

Table 7. Indicators

ID	Measure	Consisting of	Study Count
I1:	Cumulative flow diagram	BM1, BM2, BM5	6
I2:	Regression	Potentially any (eg. BM1, DM2, DM3)	9
I3:	Box-plot	Interval or ratio scale (eg. DM3)	1
I4:	Burndown chart	BM1, BM5, DM1	3
I5:	Control Chart	Interval or ratio scale (eg. DM4, DM6, DM13)	2
I6:	Utilization	DM4, DM6	4
I7:	Design debt advice func.	DM12	1
I8:	Variance	BM1, BM2, BM5	1
I9:	Due date performance	BM1, DM3	2
I10:	Relative comparison	DM6, DM7	2
I11:	Cost of delay	BM1, DM5	1
I12:	Cost model	DM9	1
I13:	Overall state	DM6	1
I14:	Histogram	DM3	1

of speed related aspects, and not, for example, quality and financial aspects, or a combination thereof.

Indicators from the literature can be shortly described as:

- Cumulative flow diagram (**I1**): Visualizes the cumulative amount of work completed over time for different phases, allowing to detect bottlenecks [24,38,26,6,36,33].
- Regression (**I2**): Analyses the data set with regression lines (e.g. to determine trends of work completion) [24,39,36,33,37,13,14,38,26].
- Box-plot (**I3**): Illustrates the distribution of the data set from measures on a ratio or interval scale [24].
- Burndown chart **I4**: Shows the number of story points remaining versus a duration of time [40,36,4].
- Control chart **I5**: Shows whether a process is under control by using control limits in relation to the mean of the data set over time [24,6].
- Utilization (**I6**): Amount of capacity in process [6,40,34,14].
- Design debt advice func. (**I7**): Shows whether corrective action is needed [29].
- Variance (**I8**): Indicates inconsistency in the flow of work items [26].
- Due date performance (**I9**): Percentage of work items delivered on time [39,33].
- Relative comparison (**I10**): The comparison of multiple elements [39,5].
- Cost of delay (**I11**): The difference in the profit after a time [4].
- Cost model (**I12**): Measures cost using inventory, waste and investment [26].
- Overall state (**I13**): The combination of individual inventories [24].
- Histogram (**I14**): Shows eg. the distribution of lead time [33].

5   Discussion

Increased attention on lean measurements: Our trend analysis has shown that the number of studies on LSD measures has drastically increased in 2010 (see Section

4.1). Pernstål et al. [42] conducted a systematic review on LSD in the time period of 1990-2010. Eleven studies are in common between Pernstål et al.'s literature review. In the time before and excluding 2010 our study has 11 sources focusing on measurements, while Pernstål et al.'s has 26 sources for the same time period. This indicates that the interest in LSD measures has drastically increased from 2010 onwards, given that the low number of measurement studies before 2010 is not related to the low number of studies on lean overall. The trend identified emphasizes the practical and research relevance of studying LSD measures.

Need for evaluation: Only 9 studies evaluated lean measures in industry, as shown in Section 4.2. Hence, the results obtained have limitations in generalizability. Future rigorous studies are needed to evaluate the effect of practitioners using lean measures, in particular with an emphasis on what LSD aims to achieve. To make the link between the intention of lean and the use of measures more explicit, we link the identified base measures, derived measures, and indicators to the lean principles (as presented in Section 2.1)

Focus in relation to lean principles: Table 8 shows a mapping of measures to principles, which also makes the purpose of the measures (and hence the information need they fulfil) explicit. *Waste elimination* is mainly related to identification of non-value added time and work in process, which is considered wasteful as long as the work is not completed and delivered. *Build quality in* is solely defect based (e.g. passed test cases and defects reported), and does not consider a wider definition of quality. *Knowledge creation* is captured on an individual and team level by capturing perceived skill capabilities. However, no means for actual skill measurement are provided. Furthermore, measures of learning over time might be important to capture, which are not mentioned in the existing lean literature, but are emphasized as a main concept for continuous improvement. *Defer commitment* has not been supported by measures at all. *Deliver as fast as possible* is well captured and supported by the identified studies. *Respect for people* is addressed by capturing their motivation, while the instrument used has not been described. *Optimize the whole* is touched on by optimizing the flow with respect to utilization of capacity. Gaps are: (1) no measures related to deferring commitment; (2) no well defined instrument for capturing respect people; (3) knowledge creation is not objectively assessed; (4) deliver fast is very well supported.

Table 8. Mapping of LSD principles (see Section 2.1) to measures (see Tables 3 to 6)

Principle	Base measures	Derived measures	Indicators
Eliminate waste	BM3, BM4, BM5, BM8	DM5, DM6, DM9	I5, I6, I10, I12
Build quality in	BM10, BM11, BM12, BM13, BM14, BM16, BM17, BM18	DM10, DM12, DM13	I7
Create knowledge	BM22	–	–
Defer commitment	–	–	–
Deliver fast	BM1, BM2, BM6, BM7, BM15, BM19	DM1, DM2, DM3, DM7	I2, I3, I4, I9, I14
Respect people	BM21	–	–
Optimize the whole	BM9, BM20	DM4, DM8, DM11	I1, I8, I11, I13

Need for well defined and reusable measurement components: Overall, we found that measures were only partially specified, not presenting all elements of the ISO 15939 model. Hence, to achieve reusable and well defined measures we envision measurement components, where a component fulfills a well specified information need related to lean principles. The components should report on indicators, derived measures, and base measures, as well as the attributes and their entities. A well defined component also ensures comparability between measures collected over time, and between organizations.

Implications: Two implications for researchers and practitioners should be highlighted in this work. Firstly, software organizations would benefit from using the measures in a repository [43], because it would allow for both bottom-up and top-down measurement program planning. Secondly, empirical studies could be carried out to elicit information needs since this mapping only uses principles. Since this study provides a basis of measures, information needs could be empirically elicited to better support an understanding of what measures are relevant. Furthermore, it would allow a greater understanding of what measures are currently used through collaboration between industry and academia.

6   Conclusion

We conducted a systematic mapping study on software measures in the context of the LSD literature. We identified 27 primary literature sources used to elicit measures using the ISO 15939 standard. Based on the studies we investigated publication trends, types of studies conducted, and base measures, derived measures, as well as indicators reported.

RQ1: Which trends can be seen in terms of number of publications and publication forums over time? We identified a significant increase in literature on LSD measures in 2010 and onwards, indicating relevance for research and practice.

RQ2: How were measures evaluated in terms of research types? The most frequent way of reporting lean measures was experience reports. Only few opinion papers, solution proposals, and validation research (lab) have been presented. Nine studies were conducted using evaluation in industry. However, these originated primarily from Scandinavia focusing on few companies, hence further studies in different contexts are needed.

RQ3: Which measures and indicators have been proposed? We identified 22 base measures, 13 derived measures and 14 indicators in the literature. By mapping measures to lean principles we found: (1) no measures related to deferring commitment; (2) no well defined instrument for capturing respect people; (3) knowledge creation was not objectively assessed; (4) deliver fast was well supported.

This study allowed to understand the state of the art in LSD measures. However, it is essential to understand the state of practice of a large population. Hence, conducting an industrial survey is the next step to take.

References

1. Dybå, T., Dingsøyr, T.: Empirical studies of agile software development: A systematic review. Information & Software Technology 50(9-10), 833–859 (2008)
2. Petersen, K.: Is lean agile and agile lean. A comparison between two software development paradigms. In: Modern Software Engineering Concepts and Practices: Advanced Approaches, pp. 19–46. IGI Global (2011)
3. Cockburn, A., Highsmith, J.: Agile software development, the people factor. Computer 34(11), 131–133 (2001)
4. Poppendieck, M.: Lean software development: an agile toolkit. Addison-Wesley Professional (2003)
5. Mujtaba, S., Feldt, R., Petersen, K.: Waste and lead time reduction in a software product customization process with value stream maps. In: Australian Software Engineering Conference, pp. 139–148 (2010)
6. Petersen, K., Wohlin, C.: Software process improvement through the lean measurement (spi-leam) method. Journal of Systems and Software 83(7), 1275–1287 (2010)
7. Dybå, T., Sharp, H.: What's the evidence for lean? IEEE Software 29(5), 19–21 (2012)
8. Morgan, J.M., Liker, J.K.: The Toyota product development system. Productivity Press, New York (2006)
9. Poppendieck, M., Cusumano, M.A.: Lean software development: A tutorial. IEEE Software 29(5), 26–32 (2012)
10. IEEE standard adoption of ISO/IEC 15939:2007 systems and software engineering measurement process. IEEE Std 15939-2008, pp. C1–C40 (2009)
11. Liker, J.K.: The Toyota Way. Esensi (2004)
12. Womack, J.P., Jones, D.T., Roos, D.: The machine that changed the world: The story of lean production–Toyota's secret weapon in the global car wars that is now revolutionizing world industry. Simon and Schuster (2007)
13. Middleton, P., Taylor, P.S., Flaxel, A., Cookson, A.: Lean principles and techniques for improving the quality and productivity of software development projects: a case study. International Journal of Productivity and Quality Management 2(4), 387–403 (2007)
14. Poppendieck, M., Poppendieck, T.: Implementing Lean Software Development: From Concept to Cash. Addison-Wesley Professional (2006)
15. Sjøberg, D.I.K., Johnsen, A., Solberg, J.: Quantifying the effect of using kanban versus scrum: A case study. IEEE Software 29(5), 47–53 (2012)
16. Staron, M., Meding, W., Karlsson, G., Nilsson, C.: Developing measurement systems: an industrial case study. Journal of Software Maintenance 23(2), 89–107 (2011)
17. Petersen, K., Feldt, R., Mujtaba, S., Mattsson, M.: Systematic mapping studies in software engineering. In: 12th International Conference on Evaluation and Assessment in Software Engineering, vol. 17, p. 1 (2008)
18. Wieringa, R., Maiden, N.A.M., Mead, N.R., Rolland, C.: Requirements engineering paper classification and evaluation criteria: a proposal and a discussion. Requir. Eng. 11(1), 102–107 (2006)
19. Kitchenham, B.A., Charters, S.: Guidelines for performing systematic literature reviews in software engineering (2007)
20. Dixon-Woods, M., Agarwal, S., Jones, D., Young, B., Sutton, A.: Synthesising qualitative and quantitative evidence: a review of possible methods. Journal of Health Services Research & Policy 10(1), B45–B53 (2005)
21. Ware, M.P., Wilkie, F.G., Shapcott, M.: The application of product measures in directing software maintenance activity. Journal of Software Maintenance 19(2), 133–154 (2007)

22. Middleton, P.: Lean software development: Two case studies. Software Quality Journal 9(4), 241–252 (2001)
23. Staron, M., Meding, W., Söderqvist, B.: A method for forecasting defect backlog in large streamline software development projects and its industrial evaluation. Information & Software Technology 52(10), 1069–1079 (2010)
24. Petersen, K.: A palette of lean indicators to detect waste in software maintenance: A case study. In: Wohlin, C. (ed.) XP 2012. LNBIP, vol. 111, pp. 108–122. Springer, Heidelberg (2012)
25. Staron, M., Meding, W., Caiman, M.: Improving completeness of measurement systems for monitoring software development workflows. In: Software Quality Days 2013, pp. 230–243 (2013)
26. Petersen, K., Wohlin, C.: Measuring the flow in lean software development. Softw., Pract. Exper. 41(9), 975–996 (2011)
27. Staron, M., Meding, W.: Monitoring bottlenecks in agile and lean software development projects – A method and its industrial use. In: Caivano, D., Oivo, M., Baldassarre, M.T., Visaggio, G. (eds.) PROFES 2011. LNCS, vol. 6759, pp. 3–16. Springer, Heidelberg (2011)
28. Janes, A., Succi, G.: To pull or not to pull. In: OOPSLA Companion 2009, pp. 889–894 (2009)
29. Heidenberg, J., Porres, I.: Metrics functions for kanban guards. In: ECBS 2010, pp. 306–310 (2010)
30. Raman, S.: Lean software development: Is it feasible? In: Proceedings of the 17th AIAA/IEEE/SAE Digital Avionics Systems Conference, DASC, vol. 1, p. C131. (1998)
31. Sutton, J.M.: Lean software for the lean aircraft. In: 15th AIAA/IEEE Digital Avionics Systems Conference, pp. 49–54 (1996)
32. Vilkki, K.: When agile is not enough. In: Abrahamsson, P., Oza, N. (eds.) LESS 2010. LNBIP, vol. 65, pp. 44–47. Springer, Heidelberg (2010)
33. Anderson, D.J.: Kanban. Blue Hole Press (2010)
34. McManus, H.: Product development value stream mapping (PDVSM) manual. Lean Aerosp Initiative (2005)
35. Taipale, M.: Huitale – A story of a finnish lean startup. In: Abrahamsson, P., Oza, N. (eds.) LESS 2010. LNBIP, vol. 65, pp. 111–114. Springer, Heidelberg (2010)
36. Kniberg, H.: Kanban and Scrum-making the most of both. Lulu.com (2010)
37. Polk, R.: Agile and kanban in coordination. In: AGILE 2011, pp. 263–268 (2011)
38. Swaminathan, B., Jain, K.: Implementing the lean concepts of continuous improvement and flow on an agile software development project: An industrial case study. In: AGILE India (AGILE INDIA), pp. 10–19. IEEE (2012)
39. Seikola, M., Loisa, H.M., Jagos, A.: Kanban implementation in a telecom product maintenance. In: EUROMICRO-SEAA 2011, pp. 321–329 (2011)
40. Prochazka, J., Kokott, M., Chmelar, M., Krchnak, J.: Keeping the spin - from idea to cash in 6 weeks: Success story of agile/lean transformation. In: ICGSE 2011, pp. 124–130 (2011)
41. Grid, C.: Measuring continuous integration capability (2008)
42. Pernstal, J., Gorschek, T., Feldt, R.: The lean gap: A review of lean approaches to large-scale software systems development. Journal of Systems and Software (2013)
43. Gencel, C., Petersen, K., Mughal, A.A., Iqbal, M.I.: A decision support framework for metrics selection in goal-based measurement programs: Gqm-dsfms. Journal of Systems and Software (2013)

Bringing Total Quality in to Software Teams:
A Frame for Higher Performance

Petri Kettunen

University of Helsinki
Department of Computer Science
P.O. Box 68, FI-00014 University of Helsinki, Finland
petri.kettunen@cs.helsinki.fi

Abstract. The current trends in most software-intensive product development organizations are in striving for high performance. Overall, software product creation has become more and more value-driven. However, from the customer and user satisfaction points of view "software" itself has no value until it is executed in some target machine (including embedded systems) producing certain results. Those outcomes (e.g., web services) bring benefits and even delight which are valued by the customers in terms of quality. In order to address those considerations, this paper proposes a software team-oriented performance analysis and improvement framework supported by provisional instrumentation. The aim is to gauge Lean software teams and organizations to advance their thinking towards the total quality perspective. The industrial cases demonstrate, how it is able to catalyst such team performance drivers and quality aims of software development under different circumstances.

Keywords: new product/service development, software-intensive systems, value, total quality, performance management.

1   Introduction

Basically every software development organization is nowadays looking for new ways to improve their performance. Compelling value creation capabilities are thus becoming competitive new product and service development (NPD, NSD) edges. Moreover, innovation is increasingly a major competitive advantage in most software business areas.

However, software product development is still often seen mostly from the producer point of view. The concept creators are supposed to know, what the customers are going to value about the new product. Those inherent traits are often problems in modern competitive environments in which the product market and customer values are uncertain and subject to rapid, even disruptive changes [1], [2], [3], [4].

Potentially much more can be achieved by stretching the development outside the typical customer and market interface boundaries seeing the product concepts and the whole NPD/NSD system in terms of producing valuable effects and benefits in the customer-space [5]. Such effects-based quality rethinking puts emphasis on

B. Fitzgerald et al. (Eds.): LESS 2013, LNBIP 167, pp. 48–64, 2013.

information systems development and design thinking as reference disciplines in addition to basic software engineering. Overall, that line of thinking brings up new challenges but more importantly new business opportunities for both incumbent and startup NPD/NSD companies.

All those needs call for more powerful tools for software-intensive enterprises to master their product development efforts with teams. The prime move towards this direction is to view the products in a larger quality perspective from the customer-space in contrast to the typical producer-space [6]. The purpose of this paper is to explicate such software-intensive NPD thinking with supporting team performance measures. Our overall research question is therefore set as follows: How can software team performance be improved with total quality thinking?

Taking that heading, the rest of this paper is organized as follows. The next Section 2 reviews software team performance in general and effects-based product development views in particular, highlighting the needs and opportunities for further quality-oriented advances. Section 3 then presents our team-oriented performance analysis and development framework, followed by certain demonstrating industrial case examples in Section 4. Section 5 discusses the proposition with implications and concluding pointers to further work in Section 6.

2 Software Product Development Performance Management

In general, the purpose of NPD process is to satisfy customer/user needs and to address business opportunities with product offerings. New product development performance can be measured from different viewpoints typically in terms of product quality, development cost and development time. Such performance indicators are for instance product technical performance, innovativeness, cost, service level, lead time, and market "fit" (attractiveness) [7]. Furthermore, the success should be measured not simply in terms of traditional project management metrics (product development project success; e.g., schedule compliance), but more in terms of the business performance (product business success; e.g., market share gains) following the release(s).

The product features and even the basic nature of the product need to be weighted from different viewpoints during the development. The more modern product creation process models attempt to achieve this with concurrent concept development and R&D phases [2], [8], [1]. Agile software development methods have adopted such principles [9].

However, often the profound problem is that the product developers tend to concentrate on just building the current product technical design at hand, neglecting or even ignoring the overall business success [10], [11], [12], [5]. In particular, the producer view is often different from the customer view [6]. Moreover, the nature and role of the product under development can be seen very differently in different disciplines (e.g., marketing and engineering) [7]. Considering software development in particular, there can be huge differences between the viewpoints. It is in particular important to realize, that software itself is not a product, but it is the service it provides or enables that brings value.

All in all, the products can be seen not only from different perspectives, but also from different scopes in conjunction to their environment. While a traditional product development view is in the core product, the possibly extended product and the complementary services could ultimately affect much more for the total customer quality and value [13], [14], [15]. Various hybrid product-service combinations are increasingly sources of competitive advantages.

In general, IT systems can also be understood as products. They provide services which bring certain benefits (e.g., in business processes) [16], [5]. One seminal example of this line of thinking is the PIOCO development model [17]. In particular, it addresses the organizational context and the total effectiveness of the IS/IT system under development from the change management perspective. Successful services fit well with their actual use context. They are then typically adaptable to the current user needs, often coupled with complementary products and services [18].

In all, there is no one universal measure of software team performance. To begin with, software teams can be seen as general work teams and their performance accordingly like dimensioned for instance by Hackman [19]. Typically software team performance is associated with productivity [20]. With traditional project teams, the basic objectives of achieving the product goals (functionality, quality) within the constraints (resources, schedule, cost) are typical measures in product and process performance dimensions. However, software development teams have usually multiple enterprise stakeholders – including the team members themselves – and consequently multiple different dimensions of performance [21], [22], [23], [24], [25]. Multivariate measures are thus usually more applicable. Prior literature has described many possible software team performance measures [26], [27]. The measures can address both the product and process, and be objective or subjective.

It follows that the performance is relative to the organizational environment of the team. Consequently, different teams may have different performance targets even within same larger organizations [24]. For instance, new feature development of existing products may be judged primarily of the throughput while more creative new product creation could be judged by the novelty of the solution.

In particular the essence of Lean is efficient creation of value (desired capabilities) at specific cost for all enterprise stakeholders [28]. The concept of value is likewise central to high performance software development [29], [30]. Value-centric product development models and value-based software engineering (VBSE) focus specifically on those aspects. This line of thinking can be further extended beyond the direct product value towards its benefits to the customers and even their customers. Software team performance in terms of value creation efficiency can be assessed with value stream mapping/analysis (VSM/A) and more generally value network analysis (VNA) methods [31], [3], [32], [33]. Different stakeholders tend to have different perspectives of the software value and use different value constructs to judge it [34]. This is in particular so with the embedded software components of software-intensive products.

In practice there are usually many ways to achieve and affect the (high) performance in software teams. Such means can stem from the processes, tools, organization, and most importantly the people in the team [35], [36], [37], [38].

Total Quality Management (TQM) is a general-purpose quality leadership and organizational development approach originating from manufacturing disciplines. It has been applied also to software organizations [39], [40]. We do not address TQM further here, but one of the key tenets of such total quality thinking is overall customer satisfaction. It covers not only the products but basically everything the organization does for the business. The principal idea is to manage the entire organization as a customer-focused integrated system with continuous improvements. The role of teams is central.

Similar standpoints of customer goal-orientation are taken for instance in the Outside-In Development (OID) and Impact Mapping methods [41], [42]. One of the main implications is then that also the software developers should be systematically supported with the key business information [43].

Building on the line of thinking reviewed above, we propose a team-oriented framework for managing software-intensive NPD performance. We adopt the fundamental philosophy of TQM that overall customer delight is the key driver across the entire product development organization. Consequently, software teams should also adopt such thinking. That principle leads to taking broader views on the products under development by seeing them in the larger quality space coupled with appropriate performance measurements. However, notably, our aim is not to apply TQM to the full in here.

3   Total Quality Oriented Team Performance Gauging Frame

The key idea of our proposal is to rescale traditional software-intensive NPD performance management and frames of reference by advancing from software team outputs towards the effects and benefits of the software-enabled products. Table 1 presents the foundational reference frame. The underlying principle is that the software-intensive product (under development) should be viewed at different levels of impacts in its use and business context. This brings the total quality in.

Table 1. Software product development performance management hierarchy

Space	LEVEL	Drivers	Focus	OBJECTIVES
Customer-User	Strategic	Megatrends	What are the desired (business) effects of the results usage?	Impacts
	Tactical	Innovation	How do the clients use the results?	Benefits
	Operational	Application	Which software capabilities (features) shall we deliver, and what results does the execution produce?	Outcomes
Producer-Supplier	PRODUCT	Technology	How do we design the software features?	Outputs

We define three such main levels: strategic, tactical, and operational. They have been chosen based on typical NPD competence and management areas [7]. In principle, we take multiple perspectives of value and quality (internal and external) into the consideration like in the Software Value Map [34]. Likewise the levels reflect the seminal Balanced Scorecard (BSC) dimensions of financial (~ strategic), customer and innovation/learning (~ tactical, ~operational), and internal processes (~product) ones. The key feature is to elevate the focus from the basic product outputs (software implementation) in the producer space to the higher levels of the customer/user space objectives. Seeing from that viewpoint, even extended products can be reconceptualized as elements of the customer value creation system. Furthermore, additional aspects of customer value and delight such as user experience and brand can be incorporated in more holistic ways here.

In addition, the time dimension should be taken into account. This is in particular with respect to the product release/delivery point (and possibly future upgrading). Like discussed in Sect. 2, software does not create value until it is executed. The resulting outcomes (results) bring then the benefits, which have longer-term impacts. In order to test and operationalize the frame proposed above, we apply design science to construct actionable artifacts. We can utilize our earlier investigations of sensing high-performing software teams with a self-assessment instrument [44], [45]. The Monitor instrument captures a wide set of team performance attributes and influencing factors. By selecting and combining a distinct subset of them here based on the ruling in Table 1, we can produce an indicative performance orientation view of the software development team. Such a self-portrait can then be analyzed with respect to how the team focuses in terms of total quality.

Table 2 presents such a view of the Monitor question items. They are categorized following the hierarchy in Table 1. The rationale part explains how the items address the focal points at each level of the hierarchy.

Table 2. Software team performance Monitor configuration

ITEM	Rationale
Strategic Level	
How important are the following aspects for you in your work? • *Working in the particular application/business domain*	Systemic impacts are understood and discovered. The software products/services are (re)shaped accordingly together with other elements of the total solutions and offerings (e.g., business model).
How do you rate the following organizational factors in your context? • *The organization is flexible and responsive to customer needs.* • *The organization is capable of continuously creating and delivering successful products.*	The whole organization is encouraged to think outside-the-box ("big picture"). The mindset is shifted from current rigidities and limitations towards leveraging the organizational strengths and capital ("can do").

Table 2. (*continued*)

How do you rate the following aspects from your point of view? • *We have a clear, compelling direction that energizes, orients the attention, and engages our full talents.*	Finding (the) most significant and meaningful problems and opportunities to be solved with software is emphasized.
Tactical Level	
How important are the following for your team? • *Doing the right things (products/services providing optimal value)* • *Thinking the total product / service / system*	The role of the software in the product solutions is comprehended. The positioning of the products with the customer/user systems is motivated.
How do you rate the following aspects from your point of view? • *We see how our products bring benefits (value).*	The importance and usefulness of the product to customer/user needs and problems are prompted ("reason for being"). The fitness of the product solution to its purpose and concept of operations is assessed.
How important are the following aspects for you in your work? • *Developing the particular product or service (innovation)*	The purpose of the product drives the software development.
Operational Level	
How do you rate the following concerns? • *How often are you able to see the software (product) in actual use?*	The actual use context and how the user operations utilize the software execution results are observed in real time.
How important are the following for your team? • *Developing user functionality*	The results-driven development is urged.
How do you rate the following concerns? • *We are uncertain about what to implement (requirements/specs).*	Providing the user results directs the software development.
Software PRODUCT Level	
How do you appraise the following team outcomes and impacts? • *Outputs meet the organizational standards and expectations.*	The software implementation is assessed against technical quality criteria (e.g., reliability, response time).
How important are the following for your team? • *The software (design) is easily upgradable and flexible for future development.*	The customer space uncertainties and opportunities are taken into account in design decisions and preparations (e.g., architectural choices). Technical debt is avoided.
How important are the following aspects for you in your work? • *Solving software engineering problems (software design)*	Technical quality can be built in. Excellence in software design is fostered.

Notably, the basic configuration presented here is not intended to be fully fixed. It can be specialized further based on the organizational context and business model aims. For instance, embedded software development organizations may emphasize systems thinking more while interactive consumer product developers could highlight user experience traits [4]. Furthermore, the underlying Monitor instrument is still under continuous improvement.

4 Case Exhibits

This section demonstrates, how the framework proposed in Sect. 3 can be operationalized. We have been utilizing the Monitor instrument earlier in various other case studies to survey software teams for high performance. We can now revisit that raw data by reviewing the data with the configuration defined in Table 2 (i.e., the original data has been collected before the frame here was composed).

There are four such case teams included here. Considering their key demographic information, the team #1 develops embedded system components in a large global company, whereas the team #2 is a dedicated software product development group in a small, domestic company. The team #3 is an embedded software development team working on mass-market consumer products in a medium-size company. The team #4 is in a domestic unit of larger company headquartered abroad. They develop components for system software products of the company.

Tables 3-6 present the Monitor data of the case teams. The tables correspond to the levels defined in Table 1. The organization of each table is as follows: The question blocks are as delineated in Table 2. The items have been extracted from the Monitor described in detail in our initial publication of the instrument [44].

The data shows the number of responses of the team self-ratings. The respondents were grossly team members. The data collection was done midcourse. All responses were anonymous. Note that some respondents skipped some questions.

Table 3. Strategic level team performance perceptions

How important are the following aspects for you in your work?	Very Impor- tant		Impor- tant		Some- what		A little		Unim- portant		n/a	
Working in the particular application/business domain												
Industrial Team #1 [1]	0	0	1	2	2	0	3	1	1	1	0	0
Industrial Team #2	0		0		1		1		2		0	
Industrial Team #3	1		3		5		2		0		1	
Industrial Team #4	1		5		4		2		2		1	
How do you rate the following organizational factors in your context?	Strong- ly Agree		Agree		Neutral		Dis- agree		Strong- ly Dis- agree		I don't know	

---

[1] The industrial team #1 utilized the Monitor two times (in some six months).

Table 3. (*continued*)

The organization is flexible and responsive to customer needs.					
Industrial Team #1	1 1	1 1	3 2	2 0	0 0	0 0
Industrial Team #2	1	2	0	0	0	1
Industrial Team #3	3	5	4	0	0	0
Industrial Team #4	1	11	3	0	0	0
The organization is capable of continuously creating and delivering successful products.					
Industrial Team #1	1 1	4 2	2 1	0 0	0 0	0 0
Industrial Team #2	0	2	1	0	0	1
Industrial Team #3	2	9	0	1	0	0
Industrial Team #4	3	9	3	0	0	0

How do you rate the following aspects from your point of view?	Strongly Agree	Agree	Neutral	Disagree	Strongly Disagree	I don't know
We have a clear, compelling direction that energizes, orients the attention, and engages our full talents.					
Industrial Team #1	- 0	- 2	- 1	- 1	- 0	- 0
Industrial Team #2 [2]	-	-	-	-	-	-
Industrial Team #3	0	8	4	0	0	0
Industrial Team #4	0	11	4	1	0	0

Table 4. Tactical level team performance perceptions

How important are the following for your team?	Key	Important	Relative	Some little	Little	I don't know
Doing the right things (products/services providing optimal value)					
Industrial Team #1	3 2	5 0	2 1	0 1	0 0	0 0
Industrial Team #2	1	4	0	0	0	0
Industrial Team #3	3	8	2	0	0	0
Industrial Team #4	1	10	4	1	0	0
Thinking the total product / service / system					
Industrial Team #1	- 2	- 2	- 0	- 0	- 0	- 0
Industrial Team #2 [2]	-	-	-	-	-	-
Industrial Team #3	1	6	5	1	0	0
Industrial Team #4	2	6	6	2	0	0

How do you rate the following aspects from your point of view?	Strongly Agree	Agree	Neutral	Disagree	Strongly Disagree	I don't know
We see how our products bring benefits (value).					
Industrial Team #1	1 0	4 2	1 1	1 1	0 0	0 0

---

[2] The version of the Monitor that the team used did not include all the items incorporated here.

Table 4. (*continued*)

	Very Important	Important	Somewhat	A little	Unimportant	n/a
Industrial Team #2	0	3	1	0	0	0
Industrial Team #3	3	7	2	0	0	0
Industrial Team #4	2	8	4	2	0	0
How important are the following aspects for you in your work?	Very Important	Important	Somewhat	A little	Unimportant	n/a
Developing the particular product or service (innovation)						
Industrial Team #1	3 1	0 1	3 1	1 0	0 1	0 0
Industrial Team #2	0	1	2	0	1	0
Industrial Team #3	3	5	3	1	0	0
Industrial Team #4	1	8	5	0	1	0

Table 5. Operational level team performance perceptions

How do you rate the following concerns?	Always	Usually	Occasionally	Seldom	Never	I don't know
How often are you able to see the software (product) in actual use?						
Industrial Team #1	2 0	0 1	1 1	1 0	3 2	0 0
Industrial Team #2	0	0	1	0	2	1
Industrial Team #3	6	3	2	1	0	0
Industrial Team #4	7	1	4	2	2	0
How important are the following for your team?	Key	Important	Relative	Some little	Little	I don't know
Developing user functionality						
Industrial Team #1	0 -	4 -	5 -	1 -	0 -	0 -
Industrial Team #2	0	2	2	1	0	0
Industrial Team #3	4	7	1	1	0	0
Industrial Team #4	4	9	3	0	0	0
How do you rate the following concerns?	Always	Usually	Occasionally	Seldom	Never	I don't know
We are uncertain about what to implement (requirements/specs).						
Industrial Team #1 [2]	- -	- -	- -	- -	- -	- -
Industrial Team #2 [2]	-	-	-	-	-	-
Industrial Team #3	0	2	4	6	0	0
Industrial Team #4	0	1	0	8	6	1

In addition, in case of the industrial teams #1 and #3, the Product Owners (PO) of the organization used the Monitor independently of the team (i.e., external view). Table 7 shows their ratings to certain items (c.f., Industrial Team #1, #3 in Tables 3-5). The industrial team #3 has two product owners serving for two different product lines.

Table 6. Software PRODUCT level team performance perceptions

How do you appraise the following team outcomes and impacts?	Key		Impor-tant		Rela-tive		Some little		Little		n/a	
Outputs meet the organizational standards and expectations.												
Industrial Team #1	3	3	5	1	2	0	0	0	0	0	0	0
Industrial Team #2	0		4		1		0		0		0	
Industrial Team #3	0		7		4		1		1		0	
Industrial Team #4	2		8		3		3		0		0	

How important are the following for your team?	Key		Impor-tant		Rela-tive		Some little		Little		I don't know	
The software (design) is easily upgradable and flexible for future development.												
Industrial Team #1	-	1	-	1	-	2	-	0	-	0	-	0
Industrial Team #2 [2]	-		-		-		-		-		-	
Industrial Team #3	1		10		1		1		0		0	
Industrial Team #4	2		10		3		1		0		0	

How important are the following aspects for you in your work?	Very Impor-tant		Impor-tant		Some-what		A little		Unim-portant		n/a	
Solving software engineering problems (software design)												
Industrial Team #1	1	1	6	2	0	1	0	0	0	0	0	0
Industrial Team #2	3		1		0		0		0		0	
Industrial Team #3	7		2		1		0		1		1	
Industrial Team #4	6		6		2		1		0		0	

Table 7. Organizational stakeholder performance perceptions (partial)

How important are the following aspects for you in your work?	Very Impor-tant	Impor-tant	Some-what	A little	Unim-portant	n/a
Working in the particular application/business domain						
Industrial Team #1 PO	0	1	0	0	0	0
Industrial Team #3 PO	0	1	1	0	0	0

How important are the following for your team?	Key	Impor-tant	Rela-tive	Some little	Little	I don't know
Thinking the total product / service / system						
Industrial Team #1 PO	0	1	0	0	0	0
Industrial Team #3 PO	1	0	1	0	0	0

How do you rate the following concerns?	Always	Usually	Occa-sionally	Seldom	Never	I don't know
How often are you able to see the software (product) in actual use?						
Industrial Team #1 PO	0	0	0	1	0	0
Industrial Team #3 PO	1	0	1	0	0	0

In essence, the Monitor views tabulated in Tables 3-7 exhibit, how the case software teams (and their product owners) perceived their product development quality performance space and focus framed in Table 1. We can now reflect their views with respect to Table 2 like follows ('*italics*' as in the respective tables):

- Table 3: Basically all teams seem their organizations to be '*flexible and responsive*' and able to develop '*successful products*'. However, there seems to be some room for clarifying the overall strategic '*direction*' in the organizations. More importantly, the '*business domain*' interests could be strengthened for the total quality thinking.

- Table 4: The software teams tend to appreciate the '*value*' of the product. This is in particular for the consumer product developers (team #3). For the B2B system product teams (#1, #2) it may be more difficult to realize the customer '*benefits*'. This could be an impediment for '*innovation*' idea generation. For the system component team (#4), the view to the '*total product*' may be somewhat limited.

- Table 5: For the system product teams (#1, #2) it may be more difficult to realize the customer perspective, if they are not able to see the whole product system in '*actual use*'. The '*user functionality*' may then remain more distant to them. However, the component team #4 members are hardly ever '*uncertain*' about their requirements, while the consumer product team (#3) perceives to be more often in doubt with their '*specs*'.

- Table 6: The '*organizational standards*' for the direct outputs of the software development may vary depending on the maturity of the organization. In case of the team #1, the organization is an established company with a long history while the team #2 and #3 are in more recent setups. The different nature and life-cycle stage of the products is also reflected in the '*design*' expectations (systems vs. fast-moving consumer products). In general, all teams tend to be motivated to '*software engineering*' (design) work.

- Table 7: The Product Owners tend to have an intrinsic motivation and be interested in the specific product area ('*application/business domain*') with a systems thinking mindset ('*total product*'). However, in case of the industrial team #1, the product owner is not often able to see the entire product system in operational '*use*', which may limit his steering assumptions and insights (even hidden).

- By and large, the software team views (Tables 3-6) can be expected to emphasize the producer space (product level) while the Product Owners (Table 7) may put more weight on the customer space (strategic, tactical, and operational levels). For instance the relative importance of the product domain ('*application/business*') suggests that.

More specifically, it is possible to profile individual teams with respect to how they perceive their quality and performance focus on the different levels of the frame in Table 1. Furthermore, this can be done with more specific lenses by masking the configuration in Table 2. Table 8 shows one such view as an example for the team #4 (repeating the respective data in Tables 3-6) focusing on the orientational mindsets. In this case the team appears to have somewhat stronger interests for the lower levels (product and operational) than the higher business level (tactical and strategic).

Table 8. Team quality focus reflections (Industrial Team #4)

How important are the following …	Very Impor- tant I Key	Impor- tant	Some- what I Rela- tive	A little I Some little	Unim- portant I Little	n/a I I don't know
Working in the particular application/business domain	1	5	4	2	2	1
Developing the particular product or service (innovation)	1	8	5	0	1	0
Developing user functionality	4	9	3	0	0	0
Solving software engineering problems (software design)	6	6	2	1	0	0

The interpretations presented above are mostly provisional done by the author alone. However, although the reasoning has been done retrospectively here, our envisioned approach is to conduct such performance analysis and improvement together with the teams. In general, drawing decisive conclusions based on survey results only is not recommended. By engaging the team into such discussions concerning its quality and performance focus, the total quality thinking can be brought into the software team systematically and consciously using the profile views (like in Table 8) as catalytic questions. In our previous studies with the Monitor, we have observed in particular that often the question items with wide ranges of different answers (even disagreements) tend to be most fruitful areas for further discussions and potential actions. Moreover, continuous improvements call for iterative rounds.

5   Discussion

This work builds on the TQM principle that customer satisfaction is everyone's goal. However, we do acknowledge the fact that TQM has an established meaning and definitions (e.g., BS 7850-1). Our intention is not to redefine that for software teams and organizations, but to facilitate achieving its goal of total customer satisfaction within software-intensive product development.

The purpose of the analysis framework constructed here (Sect. 3) is to bring that in to software teams in order for software-intensive NPD organizations to achieve high(er) performance. The design rationale is to cover broadly key areas to gauge them systematically. Such awareness will make it possible to build holistic quality navigation aids for organizational and team performance development. The general idea is to formulate catalytic questions (probes) triggering discussion and further elaborations by the team members themselves rather than being prescriptive.

The case examples in Sect. 4 illustrate, how the proposed framework can be used to in practice as a performance steering and improvement approach:

1. The software team conducts a self-assessment with the Monitor.
2. The resulting Monitor data is reviewed with the frame in Table 2.

3. The view is analyzed accordingly (Rationale column in Table 2), possibly first by an external facilitator (researcher), but most importantly by the team itself and also with its managers and even customers.
4. If considered necessary, consequent improvement actions are devised to achieve the total quality. This is usually a continuous cycle following the TQM philosophy.

The purpose of this work is not to construct a comprehensive theoretical model of software value and quality. That would require more systematic mapping of the prior research and literature like done for instance for the Software Value Map [34]. Our contribution here is to promote similar multiperspective mindset (economics, business, management, and software engineering) for practicing software teams with actionable instrument support.

Our Monitor-based approach does not give direct answers for the software teams to instruct the improvement actions. That is for the teams themselves to devise and judge. However, the general guidelines in Table 2 are expected to serve as instrumental starting points for the actual development discussions.

We do not measure here, how the team is in its performance. That must be measured otherwise like suggested in Sect. 2. In this work the idea is to charter the overall performance space expanding from the technical software outputs up to systemic quality effects. Aligned measures can then be defined for each level.

Currently the main limitation of the approach is that, in its current stage of development, it has not been validated for prediction [46]. Such external validation could be done by analyzing a larger (statistically significant) set of teams, comparing their Monitor views against their actual performances. However, the key idea of our approach is to gauge individual teams to improve their performance in the specific organization context. Local validation is thus emphasized. At the time of this writing we do not yet have such data available for the case teams (Sect. 4), though.

The indicative items included in the proposed performance orientation frame (Table 2) are based on our prior works on the software team performance development Monitor [44], [45]. The selection criteria are heuristic as explained in Table 2. There are potentially several other items, which could be incorporated. The Software Value Map method could be used to guide and refine the selection more systematically [34]. Currently our level of abstraction is higher, showing the main areas, but the instrumentation could be populated with such deeper value and quality component analysis (e.g., customer life-cycle and user experience attributes). In all, more empirical validation is needed to shape the selection. The industrial case examples in Sect. 4 demonstrate the current explanatory power and potential to drive consequent improvement actions. However, that is not a comprehensive evaluation of the framework.

Table 9 aggregates the premises and key implications of our quality-oriented performance orientation approach (c.f., Table 1). Those may serve as guidelines both in engineering management as well as for organizational development.

Table 9. Key inferences

LEVEL	Problem Definition	Desired Effects	Design Space	Measures	Core Competence
Strategic	Vision, Mission ("Dreams")	Impacts	Business problems, opportunities	Financial, marketing and sales	Systems thinking
Tactical	Needs/Goals	Benefits	Customer problems	Customer satisfaction	Customer needs elicitation
Operational	Requirements	Outcomes	Service problems	User acceptance	Service design
PRODUCT	Specs	Outputs	Software design problems, constraints	Software quality (technical), process	Software engineering, technology development

In conclusion, our proposed line of thinking for software-intensive product quality performance spaces opens up several avenues for NPD/NSD organizations. Industrial software development teams working even in larger companies could stimulate their quality mindset by taking a wider view of their product/service context. Startup companies could begin with more often at the higher levels than the often typical product level in order to recognize most valuable opportunities to serve new customers and markets. Each company should continuously manage and develop the performance portfolio of their teams accordingly. Such holistic understanding should improve the lean and agile project and portfolio management.

Following the reasoning above, we see the following avenues for further development of our propositions constructed here:

- There could be more indicating items in our software team Monitor configuration suggested here (Table 2). Some such potential ones are the following:

  — Strategic: *People know what they must do differently in the future to meet changing business needs.*
  — Tactical: *Know what our customers appreciate most in our software.*
  — Operational: *Product's usefulness to the customer(s)*

- Appropriate measures should be devised and linked to the different levels of the performance management hierarchy (Table 1). Ultimately, they should gauge the software product development to achieve the desired higher-level effects. Some potential measurement types are outlined in Table 9. Moreover, the strength of the different TQM dimensions could be measured [40].
- By analyzing more case teams and collecting also static feedback about the instrumentation by exchanging views with the teams, certain performance development patterns and decision-making rules could possibly be identified at least locally. This would systematize the rationales in Table 2.

- Market-driven and contract-driven software product development environments may differ with respect to their performance drivers (e.g., specifying software requirements). The approach should be contrasted in such different contexts.

6   Conclusion

The aim of this investigation is to build contextual and situation-aware total quality understanding of high-performing software-intensive product development based on teams. This paper takes the standpoint that software is an enabling technology. Consequently, it is not the direct output of the software development but the target execution outcome (results / services) that creates value. Possibly much more value can be created and captured by starting from the customer perspective in the first place. Even more can be achieved by stretching the development outside the typical customer and market interface boundaries. Effective outcomes then bring benefits and further (positive) impacts. The software team quality and performance should be comprehended and steered accordingly.

We have proposed an effects-driven quality and performance orientation framework with provisional instrumentation aids. It is initially devised for software teams, but ultimately the entire product development organization should be geared accordingly.

In all, by taking an advantage of all those traits in combination leads to reframing the entire product development systems of software-intensive NPD organizations with broader views on the products under development by seeing them in the larger business performance context and quality space. Like illustrated in the case examples here, we encourage software organizations to engage their teams to such total quality orienting discussions.

Acknowledgements. This work was supported by TEKES as part of the Cloud Software Program of DIGILE (Finnish Strategic Centre for Science, Technology and Innovation in the field of ICT and digital business).

References

1. Ottosson, S.: Dynamic Product Development – DPD. Technovation 24, 207–217 (2004)
2. Holman, R., Kaas, H.-W., Keeling, D.: The future of product development. The McKinsey Quarterly 3, 28–39 (2003)
3. Buschmann, F.: Value-Focused System Quality. IEEE Software 27(6), 84–86 (2010)
4. Svensson, R.B., Gorschek, T., Regnell, B., Torkar, R., Shahrokni, A., Feldt, R.: Quality Requirements in Industrial Practice – An Extended Interview Study at Eleven Companies. IEEE Trans. on Software Engineering 38(4), 923–935 (2012)
5. Alter, S.: Defining information systems as work systems: implications for the IS field. European Journal of Information Systems 17, 448–469 (2008)
6. Middleton, P., Sutton, J.: Lean Software Strategies: Proven Techniques for Managers and Developers. Productivity Press, USA (2005)

7. Krisnan, V., Ulrich, K.T.: Product Development Decisions: A Review of the Literature. Management Science 47(1), 1–21 (2001)
8. MacCormack, A., Verganti, R., Iansiti, M.: Developing Products on "Internet Time": The Anatomy of a Flexible Development Process. Management Science 47(1), 133–150 (2001)
9. Smith, P.G.: Flexible Product Development: Building Agility for Changing Markets. Jossey-Bass, San Francisco (2007)
10. Adams, D., Hublikar, S.: Upgrade Your New-Product Machine. Research Technology Management 53(2), 55–67 (2010)
11. Patton, J.: Ambiguous Business Value Harms Software Products. IEEE Software 25(1), 50–51 (2008)
12. Lynn, G.S., Morone, J.G., Paulson, A.S.: Marketing and Discontinuous Innovation: The Probe and Learn Process. California Management Review 38(3), 8–37 (1996)
13. Trott, P.: Innovation Management and New Product Development. Pearson Education, USA (2005)
14. Cusumano, M.A.: The Business of Software. Free Press, New York (2004)
15. Browning, T.R.: On Customer Value and Improvement in Product Development Processes. Systems Engineering 6(1), 49–61 (2003)
16. Hertzum, M., Simonsen, J.: Effects-Driven IT Development: Specifying, Realizing, and Assessing Usage Effects. Scandinavian Journal of Information Systems 23(1), 3–28 (2011)
17. Iivari, J., Koskela, E.: The PIOCO Model for Information Systems Design. MIS Quarterly, 401–419 (1987)
18. Posselt, T., Förstl, K.: Success Factors in New Service Development: a Literature Review. Fraunhofer Institute (2011)
19. Hackman, J.R.: Leading Teams: Setting the Stage for Great Performances. Harvard Business School Press, Boston (2002)
20. Petersen, K.: Measuring and predicting software productivity: A systematic map and review. Information and Software Technology 53, 317–343 (2011)
21. Chenhall, R.H., Langfield-Smith, K.: Multiple Perspectives of Performance Measures. European Management Journal 25(4), 266–282 (2007)
22. Jang, J.J., Motwani, J., Margulis, S.T.: IS team projects: IS professionals rate six criteria for assessing effectiveness. Team Performance Management 3(4), 236–243 (1997)
23. Stensrud, E., Myrtveit, I.: Identifying High Performance ERP Projects. IEEE Trans. Software Engineering 29(5), 398–416 (2003)
24. Berlin, J.M., Carlström, E.D., Sandberg, H.S.: Models of teamwork: ideal or not? A critical study of theoretical team models. Team Performance Management 18(5/6), 328–340 (2012)
25. Seddon, P.B., Staples, S., Patnayakuni, R., Bowtell, M.: Dimensions of Information Systems Success. Communications of AIS 2, Article 20 (1999)
26. Kasunic, M.: A Data Specification for Software Project Performance Measures: Results of a Collaboration on Performance Measurement. Technical report TR-012, CMU/SEI (2008)
27. McLeod, L., MacDonnell, S.G.: Factors that Affect Software Systems Development Project Outcomes: A Survey of Research. ACM Computing Surveys 43(4) (2011)
28. Bozdogan, K.: A Comparative Review of Lean Thinking, Six Sigma and Related Enterprise Process Improvement Initiatives. Working paper, 060531. MIT, Cambridge (2006)
29. Winter, M., Szczepanek, T.: Projects and programmes as value creation processes: A new perspective and some practical implications. International Journal of Project Management 26, 95–103 (2008)

30. Ancona, D., Bresman, H.: X-Teams: How to Build Teams that Lead, Innovate, and Succeed. Harvard Business School Press, Boston (2007)
31. Allee, V.: Value Network Analysis and value conversion of tangible and intangible assets. Journal of Intellectual Capital 9(1), 5–24 (2008)
32. Patanakul, P., Shenhar, A.: Exploring the Concept of Value Creation in Program Planning and Systems Engineering Processes. Systems Engineering 13(4), 340–352 (2009)
33. Mossman, A.: Creating value: a sufficient way to eliminate waste in lean design and lean production. Lean Construction Journal, 13–23 (2009)
34. Khurum, M., Gorschek, T., Wilson, M.: The software value map – an exhaustive collection of value aspects for the development of software intensive products. J. Softw. Evol. and Proc. 25, 711–741 (2013)
35. Sawyer, S.: Software Development Teams. Communications of the ACM 47(12), 95–99 (2004)
36. Curtis, B., Krasner, H., Iscoe, N.: A Field Study of the Software Design Process for Large Systems. Communications of the ACM 31(11), 1268–1287 (1988)
37. Sudhakar, G.P., Farooq, A., Patnaik, S.: Soft factors affecting the performance of software development teams. Team Performance Management 17(3/4), 187–205 (2011)
38. Lu, Y., Xiang, C., Wang, B., Wang, X.: What affects information systems development team performance? An exploratory study from the perspective of combined socio-technical theory and coordination theory. Computers in Human Behavior 27, 811–822 (2011)
39. Li, E.Y., Chen, H.-G., Cheung, W.: Total Quality Management in Software Development Process. The Journal of Quality Assurance Institute 14(1), 4–6, 35–41 (2000)
40. Ho, P.V.: Total Quality Management Approach to the Information Systems Development Processes: An Empirical Study. Dissertation, Virginia Polytechnic Institute and State University, USA (2011)
41. Kessler, C., Sweitzer, J.: Outside-in Software Development: A Practical Approach to Building Successful Stakeholder-based Products. IBM Press (2007)
42. Adzic, G.: Impact Mapping: Making a big impact with software products and projects. Provoking Thoughts Limited, UK (2012)
43. Fröberg, J., Cedergren, S., Larsson, S.: What Information on Business Parameters Is Required by Embedded Software Developers to Do an Effective Job? In: Cusumano, M.A., Iyer, B., Venkatraman, N. (eds.) ICSOB 2012. LNBIP, vol. 114, pp. 273–278. Springer, Heidelberg (2012)
44. Kettunen, P., Moilanen, S.: Sensing High-Performing Software Teams: Proposal of an Instrument for Self-monitoring. In: Wohlin, C. (ed.) XP 2012. LNBIP, vol. 111, pp. 77–92. Springer, Heidelberg (2012)
45. Kettunen, P.: The Many Facets of High-Performing Software Teams: A Capability-Based Analysis Approach. In: McCaffery, F., O'Connor, R.V., Messnarz, R. (eds.) EuroSPI 2013. CCIS, vol. 364, pp. 131–142. Springer, Heidelberg (2013)
46. Fenton, N.E., Pfleeger, S.L.: Software Metrics – A Rigorous and Practical Approach. International Thompson Computer Press (1996)

Improving Development Visibility
and Flow in Large Operational Organizations

Jo Ann Lane[1] and Richard Turner[2]

[1] University of Southern California, Los Angeles, CA, USA
[2] Stevens Institute of Technology, Hoboken, NJ, USA
jolane@usc.edu, rturner@stevens.edu

Abstract. In large operational systems, understanding the status of evolutionary capability development is often difficult. This is particularly true where capabilities depend on significant software components that are managed and operated as interacting subsystems. Schedules are rarely stable due to significant external drivers, thus integrated master schedules are hard to maintain and update. On-demand (pull) scheduling methods have been shown to smooth flow and maximize value across a process. The mechanics of these methods enhance visibility by forcing informed discussions on value, capability, and priority and by providing timely, relevant information to higher-level engineering organizations. This paper uses a notional information management system supporting a large health care system as an illustration of a management architecture that supports such an approach. The architecture includes a network of kanban-based scheduling systems, enhanced visualization, and employs a services approach to systems engineering that allows its work to be quantized as part of the overall development flow.

Keywords: systems engineering, software engineering, kanban, pull scheduling, systems of systems, management visibility.

1 The Story So Far…

In the summer of 2011, the US Department of Defense presented the Systems Engineering Research Center with a critical problem: how to replace complex integrated master schedules and plans and provide more effective management within a large, evolving operational system of systems. Additional concerns included the inability of scarce systems engineering (SE) resources to support schedule-driven projects, decisions made late or at a level removed from the context, and a lack of visibility into the status of system-wide capability developments—similar to issues already documented by a defense industry organizations [1]. Lean approaches based on Deming and The Toyota Production System have been deployed in manufacturing for decades and are well documented in the business and academic literature. In the last few years, however, on-demand scheduling techniques, such as the lean practice of *kanban*, have been successfully modified and adapted to support more agile, value-based scheduling in managing software projects [2, 3, 4, 5]. After considering the

B. Fitzgerald et al. (Eds.): LESS 2013, LNBIP 167, pp. 65–80, 2013.

issue, we decided to investigate the compatibility of the lean concepts with the sponsor's needs. Could they be applied to managing systems at a larger scale such as complicated systems of systems, and could they be used for systems engineering activities both at the portfolio and project levels of abstraction? Could they also be used across contracts, where non-governmental organizations were developing individual projects without close inter-project communication?

The result was an investigation into lean management, and a series of thought and simulation experiments on how to scale the kanban concept [6]. These in turn led to the need to consider systems engineering as a service, understand how communication between kanban systems could be accomplished, how to establish the comprehensive and current values for work items, how resources could be shared across kanban systems, and what types of controls were best to manage flow and protect resources [7].

It became apparent that discussions, arguments and whiteboard work were not converging, and it was necessary to apply the ideas to a specific, real environment. This paper describes an architecture for managing flow through a highly specialized information system of systems (SoS) as represented by a large health care system.

2   Concerning Kanban-Based Scheduling System Networks

In [6], we created the fundamental building block of the architecture – The Kanban-based Scheduling System (KSS). Illustrated in Figure 1, the KSS is designed to be replicable as a single system (made up of multiple KSS building blocks) or a network of such systems. Its functional requirements were to:

— Coordinate multiple levels of development activity
— Support analysis and decision making at every level
— Flexibly schedule work considering value across the system of systems
— Balance work in progress (WIP) across resources with organizational capacity to improve flow
— Make visible to all levels progress of capability development and deployment
— Establish a basis for continuous improvement in a rapidly changing environment

The fundamental concept is that each organizational entity adopts a hybrid system and organizational value-driven KSS designed by the organization to meet their specific needs. Each KSS includes a kanban board with specific and public management controls designed to integrate the KSS with others. The kanban board is a working tool used to track work and collect typical statistics such as cumulative flow diagram information. An organization with many sub-organizations may choose to have a dashboard that rolls up the information from the LSSs within it (or tasked by it) into a more informative visual tool. Such dashboards act as information radiators at all levels of development activity. The result of the system is that each KSS provides current, consistent information that flows up, down and across the organizations as needed.

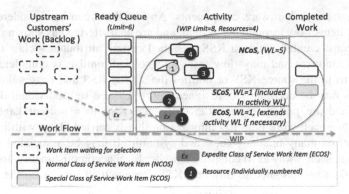

Fig. 1. The KSS Building Block [6]

Each KSS has a single backlog of unlimited length and a single acceptance queue with a capacity-informed limit. Each also has a queue where completed items are reacquired by the source KSS or forwarded to a downstream KSS. The organizational KSS may include lower-level KSSs if appropriate. Table 1 shows the template designed to characterize a KSS within the network.

Table 1. KSS Summary Template

KSS Name			
Demand:			
Work sources	Organizations that can assign work items to the KSS		
Resources:			
Dedicated	Resources under control of this KSS		
Shareable	Resources available to share on teams with other orgs		
Sourced	Organizations (KSSs) to which work items can be assigned		
Managed resources	Any specialists that are managed individually		
Activities:			
Description	WIP Limit	Resource Type	Cohesion
		Internal, Sourced, or X-discipline team	Interruptible or Must complete
Flow and Visibility:			
Additional CoS handled	CoS beyond the system-wide that are recognized by this KSS		
Additional CoS introduced	CoS defined for work this org assigns to other KSSs		
Work Selection Value Adjustments:			
Source-based	CoS-based	Resource-based	Completion-based
Goals	From GQK analysis		
Questions answered	From GQK analysis		
Data maintained/used	From GQKanalysis		
Information shared	e.g. Avg. Lead time, Avg. blocked tasks. Avg. time blocked		

2.1   Work Items

In most systems of systems, capabilities are identified at a high level. Systems engineering decomposes these into requirements, which are further decomposed into software features or hardware components. Any of these can be considered a work item. Work items flow through the system, and are characterized as shown in Table 2. A work item is created within a KSS, assigned certain attributes – class of service, value, associations – and may flow from KSS to KSS until it is complete and then either returns to the source KSS or notifies the source KSS and passes downstream. Work items may be decomposed, assigned to (or selected by) individual or multiple resources, and are pulled through the individual KSS in a normal kanban board fashion. While each work item has information that is carried along with it, its value is dependent on many factors – local and systemic. It may be associated with other work items in such a way as to comprise a higher level accomplishment – for example several work items assigned to different KSSs may actually make up the necessary features to meet a particular requirement.

Table 2. Generic Work Item

Identification	Date required	Date completed
Work Item Identifier		
Date Created	Resources Assigned	
Date Entered Current Backlog		
Provenance		
Capability Ids		
Requirement Ids		
Demand Source		
Description		
Work To Do		
Specialties Required		
Estimated Effort		
Value/Priority		
Base Value		
KSSN Class Of Service	BLOCKED	
Adjusted Class Of Service		
Adjusted Selection Value	Reason blocked	

2.2   Network Flow

Work items flow by negotiation between the KSSs, with each organization agreeing to what is essentially a service contract for the work item. Backlog mechanics operate with mutually agreed to rules as to when and how prioritization and selection take place. Value parameters and functions, Classes of Service, and service level agreements may be established as network wide or KSS controls. Network-wide controls generally take precedence over local controls. The network also communicates the status of each work item as it flows through the system.

It should be noted that this is not a value stream analysis nor model. It is, however, a scheduling system that if used correctly, may identify the type of information often sought in such analyses from the current data on the kanban boards and dashboards.

Because kanban concepts have been primarily used with single level value streams, we wanted to understand the information needed for decision making, including scheduling and flow monitoring/control, at each level of SE activity or utilization. This would allow us to construct a KSS that would support visualization of WIP and status for each specific level. It would also provide insight into the information flow required. To accomplish this, we turned to the Basili, Caldieri, and Rombach Goal-Question-Metric approach [8, 9]. For each level we defined the goals and the questions that made sense to ask in order to determine if the goals were being met. Given our research is to investigate KSSs, we decided to fully utilize the metrics available from flow and pull concepts. To acknowledge this, we affectionately referred to the results as goal-question-kanban (G-Q-K) information.

2.3   Systems Engineering as a Service?

The idea of applying SE as a service within an on-demand scheduling system is not as farfetched as it may seem to some systems engineers. It effectively merges the SE flow and the software development project flow. These services act as any other work item in the KSS. SE performs early definitional activities, like operational concepts, architecture, and functional allocation. Other activities are ongoing like incremental verification and validation. Still others are performed at the request of a project and include trade studies, specialty engineering (like safety or security), and impact assessments. All involve maintenance and evolution of long-term, persistent artifacts that support development across multiple projects.

With the knowledge in these persistent artifacts, SE can be opportunistic in applying its cross-project view and understanding of the larger environment to specific projects individually or in groups. It can also broker information between individual projects where there may be contractual or access barriers. When a system-wide issue or external change occurs, SE can ensure that the broader issue is handled in an effective and compatible way [7].

3   The Health Care System Environment

We decided to use a health care system as the target for our prototypical architecture because of its similarity to many operational defense and intelligence community. systems. The target system is a set of integrated medical information management systems. It consists of hardware, over two million lines of source code, numerous commercial-off-the shelf (COTS) software products and communications networks. Its primary goal is to support the administration and delivery of health care in networked set of hospitals and clinics in a timely and safe manner, coordinating a variety of providers and specialists.   Key overarching requirements are to ensure patient safety and protect patient information according to regulations.

The Health Care Development Organization is around 1000 engineering professionals, some of whom are out-sourced, consists of three groups. The *systems engineering group* performs analyses related to new or enhanced capabilities, requirements development and allocation, evaluations of medical devices for integration, system performance assessments and upgrade recommendations, deployed and development networks, specialty engineering, SoS-level integration and acceptance testing. *Product teams* are responsible for software maintenance and enhancement for the custom constituent systems or products; database structures and embedded procedures, COTS product tailoring, integration, and upgrades; licensed data upgrades such as pharmacy approved formularies; and, responding to issues beyond the scope of the user help desk. The *user support group* runs the help desk, site configuration management, and site installations and upgrades.

Key custom software includes user access management, patient management, pharmacy, laboratory, radiology, and patient telemetry. The constituent systems share a single database that maintains the information for all of the patients and personnel related to a given health care site. There are also interfaces to other health care systems, including custom legacy systems, COTS products, and electronic medical devices such as heart rate monitors and infusion pumps.

The current systems engineering and software engineering organizations are fully staffed with respect to development budget. When new needs or capabilities are identified, systems engineering analyzes the new needs/capabilities in terms of the given systems and decides how address them. Often multiple new needs/capabilities are analyzed together to facilitate the identification of common solutions that can support more than one need/capability as well as support performance upgrades and technology refresh. The results of the analysis activities are a set of requirements. The next step in the process is to allocate those requirements to one or more products for implementation. Figure 2 provides an example that illustrates how multiple requirements are derived from one or more needs and then mapped to the enterprise products for implementation.

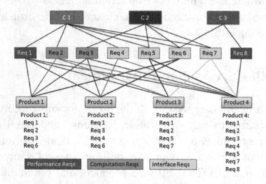

Fig. 2. Capabilities to requirements to products

Once the requirements are allocated to the products, the product teams analyze them and convert them into features and stories for implementation. Systems engineering monitors the capability "pieces" to guide their system integration and testing activities. When all of the capability requirements are implemented in the affected products and deployed, the mission capability is considered "completed."

Several issues exist. There is no visibility at the capability level showing which user stories are related to which capabilities and which products are implementing pieces of the capability. The systems engineering resources are hampered by variable, multiple tasks, and rapidly changing priorities. Software tasks become blocked waiting for systems engineering tasks to complete. As a result, started tasks are difficult to complete in a timely manner.

4   The Health Care KSS Network

The KSS Network prototype defines a 3-tiered management architecture:

1. Executive/Stakeholder Management (ESM)
2. Capability Engineering (CE)
3. Product/Domain Engineering (PDE)

Figure 3 provides an overview of the Health Care System KSS-network showing function levels, KSS elements for monitoring and control, and Dashboards for providing information from multiple KSSs.

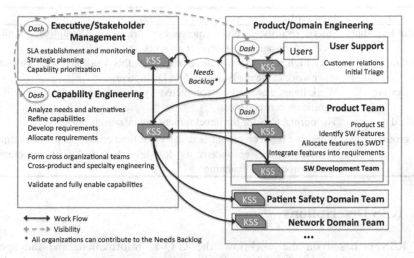

Fig. 3. Overview of KSS Network

Classes of service (CoSs) provide a variety of handling options for different types of work and affect the next work item selection value for KSSs. They may be aligned with Service Level Agreement priorities. Most CoSs are intended to ensure priority rather than force immediate execution. There are CoSs that are disruptive–that is, they can suspend current work in progress. These are associated with critical or expedited work to allow swarming of all appropriate resources to ensure completion as soon as possible. However, disruptive CoSs are minimized because they counter the normal kanban philosophy of completing work rather than interrupting it. While most CoSs are shared across the entire KSS network, individual KSSs may define additional *KSS-Specific* CoSs to handle flow specific to their types of work. Table 3 shows the COSs that apply to all the work in the KSS Network.

The calculation of the selection value of each work item depends on its inherent static value as assigned at it's creation, it's inherited value by being associated with the value the requirements and capabilities it supports, and the state of the development process (e.g. the status of capabilities, requirements and other work items). One simple calculation of this could be:

$Vt = Vinh + Vstat + Vbase$; where $Vinh$ = Sum of all the current values of the requirements the work item supports (with each requirement also includes additional value for multiple capabilities that it supports); $Vstat$ = Adjustments due to the status of work, such as additional value added for near completion of requirements or capabilities, or a negotiated value between the work item owner and the work provider (an example might be the reduction of value to group certain work items that require special handling like certification); and, $Vinit$ is the initial value defined. Regardless of the value, the item's current class of service controls the rules by which the work item may be selected.

Table 3. General Classes of Service

CoS	Description
Critical Expedite	Safety, security, or other emergency work items. <u>Disruptive</u>: requires necessary resources to stop current work and complete it.
Important	Very high priority work items such that this work takes priority over other work in the ready queue. Not Disruptive.
Date Certain	Work items that must be completed by a specific date or there will be significant consequences.
Standard	The normal CoS for the development organizations work.
Background	Work that must go on but is usually not time critical. It includes things like architectural enhancements, low-level technical debt, or research and environmental scanning

5   KSS Descriptions

Each KSS is based on the workflow, the G-Q-K information, and the special circumstances and needs of each organization of resources represented by the KSS. There are nearly as many ways to define a KSS as there are to define a system. We simply recommend processes and visualizations appropriate to our target organization. Each description includes a summary, process flow descriptions, and visualization tools.

5.1   Executive/Stakeholder Management (ESM)

The ESM level determines which proposed capabilities (or capability enhancements) are going to be approved for development. As part of this process, ESM assesses the value of the capability against its expected cost and schedule to develop. This highest-level in the KSS network is concerned primarily with the current status of identified capabilities (or needs) as represented by the development state of each "not fully deployed" but "approved for development" capability – essentially WIP. At this level, the KSS is tracking capabilities and their priority. The insight it provides should inform decisions about overall organizational strategy, resource staffing, and development funding priorities. Table 4 provides the ESM KSS Summary.

Accepting/Selecting Next Work Item. Requests for system capabilities come from the users, systems engineering groups, and strategic initiatives. There is always a backlog of ideas needs, and wants. ESM must identify the highest priority capabilities. They must balance adding new capabilities with improving existing system capabilities and maintaining the infrastructure. They must also act on critical issues regarding patient safety, infrastructure failure, and regulatory changes. The outcome of this process is sending only the highest value and most critical work to the systems engineering group to analyze and develop.

Table 4. ESM KSS Template

Executive/Stakeholder Management KSS			
Demand:			
Work sources	Needs backlog, Stakeholders, Critical Events, Strategic Plans		
Resources:			
Dedicated	IT Managers, CTO, …		
Shareable	None		
Sourced	CE		
Managed resource specialties	None		
Activities:			
Description	*WIP Limit*	*Resource Type*	*Cohesion*
Capability Analysis		Sourced (CE)	Interruptible
Capability Prioritization-CoS Assignment		Internal	Must complete
Capability Development Project		Sourced (CE)	Interruptible
Flow and Visibility:			
Additional CoS handled	None		
Additional CoS introduced	None		
Work Selection Value Adjustments			
Source-based	*CoS-based*	*Resource-based*	*Completion-based*
None	None	None	None
Goals	G1. Deploy capabilities according to value-based priorities and CoS. G2. Understand source/cause of blocked work flows G3. Strategic IT decisions based on current and projected WIPs and backlogs (examples might include investments in additional resources (hardware, tools, people) or decisions to drop lower priority capabilities). G4. Changing needs and priorities are integrated with existing strategy		
Questions answered	Q1. What capabilities are currently in progress? Q2: What capabilities are currently blocked? Q3: What capabilities are pending acceptance? Q4. Are the planned and actual values of each deployed capability tracking? Q5: Are the current WIP level for ESM activities correct? Q6. What is the average time to completion for "accepted" capabilities by CoS? Q7. What is the requirements volatility by capability? Q8. What KSSs show capacity not meeting demand? Q9: What KSSs indicate excess capacity?		
Data maintained/used	KSS1: Flow data on CE and Product Teams* KSS2: Average time to deploy capabilities for each CoS priority level KSS3: Relationships between capabilities and requirements KSS4: Status of requirement completion/deployment KSS5: % of requirements completed/deployed for each in-process capability KSS6: Status of SE tasks supporting capability acceptance decisions *Includes CFD (throughput, WIP, Lead time), backlog level, resource utilization, blocked tasks, and similar data.		
Information shared	Capabilities under development, CFDs for each Capability, Network Value Tracking,		

Some work items initiated within the ESM level are special studies related to the prioritization of capabilities and the possible combination of multiple needs into a more effective capability need. This work includes cost and schedule estimations, Ops Concept development, COTS evaluations, and other traditional early SE activities.

Allocating Resources and Team Development. ESM must understand the overall capacity, work in progress, and resource distribution across CE and PDE teams in order to determine the highest priority capabilities and decide how to meet strategic needs and balance ongoing tasks. Starting too many capability developments can lead to less effective execution, while starting too few may jeopardize stakeholder satisfaction. This organization must work closely with the CE organization and User Support to map the landscape reflected in the needs backlog.

Completion and Disbursement. While the decision to deploy is a systems engineering or PDE decision, the declaration of a capability being "finished" (i.e. fully implemented and deployed) is usually reserved for the ESM.

KSS review at this level examines the work in progress, demand, capacity, and performance to ensure it is focused on achieving capabilities and handling critical events. Resource management, including budgeting, requires an understanding of how development resources are being utilized throughout the system, what is in the backlog of desired capabilities, and areas where there is excess capacity or capacity is insufficient for the projected demand. Budgeting is a factor in determining how much demand is realistic regardless of capacity. Strategic changes to resource mix across the SoS may be needed through hiring, contracting, or moving resources.

5.2   Capability Engineering (CE)

CE represents all capability-related SE activities, specialty SE support for product teams, including software system engineering tasks, where software is a key component in the requirements allocation. CE is responsible for creating capability descriptions that incorporate the needs identified and prioritized by the ESM level. CE must balance the various SE resources as they work with both internal activities and lead cross-organizational teams in CE-related activities. Decisions and scheduling of the SE resources must include front-end and ongoing architectural work as well as supporting development, integration, verification and validation with product teams.

The CE KSS represents multiple levels of activity and may choose to break into multiple KSSs as the complexity grows. However, the initial concept is a single KSS that handles a variety of different activities. First, the CE must respond to the ESM requests for analysis and SE support to ESM decision activities and for the development of capabilities that are the highest priority to the SoS. The CE also provides SoS analysis support to the various PDE Teams and manages the limited number of SoS specialty engineering resources. Given the goals associated with this level, both the kanban board and the dashboard will be somewhat "busy" in terms of information. Table 5 presents the CE KSS template.

Accepting/Selecting Next Work Item. As requests come in for systems engineering services, they are accepted, roughly estimated, possibly broken into smaller tasks, and valued. An additional CoS is assigned as necessary and then the work items are added to the backlogs for the appropriate resource. Queue length limits are usually maintained for backlogs, and the level of the queue in terms of a percentage is a reasonable measure of demand.

Allocating Resources and Team Development. Many CE tasks will require a team with expertise in one or more specialty engineering areas or may require collaborative support from one or more PDE Team SEs. The CE negotiates with the appropriate teams for the specific resources they need. CoS, nearness to completion of the requirement, and other factors are considered. For requests from software teams, the special software CoS is applied as described in the summary. Capability Requirements Development work items are created, sourced to the various PDE Teams, and tracked to completion. Any negotiation required is accomplished before CE or the PDE Team accepts the work.

Completion and Disbursement. As CE completes ESM analysis work items, they are delivered directly to the ESM and identified as "done" on both the ESM and CE boards. Analysis tasks from PDTs are handled the same way. Work sourced to the PDE Teams may be completed and deployed by the PDE Team. The PDE Team will share data to update the CE KSS and Dashboard. There could be an activity to provide requirement completion verification and validation within the CE KSS, but in this initial concept, it is handled within PDE. Data is passed to the ESM dashboard.

KSS Review. Walking the CE KSS involves tracking the work in progress, identifying flow problems and blockages, resolving resource issues and blockages, and monitoring the demand queue so that when resources are available the next most valuable piece of work is accepted. The review tracks the WIP-level and demand for specialty resources to avoid blockage, overwork, or underutilization. Work items should be scanned for adjustment to work value or priority on completion-based criteria. Technical or PDE Team issues should be reviewed, and often it is good to include members of critical PDE Teams in the review.

5.3   Product/Domain Engineering (PDE)

At the PDE level, there are separate KSSs for each product or domain team in the enterprise. The PDE KSSs are similar to those used in many software development organizations today, with the added requirement for systems engineering within the product or domain scope. Constituent systems/products need to provide information to higher level KSSs and dashboards all the way to the ESM level.

The User Support (US) Team operates at the PDE level because it interfaces with the product and domain teams. There are occasions, however, when it influences the needs backlogs, or when it uncovers an issue (e.g. patient safety or privacy) that requires engagement with ESM and CE to handle the solution. Each product or domain team is responsible for responding to problems the US team can't handle.

Each product team creates its own organization. If outsourced, contractual requirements and its corporate governance influence the KSS implementation. For example, if the company operating the product team uses a matrix organization for SE, they may create a separate KSS for the SE resources that might cross product team boundaries. If the SE resources are each dedicated to a specific product, then their tasks can be included in the product or the software development KSS.

Table 5. CE KSS Template

Capability Engineering KSS			
Demand:			
Work sources	ESM, PDT, Internal		
KSS Resources:			
Dedicated	SoS SEs, Specialist SoS SEs (performance, algorithms, interface, security…)		
Shareable	Most		
Sourced	PDE Teams		
Managed resources	Specialty SoS SEs (performance, algorithms, interface, security…)		
Activities:			
Description	*WIP Limit*	*Resource Type*	*Cohesion*
Capability Analysis		X-discipline team	Interruptible
Operational Concept Development		Internal, X-discipline team	Interruptible
Capability Requirements Creation		Internal, X-discipline team	Interruptible
Capability Requirement Development		Sourced	Interruptible
Special Engineering Services		Internal (managed)	Interruptible
Flow and Visibility:			
Additional CoS handled	Software Service CoS: One of the issues identified was the amount of time product tasks were blocked waiting for SoSE (CE) support. This CoS is applied to all Specialty Engineering Services work items from PTs with significant software components. The CoS is not interruptible and provides a guaranteed WIP capacity. Resource reallocation is allowed to meet this CoS.		
Additional CoS introduced	None		
Work Selection Value Adjustments			
Source-based	*CoS-based*	*Resource-based*	*Completion-based*
None	None	None	Value of work items associated with requirements or capabilities within 15% of completion are raised by 10% at selection cadence points
Goals	G1. Cost-effective, timely alternatives identified for new capabilities/enhancements G2. Adaptable, flexible, multi-purpose solutions for new capabilities/enhancements G3. Specialty engineering responses to software teams' SE requests do not create excessive delays in capability development G4. Provide quick response to changing needs and priorities		
Questions answered	Q1. What work is currently blocked? Q2. What is the % of capabilities that are deployed within the desired timeframe? Q3. What is the predicted time to completion for "accepted" CE tasks (by class of service)? Q4. Where is capacity not meeting demand (by capability specialty engineering discipline)? Q5: Where is there excess capacity (by capability specialty engineering discipline)? Q6: What is the age of items in the CE backlog queues? Q7. What are the current CE WIP levels? Q8. What are the current CE backlog levels? Q9. What is the balance between CE WIP and CE backlog?		
Data maintained/used	KSS1: Number/status of tasks in product-level queues (analysis, backlog, WIP, blocked) KSS2: Number of tasks in product-level queues blocking other tasks (e.g., dependent tasks) KSS3: Relationships between capabilities, requirements, and features at product level KSS4: Percentage of each in-process requirement already completed/deployed KSS5: Average User Support request task completion time		
Information shared	Requirements allocation, status and deployment data; CE and PDE flow information		

User and site support personnel interact directly with the users and other operational stakeholders for the system of systems. They provide insight and triage for user requests; they aggregate and categorize desired capabilities or required maintenance actions, and forward them for resolution to the CE or PDE Teams as appropriate.

The *US KSS* is set up to manage the resources of the personnel handling the triage function and to identify critical issues rapidly. They track issues to completion and support information requests on the status of specific issues. This KSS is modeled on the system developed by Joshua Bloom at The Library Corporation, and the authors appreciate his support in this research. Table 6 provides the US KSS Template.

Accepting/Selecting Next Work Item. US is the connection between the development system and the user population. Many user calls do not require development and are managed through the US KSS alone. Tickets for problems that require technical development work are written up and entered into the KSS demand queue. Initial estimations are of the "t-shirt size" variety and tickets are classified according to product, domain or other attribute. Any tickets critical to patient safety or require expedited activity are immediately handed off to the ESM, CE, and PDE teams to swarm and resolve quickly. Otherwise, initial classes of service are assigned.

Allocating Resources and Team Development. Once a ticket is entered into the demand queue, it is determined to be product specific and sent to a PDE team, it is determined to involve multiple products/domains and is entered into the ESM needs backlog as a systems of systems capability issue, or, it is not immediately understood and so sent to the SoS team to analyze and recommend action. All such tickets are maintained in the KSS as in-process work and tracked through the system to completion so US can provide feedback on its status to users.

Table 6. User Support KSS Template

User Support KSS			
Demand:			
Work sources	User requests		
Resources:			
Dedicated	Help Desk Personnel, SW/System Engineers		
Shareable	None		
Sourced	PDE Teams, CE		
Managed resource specialties	SW/System Engineers may be handled as managed resource specialists		
Activities:			
Description	*WIP Limit*	*Resource Type*	*Cohesion*
Call Reception and triage		Internal	Must complete
Secondary ticket review		Internal	Interruptible
Ticket assignment		Internal	Interruptible
Flow and Visibility:			
Additional CoS handled	None		
Additional CoS introduced	None		
Work Selection Value Adjustments			
Source-based	*CoS-based*	*Resource-based*	*Completion-based*
None	None	None	None
Goals	Not yet addressed		
Questions answered	Not yet addressed		
Data maintained	Not yet addressed		
Information shared	Not yet addressed		

Completion and Disbursement. When PDE Team or CE development work is done, the US advises the ticket requestor(s) the ticket has been resolved and provides a resolution to the user: a software patch, workaround, or fix deployment date.

KSS Review is focused on the ability to effectively triage and assign tickets. Surveillance of the status of the technical work that entered through the US KSS provides a measure of response time to user requests and may be accompanied by user satisfaction information. Because of the rapidity with which most help desk activities occur, the dashboard provides the information of a kanban board.

The *PDE Product Teams* are responsible for one or more of the Health Care System products. The teams include systems engineers, specialty engineers, software engineers, hardware engineers, and often subject matter experts that support feature determination and development. System of system capabilities may require multiple product teams to create or enhance features, implement similar features in different ways, or collaborate to develop a common solution for the specific systems. If CE is the heart of the system of systems, the product team is the arms and legs.

A PT KSS is focused on maintaining the product at a high level of effectiveness and evolving it to support system capabilities as well as product capabilities. There is always some tension among the new feature development, older feature enhancement, and typical maintenance that is required in a technology and safety critical environment. The KSS uses the various CoS defined for the system to manage flow so that major capability developments proceed at a reasonable pace without significant impact on ongoing project level work. Table 7 provides the PT KSS Template.

Accepting/Selecting Next Work Item. Selection at this level is all about balancing: the capacity with the demand, new work with ongoing activity, and SoS value with product value. While selection decisions are supported by the inherited value determination and CoSs, the product teams still negotiate the flow. The sourcing customers and PT members look at the mix of tasks in the demand queue, evaluating each according to the system values, product values and resources available, as well as considering what items represent the final parts of a requirement or capability.

Allocating Resources and Team Development. Most of the PT work is performed by groups of resources, often in a multi-discipline project team. Individual SE resources must also be available to participate in the cross-discipline/cross-system teams used in the CE in capability analysis, so there may be a reason to apply some sort of Project-level CoS that reserves some capacity for supporting those activities.

Completion and Disbursement. Since PTs are responsible for integration, V&V and deployment, their kanban board addresses these activities. Data on status, acceptance and availability for inclusion of the various work items in completing capability implementation is always provided upstream to the sourcing KSS.

KSS Review. Walking the kanban board and reviewing the dashboard at the product level consists of looking for blocked work—resource conflict issues, sourcing delays, and rework are the main sources here. If the PT cannot complete work items within the established statistical bounds, changes must be made quickly to balance demand.

Table 7. Product Team KSS Template

Product Team			
Demand:			
Work sources	US, CE, Internal, other PDE Teams		
Resources:			
Dedicated	SEs, HW and SW developers		
Shareable	SEs		
Sourced	SW Developers (SDPT), Specialty Engineers (CE), Domain Specialists		
Managed resource specialties	Varies by team		
Activities:			
Description	*WIP Limit*	*Resource Type*	*Cohesion*
Requirements analysis & feature definition		Internal, X-discipline team	Interruptible
Feature development and integration		Internal, Sourced	Interruptible
Requirements V&V		Internal, Sourced	Interruptible
Deployment		Internal, Sourced	Must complete
Flow and Visibility:			
Additional CoS handled	Software Service CoS: One of the issues identified was the amount of time product tasks were blocked waiting for SoSE (CE) support. This CoS is applied to all Specialty Engineering Services work items from software PTs. The CoS is not interruptible and provides a guaranteed WIP capacity. Resource reallocation is allowed to meet this CoS.		
Additional CoS introduced	Certification required – Applies where work is bundled to prevent costly recertification.		
Work Selection Value Adjustments			
Source-based	*CoS-based*	*Resource-based*	*Completion-based*
Varies by team	Varies by team	Varies by team	Support to work associated with requirements or capabilities within 15% of completion are raised by 10% at selection cadence points
Goals	G1. Capability-allocated requirements are developed and deployed according to value G2: Product requirements/features allocated to increments and spins based on value G3. Product team responds quickly to changing product needs and priorities G4. Minimize workflow disruptions in product increments and spins G5. Minimize rework due to poorly understood capability requirements G6. Product team provides timely responses to user support issues/problems		
Questions answered	Q1. Value of product-level work currently blocked? Q2. What is the % of requirements completed within the desired timeframe? Q3. Where is PT capacity not meeting demand? Q4. Where is there excess PT capacity? Q5. How often is the average item age in product backlogs outside expected levels? Q6. What are the current product-level WIP levels? Q7. What are the current product-level backlog levels? Q8. What is the product-level response time to SW requests?		
Data maintained	KSS1: Flow data on Product Team* KSS2: Number/status of tasks in demand queues KSS3: Number of tasks in product-level activities that are blocking other tasks KSS4: Relationships between capabilities, requirements, and features at product level KSS5: Percentage of each in-process requirement already completed/deployed KSS6: Average User Support request task completion time *Includes CFD (throughput, WIP, Lead time), backlog level, resource utilization, blocked tasks, and similar data.*		
Information shared	Flow data on Product Team*		

6   Conclusions and Further Research

Much of this work has been engaged in thinking through the various scenarios that exist in highly complex system development, sustainment and evolution. The team is convinced of the validity, and is moving forward with the research, pending further funding. We have begun to develop simulations of this KSS instantiation, and have initiated conversations with major aerospace companies to support a multi-stage analysis, investigation and piloting of the concept.

Acknowledgements. This material is based upon work supported, in whole or in part, by the U.S. Department of Defense through the Systems Engineering Research Center (SERC) under Contract H98230-08-D-0171. SERC is a federally funded University Affiliated Research Center managed by Stevens Institute of Technology. Addressing the problems also required support from practitioners and experts. A volunteer industrial working group provided their experience to the research. Of particular value were David Anderson, Curt Hibbs, Suzette Johnson, Don Reinertsen, and Jim Sutton.

References

1. NDIA-National Defense Industrial Association. Top Systems Engineering Issues In US Defense Industry. Systems Engineering Division Task Group Report (September 2010), http://www.ndia.org/Divisions/Divisions/SystemsEngineering/Documents/Studies/Top%20SE%20Issues%202010%20Report%20v11%20FINAL.pdf
2. Poppendiek, M.: Implementing Lean Software Development. Addison Wesley, Boston (2007)
3. Larman, C., Vodde, B.: Scaling Lean & Agile Development. Addison Wesley, Boston (2009)
4. Anderson, D.: Kanban: Successful Evolutionary Change for Your Technology Business. Blue Hole Press, Sequim (2010)
5. Reinertsen, D.G.: The Principles of Product Development Flow. Celeritas Publishing, Redondo Beach (2010)
6. Turner, R., Madachy, R., Ingold, D., Lane, J.: Improving Systems Engineering Effectiveness in Rapid Response Development Environments. In: Proceedings of the International Conference on Software and System Process 2012 (2012)
7. Turner, R., Madachy, R., Ingold, D., Lane, J., Anderson, D.: Effectiveness of kanban approaches in systems engineering within rapid response environments. In: Proceedings of the Conference on Systems Engineering Research 2012, Procedia Computer Science, vol. 8. Elsevier (March 2012)
8. Basili, V., Weiss, D.: A Methodology for Collecting Valid Software Engineering Data. IEEE Transactions on Software Engineering 10(3), 728–738 (1984)
9. Basili, V.R., Seaman, C.: Metric-Based Quality Management. Software Engineering for Embedded Systems Series, Fraunhofer IESE, Kaiserslautern, Germany (2010)

A Brief History of Budgeting: Reflections on Beyond Budgeting, Its Link to Performance Management and Its Appropriateness for Software Development

Garry Lohan

J.E. Cairnes School of Business and Economics
NUI Galway, Newcastle Road, Ireland
garry.lohan@nuigalway.ie

Abstract. Beyond Budgeting is an innovation from the management accounting literature that seeks to improve performance and manage organisations through flexible sense-and-respond type mechanisms, rather than the more rigid traditional command-and-control models. This contemporary thinking in management accounting resonates strongly with contemporary thinking in information systems development (ISD). In particular, the Beyond Budgeting model shares many similarities with agile software development (ASD) with both having a distinctly agile and flexible foundation. This paper discusses the history of Beyond Budgeting, its relationship with performance management and its appropriateness for the field of software development.

Keywords: Beyond Budgeting, Budgeting, Performance Management, Agile Methods.

1   Introduction

Budgeting is regarded as the cornerstone of the management control process [1, 2] and is one of the most extensively researched topics in management accounting [1-5]. The management accounting literature identifies multiple uses for budgets in organisations, such as performance management and evaluation, strategy implementation, and strategy formation, etc. yet, despite the fact that budgeting is so widely used, recent years have seen the traditional, annual budget subjected to much adverse criticism [6, 7]. Practitioners express concerns about the entire budgeting process, arguing that budgets impede the allocation of organisational resources to their best uses and encourage myopic decision making and other dysfunctional budget games [1]. Tensions exist within firms regarding the importance of, and reason to budget [4]. For example, firms that face competitive conditions find the budget important for communication of goals and strategy formation but the same competitive conditions negatively affect the importance of budgets for performance evaluation. Although relatively few organisations are planning to abandon the annual budget, it is widely accepted that the traditional budgeting model is cumbersome and ineffective [6]. The major criticisms are that traditional budgeting is incapable of meeting the demands of the competitive environment in the information age, it is

B. Fitzgerald et al. (Eds.): LESS 2013, LNBIP 167, pp. 81–105, 2013.

cumbersome and too expensive, and the extent of "gaming the numbers" has risen to unacceptable levels [8]. Ekholm and Wallin [6], Dugdale and Lyne [9] and Hansen et al. [1] identify the following criticisms relating to the annual budget process.

- Budgets are time-consuming to put together.
- Budgets constrain responsiveness and are often a barrier to change.
- Budgets are rarely strategically focused and often contradictory.
- Budgets add little value, especially given the time required to prepare them.
- Budgets concentrate on cost reduction and not value creation.
- Budgets strengthen vertical command-and-control.
- Budgets do not reflect the emerging network structures that organisations are adopting.
- Budgets encourage gaming and perverse behaviour.
- Budgets are developed and updated too infrequently, usually annually.
- Budgets are based on unsupported assumptions and guesswork.
- Budgets reinforce departmental barriers rather than encourage knowledge sharing.
- Budgets make people feel undervalued.

Others are also starting to take a closer look at the budgeting process and are beginning to question its value [10-13]. A series of articles in the MIT Sloan Management Review has called for a new approach to strategic management [14-17]. A "pragmatic, coherent approach to thinking about change" is called for [18]. McFarland [18] suggests that strategic planning managers should follow the example from the software community, who realised the problems with the traditional systems development models and invented new development processes (agile methods) to confront the new realities facing them. He says that "the insights upon which new software development approaches are based may point the way for the development of newer, faster and more effective strategy-making processes".

In the next section we take a look at the evolution of budgeting, beginning with the traditional management process. Section 3 discusses the introduction of the Beyond Budgeting model and its theoretical underpinnings. We then explore the need for Beyond Budgeting in ASD before looking at existing research on Beyond Budgeting and conclude with some observations on past and future trends.

2   Evolution of Budgeting

2.1   Traditional Budgeting Process

A budget process is defined as a system of rules governing the decision making that leads to a budget, from its formulation, through its approval, to its execution (Figure 1) [19]. The budgeting process frequently consumes six months of management time in negotiations, planning and target-setting [7].   The process begins with a formulation of the mission statement and strategic plans of the organisation for the year. Once these are in place, budget packs are sent out from corporate centre to operating divisions and an entire process of meetings and negotiations begin [8]. Once the budget is agreed upon, regular reports are required by the corporate centre to enable senior executives to control performance.

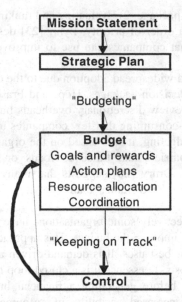

Fig. 1. The Traditional Budgeting Process

2.2 Approaches to Budgeting

The previous paragraph described the conventional approach to budgeting. This is typically an incremental budget which means that existing operations and the current budgeting allowance for existing activities are taken as the starting point for preparing the next annual budget [20]. The base is then adjusted for changes which are expected to occur during the new budget period. The major disadvantage of the incremental approach is the majority of expenditure, which is associated with the 'base level' of activity, remains unchanged. Past inefficiencies and waste inherent in the current way of doing things is perpetuated.

An approach that emerged in the late 1960s as an attempt to overcome the limitations of incremental budgeting is Zero-based budgeting (ZBB) or priority-based budgeting [20]. ZBB was used as a means for organisations to adapt to a changing environment where resources are becoming scarce, profits are being threatened, and changes are occurring with increasing frequency [21]. By acknowledging that organisations have traditionally accepted existing plans and expenditure as necessary, without examination [22], ZBB requires that all activities are justified and prioritised before decisions are taken relating to the amount of resources allocated to each activity [20]. It works from the premise that projected expenditure for existing programmes should start from base zero, with each year's budget being compiled as if the programmes were being launched for the first time. ZBB is applicable to all "actionable or discretionary" activities or costs for which a cost/benefit relationship (however subjective) can be identified [23]. Examples include R & D, advertising and training costs. It involves three stages: 1) Creating a decision package (which is a representation of the operation of a particular program) and describing each organisational activity in that package. 2) Evaluating and ranking each package and 3) allocating resources based on order of priority. Pyhrr [23] describes it as more of a "general management tool that companies can use to improve planning, budgeting, and operational management".

The process never achieved widespread adoption due to the costs and time required to identify and evaluate the decision packages. Hope and Fraser [8] acknowledge its usefulness as an exercise to review discretionary overheads but say that the "process was so bureaucratic and time-consuming that few companies used it more than once. Moreover, like traditional budgeting, it was based on the organisational hierarchy. It thus reinforced functional barriers and failed to focus on the opportunities for improving business process". Drury [20] suggests that many organisations tend to approximate the principles of ZBB rather than applying the full-scale approach outlined in the literature.

To manage costs more effectively some organisations have adopted activity-based budgeting (ABB) as a way to improve the budget. This approach aims to promote the allocation of resources to their best uses. It is demand driven and the focus is on the level of activity and related costs. In essence it is a closed loop model which creates an operationally feasible budget before generating a financial budget. The analysis of resource capacity and the increased visibility of resource consumption enable organisations to identify capacity issues and make adjustments earlier in the budgeting process than under traditional budgeting processes. Hansen et al. [1] describe the ABB-approach as marrying "a more complete operational model with a detailed financial model." The resulting closed loop model yields operationally feasible budgets with activity and resource consumption highly visible and sources of imbalance or inefficiencies identified. The transparency of the activity-based budget potentially promotes the allocation of resources to their best uses in line with organisational priorities, decreases the scope for political gaming, enhances decision making and performance evaluation, and improves operational flexibility. Despite its merits, ABB has been criticised for being only a marginal refinement of traditional management budgeting techniques [24]. Researchers have highlighted the complexities involved in ABB in practice, the behavioural problems associated with its implementation, large implementation costs and the managerial resistance they can invoke [25].

While budgeting continues to be a major performance control mechanism in organisations, there is evidence that the role of budgeting is changing [8, 26]. Traditionally, performance management models (PMMs) were designed to facilitate performance measurement by budgetary targets. As the role of the budget changes to adapt to modern turbulent business environments, the design of the PMMs and measurements will also change. There have been numerous calls for organisations to move beyond using traditional budgeting processes and budgeting techniques for performance management in modern turbulent operating environments [8, 11].

3   Budgeting and Performance Management Models

Budgeting has a strong connection to performance management within an organisation. Traditionally the budget set the goals early in the year and performance was measured against those goals. Otley (1999) links PMMs to 'overall control systems' which he reminds his readers go 'beyond the measurement of performance to the management of performance' [2]. PMMs and frameworks developed by academics such as Ferreira and Otley (2009) and Broadbent and Laughlin (2009) are generic in their construction and encompass the whole spectrum of operating environments, from command-and-control to a more decentralised environment. While PMMs are complex and intertwined, research had tended to ignore the interdependencies between the differing controlling mechanisms and concentrate on simplified and partial areas of the overall PMM. Ferreira and Otley (2009) and Broadbent and Laughlin (2009) have worked on conceptualising performance management and distinguishing it from performance measurement. Their research frameworks are especially useful when researchers seek to gain an insight into the types of performance management techniques being utilised by organisations.

The literature in the area of PMMs increasingly recognises the need for research to be based on more coherent theoretical foundations [3, 27-29]. The tendency to focus only on specific aspects of control systems, as opposed to a more comprehensive and integrated approach has led to spurious findings, ambiguity and a potential for conflicting results [27]. There have been calls for a more integrated approach that includes the interdependency between different control mechanisms operating at the same time in the same organisation [30].

In outlining a research framework for performance management models Otley [2] highlight five central issues of performance management system design:

- Key organisational objectives and the processes and methods involved in assessing the level of achievement of these objectives.
- The process of formulating and implementing strategies and plans, as well as the performance measurement and evaluation processes with their implementation.
- The process of setting performance targets and the levels at which such targets are set.
- The rewards systems used by the organisations and the implications of achieving or failing to achieve performance targets.
- The types of information flows required to provide adequate monitoring of performance and to support learning.

Ferreira and Otley [28] expanded this model into 12 questions which they believe give significant insight into the various aspects of PMMs design.

- What is the vision and mission of the organisation and how is this brought to the attention of managers and employees? What mechanisms, processes and networks are used to convey the organisations overarching purposes and objectives to its members?
- What are the key factors that are believed to be central to the organisation's overall future success and how are they brought to the attention of managers and employees?
- What is the organisation structure and what impact does it have on the design and use of performance management systems (PMSs)? How does it influence and how is it influenced by the strategic management process?

- What strategies and plans has the organisation adopted and what are the processes and activities that it has decided will be required for it to ensure its success? How are plans adapted, generated and communicated to managers and employees?
- What are the organisation's key performance measures deriving from its objectives, key success factors, and strategies and plans? How are these specified and communicated and what role do they play in performance evaluation? Are there significant omissions?
- What level of performance does the organisation need to achieve for each of its key performance measures (identified in the above question), how does it go about setting appropriate performance targets for them, and how challenging are those targets?
- What processes, if any, does the organisation follow for evaluating, individual, group, and organisational performance? Are performance evaluations primarily objective, subjective or mixed and how important are formal and informal information and controls in these processes?
- What rewards - financial and/or non-financial - will managers and other employees gain by achieving performance targets or other assessed aspects of performance (or, conversely, what penalties will they suffer by failing to achieve them)?
- What specific information flows, -feedback and feed-forward - systems and networks has the organisation in place to support the operation of its PMSs?
- What type of use is made of information and of the various control mechanisms in place? Can these uses be characterises in terms of various typologies in the literature? How do controls and their uses differ at different hierarchical levels?
- How have the PMSs altered in light of the change dynamics of the organisation and its environment? Have the changes in PMSs design or use been made in a proactive or reactive manner?
- How strong and coherent are the links between the components of PMSs and the ways in which they are used (as denoted by the above eleven questions)?

This framework was developed with underlying theory and logical reasoning and at first glance may appear to be a normative framework. This is not the case; according to Ferreira and Otley it is:

"Used to facilitate the description of PMMs design and use in practice, without any prior assumption as to whether the existence or absence of a particular feature is a good or bad thing. They are put forward as a heuristic tool to facilitate the rapid description of significant aspects of PMMs design and operation."

When looking at performance management models it is possible to use Ferriera and Otley's framework to examine the performance management systems of both traditional command-and-control hierarchical organisations, which can be placed at one end of Malone's [31] decentralisation continuum, and also decentralised and adaptive organisations which are placed at the other end (Figure 2). Some scholars believe that organisations are continuously alternating between command-and-control management and more decentralised adaptive management models (cf. Barley and Kunda, 1992), highlighting that different economic environments require different performance management models. Barley and Kunda (1992) suggest that over the past 150 years American organisations in particular, have constantly shifted from rational (command-and-control, coercive) models to normative (adaptive, employee empowering) models of control. Their argument stems from a study of economic expansion and contraction and the view that the introduction of normative management techniques came during times of economic contraction, while rational techniques were introduced during times of expansion. While there may be a pattern in the management techniques used in different economic environments, it is difficult to see how this amounts to cyclical forms of management. The evidence suggests that organisations are continuously seeking innovative ways of managing. So while rational techniques may be introduced during times of expansion, there is no indication that the normative techniques already in use are being discarded. Therefore, this article agrees with the dominant view in management, i.e. that organisations are progressively moving from rational to normative management controls. Management scholars such as Hope and Fraser (2003) and McFarland (2008) suggest that today's organisations need to move from the traditional hierarchical command-and-control model based on the yearly budgeting process to a more adaptive decentralised model in order to incorporate the required agility in their PMMs to compete in a post modern business environment.

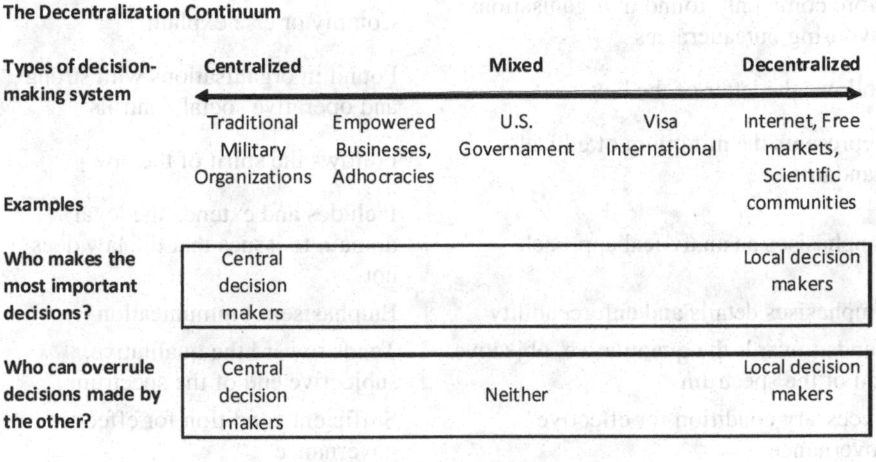

The Decentralization Continuum

Types of decision-making system	Centralized		Mixed		Decentralized
Examples	Traditional Military Organizations	Empowered Businesses, Adhocracies	U.S. Government	Visa International	Internet, Free markets, Scientific communities
Who makes the most important decisions?	Central decision makers				Local decision makers
Who can overrule decisions made by the other?	Central decision makers		Neither		Local decision makers

Fig. 2. Malone's Decentralisation Continuum

3.1 Spectrum of Performance Management: Principles vs. Rules

Baker and Mills' [32] notion of the "chief programmer team", in which one person (the chief programmer) makes all decisions, and Weinberg's [33] concept of the "egoless programming team", where decision making is distributed among team members, are instances of control through structure- through centralisation and through decentralisation, respectively. The issue of centralisation versus decentralisation is likely to be more important in a software development team context to the extent the developers view themselves as professionals; it is increasingly recognised that professional conduct in a variety of disciplines involves more than merely "following the rules" [34].

Arjoon [35] discusses a rules-based vs. a principles-based approach for organisational governance (Table 1) stating that: "the casuistic [rules-based] approach attempts to develop rules for each specific situation, while the principles-based approach provides general principles to apply to a variety of individual cases and situations". Due to the organic nature of software development, a principle-based approach to performance management and governance is seen as more effective than a rules based-approach [36-38].

Table 1. Rules-based Vs. Principles-based Approaches

Rules-Based	Principles-based
Complies with a specific set of procedural requirements (e.g., checklist of do's and don'ts)	Emphasises "doing the right thing" by appropriate means
Comply or else	Corporate behaviour is guided by a focus on end results (objectives-orientated)
More commonly found in organisations favouring bureaucracies	Comply or else explain
Follows the letter of the law	Found in organisations with strong and operative social controls
Represents the minimum of ethical standards	Follows the spirit of the law
Emphasises an analytical approach	Includes and extends the legal domain to issues that the law does not
Emphasises details and enforceability	Emphasises communication
Tends towards the quantitative, objective end of the spectrum	Tends toward the qualitative, subjective end of the spectrum
Necessary condition for effective governance	Sufficient condition for effective governance
Requires constant monitoring	Develops over a longer term
Focuses on detection	Focuses on prevention
Tends to be fear-driven	Tends to be values-driven
More explicit, detailed, prescriptive	More implicit, broad
Tends to consider issues in black and white	Considers issues in the "gray" areas
Promotes blind obedience	Promotes alignment with values
Mandatory	Discretionary
Easier to implement	More difficult to implement
Addresses proximate causes	Addresses ultimate causes

4   The Beyond Budgeting Model

There has been a move from the bureaucratic, hierarchical organisation, considered ineffective in the context of increased competition brought about by globalisation, deregulation, the emergence of powerful developing economies, and development in information technologies, towards flatter, leaner and more responsive structures [39]. As discussed earlier, many have questioned the industrial era management and government systems, and there are calls for a new model for the knowledge economy [18, 40]. Others have questioned the budgeting process and its value in the post industrial era [9, 12, 41-45]. There have been calls for a more integrated approach to performance management which includes the interdependency between different control mechanisms operating at the same time in the same organisation [30]. The problems with budgeting in practice [1] led to a series of articles and a book by Hope and Fraser [8, 46-50] arguing that organisations should abandon traditional budgeting.

Beyond Budgeting originated from a research collaboration between the European Consortium for Advanced Manufacturing-International (CAM-I)[1] and the Beyond Budgeting Round Table (BBRT). It consists of a set of six leadership principles and six process principles that aim to allow companies move past budgeting to a more value enhancing management process [8]. The Beyond Budgeting model proposes replacing the rigid annual budget-based performance evaluations with performance evaluations based on relative performance contracts with hindsight [1]. The model focuses on the connections between performance management and strategy. It advocates the use of methods such as rolling forecasts, balanced scorecards [51] and relative performance evaluation [52] with hindsight [53] as a way to motivate and empower employees. The objective is to engender a philosophy of doing what is best for the firm in light of current circumstances and to promote teamwork [1]. Many of the principles of the Beyond Budgeting model have their own individual theoretical grounding, (e.g. control theory, goal setting theory, rewards theory –group/individual) and the main premises of the model such as relative performance evaluation, empowerment, resource allocation and planning/control are also well grounded in theory. The Beyond Budgeting model as a single, coherent holistic model embraces McGregor's theory Y [54] management principles.

The model aims to promote a set of principles that lead to more dynamic processes and front-line accountability. The six leadership principles and six process principles of Beyond Budgeting support each other in a holistic model. The relative importance of each principle might vary depending on the business in question [41]. The interest in Beyond Budgeting continues to grow with more and more organisations looking to leverage the principles to improve their own performance. There is a steady stream of case study materials and books being written that give first-hand accounts of organisations that have introduced the Beyond Budgeting model [8, 13, 41, 55]. Many organisations that have previously used the traditional "command-and-control" management model are now looking at the Beyond Budgeting model as a way to sustain superior competitive advantage.

---

[1] http://www.cam-i.org/)

Table 2. The Beyond Budgeting Management Model (Source: [41])

The Beyond Budgeting Management Model			
Leadership Principles		**Process Principles**	
Customers:	Focus everyone on improving customer outcomes, *not on hierarchical relationships*	**Goals:**	Set relative goals for continuous improvement; *do not negotiate fixed performance contracts*
Organization:	Organize as a network of lean, accountable teams, *not around centralized functions*	**Rewards:**	Reward shared success based on relative performance, *not on meeting fixed targets.*
Responsibility:	Enable everyone to act and think like a leader, *not merely follow the plan*	**Planning:**	Make planning a continuous and inclusive process, *not a top down annual event*
Autonomy:	Give teams the freedom and capability to act; *do not micro-manage them*	**Controls:**	Base controls on relative indicators and trends, *not variances against a plan*
Values:	Govern through a few clear values, goals and boundaries, *not detailed rules and budget*	**Resources:**	Make resources available as needed, *not through annual budget allocations*
Transparency:	Promote open information for self-management; *do not restrict it hierarchically*	**Coordination:**	Coordinate interactions dynamically, *not through annual planning cycles*

4.1   Theoretical Foundations of Beyond Budgeting

There has are many differing views as to what a theory must contain or what constitutes a theoretical contribution [56, 57]. Dictionary definitions show that the word theory can take on many meanings including an "idea or set of ideas about something" a "conception or mental scheme of something to be done, or the method of doing it; a systematic statement of rules or principles to be followed" a "mental view" or "contemplation" [58]. Gregor [57] uses the word theory to mean conjectures, models, frameworks, or bodies of knowledge. Gregor [57] analyses theory development in information systems and proposes a taxonomy of theory types. Her theory type III is a theory for prediction, that is, the distinguishing attributes of the theory are that it says what is and what will be. The theory provides predictions and has testable propositions but does not have well developed justificatory causal explanations. The Beyond Budgeting model as used in the context of this research belongs to Gregor's Type III theory, predictive theory, or what is referred to in the budgeting literature as normative theory. Traditional budgeting techniques springing from normative budget theory are Zero-Based Budgeting (ZBB), Management by Objectives (MBO), Target Based Budgets and Planned Programming Budgets (PBB). Normative theory is advice based on observations and its proposed solutions may be based on values rather than observations. It sets attractive goals and guides for behaviour [59]. Cushing [60] says of normative theory that it: "provides predictions that "things will be better" if its prescriptions are followed."

Beyond Budgeting practitioners also embrace the Theory Y management model. The Theory Y model [54] has been widely adopted in the management literature as the preferred management model [61]. Theory Y argues that management is more than simply giving orders and coercing obedience; it is a careful balancing of the needs of the organisation and the needs of the individual [54] as defined by Abraham Maslow's hierarchy of needs. Modern technological industries present managers with the kinds of challenges McGregor foresaw: employees requiring greater flexibility and understanding from managers in order to produce quality products and to find creative solutions to various problems [61].

Another theoretical consideration for the Beyond Budgeting model is that it is to be employed as a coherent model [8, 41]. The model is developed from experience and case study research and has a large body of scientifically established knowledge underlying many of its main premises. There is substantial research relating to relative [52, 62] and subjective [63] performance evaluations, fixed budget-based performance contracts [7] and decentralisation [64], along with the main tenets of each principle (Table 3).

Table 3. Theoretical Underpinnings of Beyond Budgeting

Beyond Budgeting Principles		Underlying Theory	Key Articles Contributing to the Theory
Leadership Principles			
Customers:	Focus everyone on improving customer outcomes, *not on hierarchical relationships.*	Customer Focus	[65-70]
Organisation:	Organise as a network of lean, accountable teams, *not around centralised functions.*	Decentralisation	[71-74]
		Accountability	[75-77]

Table 3. (*continued*)

Responsibility:	Enable everyone to act and think like a leader, *not merely follow the plan.*	Empowering Leadership	[78-81]
Autonomy:	Give teams the freedom and capability to act; *do not micromanage them.*	Team Empowerment	[82-84]
Values:	Govern through a few clear values, goals and boundaries, *not detailed rules and budgets.*	Governance	[54, 85, 86]
Transparency:	Promote open information for self-management; *do not restrict it hierarchically.*	Transparency	[87-90]

Process Principles

Goals:	Set relative goals for continuous improvement; *do not negotiate fixed performance contracts.*	Goal Setting	[91-93]
Rewards:	Reward shared success based on relative performance, *not on meeting fixed targets.*	Relative Performance Evaluation	[52, 94-96]
Planning:	Make planning a continuous and inclusive process, *not a top down annual event.*	Continuous Planning	[8, 97-99]
Controls:	Base controls on relative indicators and trends, *not variances against a plan.*	Control	[100-102]
Resources:	Make resources available as needed, *not through annual budget allocations.*	Dynamic Capabilities and Resource-based View of the Firm	[103-105]
Coordination:	Coordinate interactions dynamically, *not through annual planning cycles.*	Coordination	[106-109]

4.2   Budgetary Concerns in Software Development

In software development projects, costs are indirectly estimated by first providing feature estimates to aid in release planning [110]. Once there is a consensus on the release plan and other associated costs are known a project cost baseline or budget can be aggregated from cost per iteration estimates. This baseline will need to be revisited at various stage gates and recalculated based on changes to the release plan. Customers can authorise additional funds for extra functionality at any stage of the project. In this way, development methods, such as agile methods, address the issue of cost overrun by allowing a scope change rather than a cost overrun for the project. If a budget is in place agile methods allow for project completion within budget by reducing the functionality if needed. Being agile though, implies ongoing scope definition which makes it difficult to fix the project's budget [111]. This leads to problems associated with ISD contracts as actual development costs are imperfectly known by both supplier and customer [112]. Some of the issues associated with agile development contracts such as risk exposure, opportunism, lack of trust, etc. are addressed by putting in place formal contracts. Examples of such contracts are, fixed price contracts, target cost contracts, profit sharing contracts, progressive contracts, time and materials contracts and the PS2000 (a Norwegian iterative development contract). These are not always possible to put in place and in cases where they are in place they can result in the power of an agile development methodology not being fully realised [113].

A more suitable alternative or addition to a contract may be cost accounting techniques, which track value added. There are also a number of mechanisms from management accounting for measuring cost performance and value associated with a project. Traditional cost management relies on cost accounting techniques to predict metrics such as return on investment (ROI), payback period or net present value (NPV) and to prepare project budgets. While it is difficult to fix a project's budget at the onset for ASD, there are techniques that may be used to measure the project performance during development. Stepanek [111] introduces techniques such as scoping studies, feature trade-off and triage. Anderson [114] proposes what he calls throughput accounting, which assumes fixed costs and measures efficiency as value delivered. He makes the argument that lean manufacturing does not use cost accounting anymore because it is inward thinking, caused by managers focusing on reducing cost per unit, not on increasing customer value. Sliger and Broderick [110] and Alleman et al. [115] advocate the use of AgileEVM (earned value management) as a way to measure cost performance. These cost accounting techniques may be useful but only serve to highlight the problems associated with traditional budgeting in ISD and ASD in particular. While the Beyond Budgeting model can cater for traditional ISD, it is regarded as a complement [116] to ASD. It is widely recognised that no two projects are the same and a case by case analysis will need to be conducted to find the optimum budgeting, costing and performance measurement model for each individual project. However, as certain projects will need to be completed with full functionality regardless of the budget [117], the value of the budget and project estimation process for ASD projects is questionable.

4.3   The Need for a New Budgeting Model for Agile Software Development

The business value of IT and the relationship between IT investment and organisational outcomes has received a lot of attention in recent years. There is an increasing amount of literature advocating the alignment of IS strategy and processes with business strategy [118-122]. Creating complementarities [116], partnerships and cross-unit synergies [123-125] has become increasingly important for organisations operating in a modern environment with increased complexity and uncertainty [126]. The traditional SDLC waterfall method shared many of the characteristics, and worked well within, the traditional strategic planning model (Figure. 3).

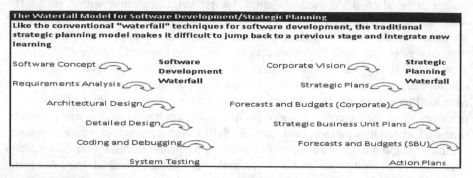

Fig. 3. The waterfall model for ISD and Planning (Source: [18])

Traditional management models rely on traditional accounting processes such as yearly budgets, quarterly and annual reporting [1, 127]. For most firms the information technology IT/IS budget represents a major element in the overall firm budget. IT budgets include expenditures directly associated with a firm's IT function, i.e., for staff salaries, payments to vendors and service firms, hardware/software purchases, training and new development associated with systems and application software portfolios [128]. There is still some debate among practitioners and academics as to the value of IT/IS investment and the extant literature has shown mixed results in establishing a relationship between IT/IS investment and firm performance [129]. Recent research findings suggest that IT/IS budget levels are positively associated with subsequent firm performance and shareholder returns [128]. Research has also shown that a firm's ability to effectively leverage its IT/IS investments by developing a strong IT capability can result in improved firm performance [130]. IT capability includes the information systems development projects. Although the completion of a business-critical project is likely to be supported by senior management whether or not budget goals are being met [117], in a modern, turbulent and competitive business environment the money being spent on IS projects is still a serious cause for concern. Many organisations are making large investments in information systems designed to deliver significant performance gains.

Success in IS project development is often a necessary prerequisite for realising these gains in organisational performance [117]. However, software development projects are continuously running over budget. Budget performance in ISD is generally the primary concern of the project manager, rather than the business investment appraisal team (project sponsor) [117]. The effective application of project management is predicated upon accurate estimates of the project budget and schedule. Estimating the development effort for a software system is a long standing problem in software project management. The often-quoted Standish Group's Chaos report from 1994[2] and subsequent updated reports have reported huge project cost overruns. Although The Standish findings have been questioned [131-133] others have shown that the software industry finds it difficult to provide accurate estimates of development cost. A review of estimation accuracy studies [134] reports that software projects have on average a cost overrun of 30-40% and most projects (60-80%) encounter effort and/or schedule overruns. Indeed software cost estimation has been described as more of an art than a science [135]. The difficult to predict development costs and technology trends make the utilisation of a traditional budgeting process questionable.

This traditional budgeting model has been questioned since the 1960s but numerous unsuccessful attempts have been made to replace it and it continues to be used widely despite its obvious shortcomings. According to McFarland [18]: "The strategic planning model is due for a "new release," one that enables companies to keep pace with changing environments, quickly create and adapt strategy and empower people throughout the organisation to make effective choices." This article goes on to say "Around the same time that managers were losing confidence in strategic planning, software development went through its own crisis, as the demand for faster design and integration of increasingly robust systems began to make the traditional "waterfall" approach to software development obsolete. The crisis in software prompted a few visionaries to rethink how software gets built. They didn't abandon a process approach to the problem; rather, they invented new development processes, such as rapid application development, extreme programming and agile software development, to confront the new realities."

With intellectual capital forming the greater part of company market value today [8] the question is how to develop and leverage human capital in support of business needs? [136]. The Beyond Budgeting model aims to leverage human capital by releasing the potential of employees through a different management model. This model uses tools such as the balanced scorecard [51, 121], rolling forecasts and key performance indicators to conduct performance evaluations based on relative performance contracts with hindsight [1]. Agile methods share many conceptual similarities with the Beyond Budgeting model and are a response to the same problems that triggered the Beyond Budgeting movement [41]. Beyond Budgeting and agile methods are complementary, conceptually similar and offer the best option for the agility [137], adaptability, and responsiveness [136, 138] required from the IT/Finance alignment in order to operate competitively in a contemporary business environment.

---

[2] www.standishgroup.com

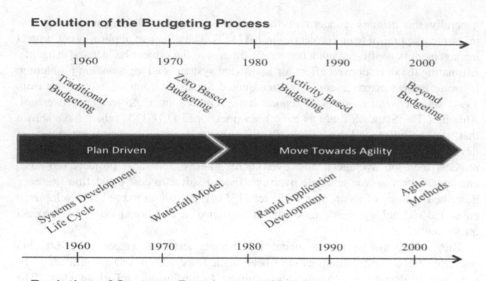

Fig. 4. Evolution of Budgeting and Systems Development

The emergence of the Beyond Budgeting concept coincided with the emergence of agile methods and both concepts share many similarities with both having a distinctly agile or adaptive perspective [36, 41, 139, 140] (Figure 4). The common thread across both agile methods and Beyond Budgeting is that the inability to do adequate planning in uncertain environments makes upfront estimation/budgeting less useful. Beyond Budgeting is orientated towards fast changing operational environments and utilises a sense-and-respond type of control mechanism, which allows an organisation to keep pace with fast changing environments [8, 46-50]. The goals of the Beyond Budgeting model are to sustain superior competitive performance while agile software development is about rapidly delivering business value. The Beyond Budgeting model has been shown to benefit organisations through faster response, innovative strategies, lower costs and more loyal customers [10, 11, 13].

5   Beyond Budgeting in Practice

One of the more prominent organisations using the Beyond Budgeting model is the large Norwegian oil and gas company, Statoil. Bogsnes [41] describes in detail his experience with implementing Beyond Budgeting in Statoil. He cites many of the same reasons for abandoning traditional budgeting and moving to the Beyond Budgeting model that are stated in the introduction section of this paper, i.e. traditional budgets are time consuming, they add little value and they are a barrier to change, etc. Bogsnes also noted that Statoil has always been a value-driven organisation that trusted its employees and gave them a wide range of responsibilities [41 pp 104]. He believed that this culture was instrumental in preparing Statoil for the

Beyond Budgeting journey. While acknowledging that the implementation process is ongoing and there are many barriers to change, Bogsnes shows that Statoil has made significant progress towards removing the traditional command-and-control processes and moving to a dynamic management model [41 pp 104]. Ostergren and Stensaker [141] also studied the use of Beyond Budgeting in a similar environment. Although their study did not specifically name the organisation, the study was also conducted in a large Norwegian oil and gas company. Their study concentrated on how the implementation affected the practices and process of 2 major divisions within the organisation. They conclude that the Beyond Budgeting model is well received within the organisation but also suggest that there are challenges to implementation. Firstly that the competition between groups advocated by the Beyond Budgeting model may lead to top managers pushing divisional managers excessively, secondly, that although gaming associated with traditional budgeting may have disappeared, new games may arise surrounding dynamic resource allocation and finally that employees may need high levels of competency and flexibility to be able to transfer easily to high activity projects. Ostergren and Stensaker [141] argue that ideological concerns may arise further into the implementation process as the Beyond Budgeting model may be understood to be a change from the Scandinavian decentralised ideology to a more centralised contract-based ideology. While the work of Hope and Fraser [8] and Bogsnes [41] highlight the many potential benefits of Beyond Budgeting, Ostergren and Stensaker [141] show that there are areas of concern still to be addressed. These findings highlight the need for further research into the affects of Beyond Budgeting as the model gains traction within industry. Lohan et al. [38, 142] operationalised the Beyond Budgeting model and used it as a lens to examine ASD teams. Their findings suggest that while Beyond Budgeting resonates strongly with ASD, many legacy practices are still in place which hinder the use of ASD techniques. They find that organisations are slowly changing their processes to align with ASD methods but some areas of concern remain. A list of recommendation was produced from their studies which are aimed at ASD teams; however they also find that organisations wishing to become truly agile must implement changes from both the bottom up and the top down.

6   Conclusion

While a central argument of this study is that there is a need for a change in the management and structure of organisations necessitated by a paradigm shift from the age of Taylorism to the information-age [143], it is worth noting that others believe this may not actually be a paradigm shift and may be part of a cyclical change of managerial discourse brought about by the expansion and contraction of economies. Barley and Kunda [144] produce a strong argument in this regard, stating that "Rather than having progressed steadily from coercive to rational and then to normative conceptions of control, managerial discourse may have elaborated in surges of rhetoric that alternately celebrated normative and rational forms of control". They show how management rhetoric has followed the path of economic expansion and contractions from the 1870s until the 1990s, highlighting how economic contraction led to periods of normative influence (industrial betterment of the 1870s, human relations of the 1930s and organisation culture of the 1980s) and economic expansion led to periods of rational influence (Taylorism/scientific management of the 1900s and systems rationalism of the 1950s). While the arguments of Barley and Kunda [144] are well presented, they state that their thesis is based on ideology rather than practice and recognise that they are in the minority with regard to their stance on the evolution of management discourse and the move towards normative forms of control. Nevertheless, for future research this may have implications for the Beyond Budgeting model as a normative management model. Should, as predicted by Barley and Kunda (1992), organisations wish to revert back to rational control models in line with an economic expansion then the Beyond Budgeting model may not gain further traction. However, advocates of the model suggest that the model is suited for organisations wishing to utilise employee knowledge, that there are inbuilt transparency and accountability mechanisms which allow employee autonomy within boundary operating conditions [41]. The studies by Hope and Fraser [8] show that the benefits of using Beyond Budgeting will be evident regardless of economic expansion or contraction. The model is designed for the information age and as pointed out by Barley and Kunda [144], it will only be with the benefit of hindsight that that we can see whether management discourse during this age reverts back towards a rational form of control as their hypothesis suggests.

There are, however, some considerations to be made regarding the implementation of Beyond Budgeting regardless of the economic environment. The model is designed to support front-line employees and shift the power for decision making further down the organisation. This may not always happen in practice. For example, Ostergren and Stensaker [141] found that in an organisation that had implemented Beyond Budgeting the controllers are perceived to be more powerful and that power has shifted upwards in the organisation. There is an increased centralisation of target setting while simultaneously there has been increased decentralisation regarding how these targets are reached by sub-divisions. They also note that while none of those they interviewed expressed any concern over an ideological clash; this may become an issue later in the implementation process, when the implications of the new system become more evident.

In the meantime we know that Drucker [143] is correct insofar as the information age has caused a major evolutionary shift in the management and structure of organisations. While it remains to be seen whether organisations revert back towards rationalism, thereby reducing the use of normative management models such as Beyond Budgeting, we know for sure that ASD methods are now an embedded part of the ISD discipline. The question remains, whether ISD methods such as agile methods will be tailored to suit more traditional PMMs or whether organisations will continue to implement normative models such as Beyond Budgeting thereby potentially improving the use of ASD methods?

Acknowledgements. This work was supported, in part, by Science Foundation Ireland grant 10/CE/I1855 to Lero - the Irish Software Engineering Research Centre (www.lero.ie).

References

1. Hansen, S.C., Otley, D.T., Van der Stede, W.A.: Practice developments in budgeting: An overview and research perspective. Journal of Management Accounting Research 15(1), 95–116 (2003)
2. Otley, D.T.: Performance management: a framework for management control systems research. Management Accounting Research 10(4), 363–382 (1999)
3. Covaleski, M.A., et al.: Budgeting research: Three theoretical perspectives and criteria for selective integration. Journal of Management Accounting Research 15(1), 3–49 (2003)
4. Hansen, S.C., Van der Stede, W.A.: Multiple facets of budgeting: an exploratory analysis. Management Accounting Research 15(4), 415–439 (2004)
5. Van der Stede, W.A.: Measuring tight budgetary control. Management Accounting Research 12(1), 119–137 (2001)
6. Ekholm, B.-G., Wallin, J.: Is the annual budget really dead? European Accounting Review 9(4), 519–539 (2000)
7. Jensen, M.C.: Paying People to Lie: the Truth about the Budgeting Process. European Financial Management 9(3), 379–406 (2003)
8. Hope, J., Fraser, R.: Beyond Budgeting: How Managers can Break Free from the Annual Performance Trap. Harvard Business School Press, Boston (2003)
9. Dugdale, D., Lyne, S.: Budgeting. Financial Management, 32–35 (March 2006)
10. Libby, T., Lindsay, R.M.: Beyond Budgeting or Better Budgeting? Strategic Finance 89(2), 46–51 (2007)
11. Neely, A., Bourne, M., Adams, C.: Better budgeting or beyond budgeting. Measuring Business Excellence 7(3), 22–28 (2003)
12. Schmidt, J.A.: Is it time to replace traditional budgeting? Journal of Accountancy 174(4), 103–107 (1992)
13. McVay, G.J., Cooke, D.J.: Beyond Budgeting in an IDS: the Park Nicollet experience. HFM (Healthcare Financial Management) 60(10), 100–110 (2006)
14. Mintzberg, H., Simons, R., Basu, K.: Beyond Selfishness. MIT Sloan Management Review 44(1), 67–74 (2002)
15. Mintzberg, H., Westley, F.: Decision Making: It's Not What You Think. MIT Sloan Management Review 42(3), 89–93 (2001)
16. Gosling, J., Mintzberg, H.: The Education of Practicing Managers. MIT Sloan Management Review 45(4), 19–22 (2004)
17. Quy Nguyen, H., Mintzberg, H.: The Rhythm of Change. MIT Sloan Management Review 44(4), 79–84 (2003)
18. McFarland, K.R.: Should You Build Strategy Like You Build Software? MIT Sloan Management Review 49(3), 69–74 (2008)
19. Ehrhart, K.-M., et al.: Budget processes: Theory and experimental evidence. Games and Economic Behavior 59(2), 279–295 (2007)
20. Drury, C.: Management and Cost Accounting. South-western, London (2008)
21. Duffy, M.F.: ZBB, MBO, PPB and Their Effectiveness Within the Planning/Marketing Process. Strategic Management Journal 10(2), 163–173 (1989)
22. Pyhrr, P.A.: Zero-base budgeting. Harvard Business Review 48(6), 111–121 (1970)
23. Pyhrr, P.A.: Zero-base budgeting: where to use it and how to begin. Advanced Management Journal 41(3), 4 (1976)

24. Major, M.: Activity-based management accounting: A critical review. In: Hopper, T., Northcott, D., Scappens, R. (eds.) Issues in Management Accounting. Pearson Education, Harlow (2007)
25. Major, M., Hopper, T.: Managers divided: Implementing ABC in a Portuguese telecommunications company. Management Accounting Research 16(2), 205–229 (2005)
26. Otley, D.T., Pollanen, R.M.: Budgetary criteria in performance evaluation: A critical appraisal using new evidence. Accounting, Organizations and Society 25(4-5), 483–496 (2000)
27. Chenhall, R.H.: Management control systems design within its organizational context: findings from contingency-based research and directions for the future. Accounting, Organizations and Society 28(2-3), 127–168 (2003)
28. Ferreira, A., Otley, D.T.: The design and use of performance management systems: An extended framework for analysis. Management Accounting Research 20(4), 263–282 (2009)
29. Broadbent, J., Laughlin, R.: Performance Management Systems: A Conceptual Model. Management Accounting Research 20(4), 283–295 (2009)
30. Abernethy, M.A., Brownell, P.: Management Control Systems in Research and Development Organizations: The Role of Accounting, Behavior and Personnel Controls. Accounting, Organizations and Society 22(3-4), 233–248 (1997)
31. Malone, T.W.: Is empowerment just a fad? Control, decision making, and IT. Sloan Management Review 38(2), 23–35 (1997)
32. Baker, F.T., Mills, D.H.: Chief Programmer Teams. Datamation 19(12), 58–61 (1973)
33. Weinberg, G.: The Psychology of Computer Programming. Van Nostrand Reinhold, New York (1971)
34. Davis, M.: Professional responsibility: Just following the rules? Business and Professional Ethics Journal 18(1), 65–88 (1999)
35. Arjoon, S.: Striking a Balance Between Rules and Principles-Based Approaches for Effective Governance: A Risks-Based Approach. Journal of Business Ethics 68(1), 53–82 (2006)
36. Poppendieck, M., Poppendieck, T.: Leading Lean Software Development: Results Are Not the Point. Addison-Wesley, Upper Saddle River (2010)
37. Larman, C., Vodde, B.: Scaling Lean & Agile Development. Addison-Wesley, Upper Saddle River (2008)
38. Lohan, G., Conboy, K., Lang, M.: Beyond Budgeting and agile software development: A conceptual framework for the performance management of agile software development teams. In: International Conference on Information Systems, St Louis (2010)
39. Berry, A.J., et al.: Emerging themes in management control: A review of recent literature. The British Accounting Review 41(1), 2–20 (2009)
40. Manville, B., Ober, J.: Beyond Empowerment: Building a Company of Citizens. Harvard Business Review 81(1), 48–53 (2003)
41. Bogsnes, B.: Implementing Beyond Budgeting: Unlocking the Performance Potential. J. Wiley & Sons, New Jersey (2009)
42. Howell, R.A.: Turn Your Budgeting Process Upside Down. Harvard Business Review 82(7/8), 21–22 (2004)
43. Cassell, M.: Budgeting and more. Management Accounting: Magazine for Chartered Management Accountants 77(8), 22 (1999)
44. Kennedy, A., Dugdale, D.: Getting the most from BUDGETING. Management Accounting: Magazine for Chartered Management Accountants 77(2), 22 (1999)

45. O'Brien, R.: Living with budgeting. Management Accounting: Magazine for Chartered Management Accountants 77(8), 22 (1999)
46. Fraser, R.: Figures of hate. Financial Management, 22–25 (February 2001)
47. Hope, J., Fraser, R.: Take it Away. Accountancy 123(1269), 50–51 (1999)
48. Hope, J., Fraser, R.: New ways of setting rewards: The Beyond Budgeting model. California Management Review 45(4), 104–119 (2003)
49. Hope, J., Fraser, R.: Who needs budgets? Harvard Business Review 81(2), 108–115 (2003)
50. Hope, J., Fraser, R.: Who needs budgets? Response. Harvard Business Review 81(6), 132 (2003)
51. Kaplan, R.S., Norton, D.P.: The Balanced Scorecard–Measures That Drive Performance. Harvard Business Review 70(1), 71–79 (1992)
52. Dye, R.A.: Relative performance evaluation and project selection. Journal of Accounting Research 30(1), 27–52 (1992)
53. Demski, J.S.: An Accounting System Structured on a Linear Programming Model. Accounting Review 42(4), 701 (1967)
54. McGregor, D.: The human side of enterprise. McGraw-Hill, New York (1960)
55. Østergren, K., Stensaker, I.: Management Control without Budgets: A Field Study of 'Beyond Budgeting' in Practice. European Accounting Review 20(1), 149–181 (2011)
56. Whetten, D.A.: What Constitutes a Theoretical Contribution? Academy of Management Review 14(4), 490–495 (1989)
57. Gregor, S.: The nature of theory in information systems. MIS Quarterly 30(3), 611–642 (2006)
58. OED. Oxford English Dictionary (2010) (April 09, 2009), http://dictionary.oed.com (cited November 9, 2010)
59. Rubin, I.S.: Budget Theory and Budget Practice: How Good the Fit? Public Administration Review 50(2), 179–189 (1990)
60. Cushing, B.E.: Frameworks, Paradigms, and Scientific Research in Management Information Systems. Journal of Information Systems 4(2), 38–59 (1990)
61. Bobic, M.P., Davis, W.E.: A Kind Word for Theory X: Or Why So Many Newfangled Management Techniques Quickly Fail. Journal of Public Administration Research Theory 13(3), 239–264 (2003)
62. Janakiraman, S.N., Lambert, R.A., Larcker, D.F.: An Empirical Investigation of the Relative Performance Evaluation Hypothesis. Journal of Accounting Research 30(1), 53–69 (1992)
63. Baiman, S., Rajan, M.V.: The Informational Advantages of Discretionary Bonus Schemes. Accounting Review 70(4), 557–579 (1995)
64. Brickley, J.A.: Managerial Economics and Organizational Architecture. McGraw-Hill, Boston (2004)
65. Caker, M.: Customer focus - An accountability dilemma. European Accounting Review 16(1), 143–171 (2007)
66. Deshpande, R., Farley, J.U., Webster Jr., F.E.: Corporate culture, customer orientation, and innovativeness in Japanese firms: A quadrad analysis. Journal of Marketing 57(1), 23–37 (1993)
67. du Gay, P., Salaman, G.: The Cult(ure) of the Customer. Journal of Management Studies 29(5) (1992)
68. Gulati, R.: Silo busting. Harvard Business Review, 98–108 (2007)
69. Levitt, T.: Marketing Myopia. Harvard Business Review 38(7), 173–181 (1960)

70. Lohan, G., Conboy, K., Lang, M.: Examining Customer Focus in IT Project Management: Findings from Irish and Norwegian case studies. Scandinavian Journal of Information Systems 23(2) (2011)
71. Glew, D.J., et al.: Participation in organizations: A preview of the issues and proposed framework for future analysis. Journal of Management 21(3), 395 (1995)
72. Inkson, J.H.K., Pugh, D.S., Hickson, D.J.: Organization context and structure: An abbreviated replication. Administrative Science Quarterly 15(3), 318–329 (1970)
73. Mendelson, H.: Organizational architecture and success in the information technology industry. Management Science 46(4), 513 (2000)
74. Radner, R.: Hierarchy: The economics of managing. Journal of Economic Literature 30(3), 1382 (1992)
75. Frink, D.D., Ferris, G.R.: Accountability, impression management, and goal setting in the performance evaluation process. Human Relations 51(10), 1259–1283 (1998)
76. Schlenker, B.R., Weigold, M.F.: Self-identification and accountability. In: Giacalone, R.A., Rosenfeld, P. (eds.) Impression Management in the Organization, pp. 21–43. Lawrence Erlbaum, Hillsdale (1989)
77. Tetlock, P.E.: Accountability: The neglected social context of judgment and choice. In: Cummings, L.L., Staw, B.M. (eds.) Research in Organization Al Behavior, pp. 297–332. JAI Press, Greenwich (1985)
78. Cox, J.F., Sims, H.P.J.: Leadership and Team Citizen Behavior: A Model and Measures. Advances in Interdisciplinary Studies of Work Teams 3, 1–41 (1996)
79. Faraj, S., Sambamurthy, V.: Leadership of information systems development projects. IEEE Transactions on Engineering Management 53(2), 238–249 (2006)
80. Pearce, C.L., Sims, H.P.J.: Vertical versus shared leadership as predictors of the effectiveness of change management teams: An examination of aversive, directive, transactional, transformational, and empowering leadership behaviors. Group Dynamics 6(2), 172–197 (2002)
81. Srivastava, A., Bartol, K.M., Locke, E.A.: Empowering leadership in management teams: Effects on knowledge sharing, efficacy, and performance. Academy of Management Journal 49(6), 1239–1251 (2006)
82. Breaugh, J.A.: The Measurement of Work Autonomy. Human Relations 36(6), 551–570 (1985)
83. Kirkman, B.L., Rosen, B.: A model of work team empowerment. In: Woodman, R.W., Pasmore, W.A. (eds.) Research in Organizational Change and Development, pp. 131–167. JAI Press, Greenwich (1997)
84. Thomas, K.W., Velthouse, B.A.: Cognitive elements of empowerment: An interpretive model of intrinsic task motivation. Academy of Management Review 15(4), 666–681 (1990)
85. Bostrom, R.P., Heinen, J.: MIS Problems and Failures: A Sociotechnical Perspective; Part 1: The Causes. MIS Quarterly 2(3), 17–32 (1977)
86. Schein, E.H.: Organizational culture and leadership, 3rd edn. Jossey-Bass, San Francisco (2004)
87. Ang, C.-L., Davies, M., Finlag, P.N.: Measures to Assess the Impact of Information Technology on Quality Management. International Journal of Quality & Reliability Management 17(1), 42–66 (2000)
88. Beech, N., Crane, O.: High Performance and a Climate of Community. Team Performance Management 5(3), 87–102 (1999)
89. Berggren, E., Bernshteyn, R.: Organizational Transparency Drives Company Performance. Journal of Management Development 26(5), 411–417 (2007)

90. O'Toole, J., Bennis, W.: What's needed next: A culture of candor. Harvard Business Review 87(6), 54–61 (2009)

91. Abdel-Hamid, T.K., Sengupta, K., Swett, C.: The Impact of Goals on Software Project Management: An Experimental Investigation. MIS Quarterly 23(4), 531–555 (1999)

92. Latham, G.P., Locke, A.E.: Self-regulation through goal setting. Organizational Behavior and Human Decision Processes 50(2), 212–247 (1991)

93. Thompson, K.R., Hochwarter, W.A., Mathys, N.J.: Stretch targets: What makes them effective? Academy of Management Executive, 48–60 (1997)

94. Gibbons, R., Murphy, K.J.: Relative performance evaluation for chief executive officers. Industrial & Labor Relations Review 43, 30-S–51-S (1990)

95. Holmstrom, B.: Moral hazard in teams. The Bell Journal of Economics 13(2), 324–340 (1982)

96. Irlenbusch, B., Ruchala, G.K.: Relative rewards within team-based compensation. Labour Economics 15(2), 141–167 (2008)

97. Grant, R.M.: Strategic planning in a turbulent environment: Evidence from the oil majors. Strategic Management Journal 24(6), 491–517 (2003)

98. Hamel, G., Prahalad, C.K.: Strategic Intent. Harvard Business Review 83(7), 148–161 (2005)

99. Mintzberg, H.: The fall and rise of strategic planning. Harvard Business Review 72(1), 107–114 (1994)

100. Kirsch, L.J.: The management of complex tasks in organizations: Controlling the systems development process. Organization Science 7(1), 1–21 (1996)

101. Ouchi, W.G.: A conceptual framework for the design of organisational control mechanisms. Management Science 25(9), 833–848 (1979)

102. Simons, R.: Control in an Age of Empowerment. Harvard Business Review 73, 80–88 (1995)

103. Barney, J.B.: Firms Resources and Sustained Competitive Advantage. Journal of Management 17(1), 99–120 (1991)

104. Haeckel, S.H.: Adaptive enterprise design: The sense-and-respond model. Planning Review 23(3) (1995)

105. Teece, D.J., Pisano, G., Shuen, A.: Dynamic capabilities and strategic management. Strategic Management Journal 18(7), 509–533 (1997)

106. Crowston, K.: A coordination theory approach to organizational process design. Organization Science 8(2), 157–175 (1997)

107. Gosain, S., Malhotra, A., El Sawy, O.A.: Coordinating for flexibility in e-business supply chains. Journal of Management Information Systems 21(3), 7–45 (2004)

108. March, J.G., Simons, H.A.: Organizations. John Wiley & Sons, New York (1958)

109. Van De Ven, A.H., Delbecq, A.L.: Determinants of coordination modes within organizations. American Sociological Review 41(2), 322–338 (1976)

110. Sliger, M., Broderick, S.: The Software Project Manager's Bridge to Agility. Addison-Wesley, Upper Saddle River (2008)

111. Stepanek, G.: Software project secrets, why software projects fail. Springer, New York (2005)

112. Wang, E.T.C., Barron, T., Seidmann, A.: Contrasting Structures for Custom Software Development: The Impacts of Informational Rents and. Management Science 43(12), 1726–1744 (1997)

113. Jamieson, D., Vinsen, K., Callender, G.: Agile procurement and dynamic value for money to facilitate agile software projects. In: 32nd Euromicro Conference on Software Engineering and Advanced Applications (SEAA) - Proceedings, pp. 248–255 (2006)

114. Anderson, D.: Agile Management for Software Engineering: Applying the Theory of Constraints for Business Results. Prentice Hall, London (2003)
115. Alleman, G.B., Henderson, M., Seggelke, R.: Making agile development work in a government contracting environment - Measuring velocity with earned value. In: Proceedings of the Agile Development Conference, pp. 114–119 (2003)
116. Milgrom, P., Roberts, J.: Complementarities and Fit - Strategy, Structure, and Organizational-Change in Manufacturing. Journal of Accounting & Economics 19(2-3), 179–208 (1995)
117. Yetton, P., et al.: A model of information systems development project performance. Information Systems Journal 10(4), 263–289 (2000)
118. Reich, B.H., Benbasat, I.: Factors that influence the social dimenion of alignment between business and information technology objectives. MIS Quarterly 24(1), 81–113 (2000)
119. Sabherwal, R., Chan, Y.E.: Alignment Between Business and IS Strategies: A Study of Prospectors, Analyzers, and Defenders. Information Systems Research 12(1), 11 (2001)
120. Slaughter, S.A., et al.: Aligning software processes with strategy. MIS Quarterly 30(4), 891–918 (2006)
121. van der Zee, J.T.M., de Jong, B.: Alignment Is Not Enough: Integrating Business and Information Technology Management with the Balanced Business Scorecard. Journal of Management Information Systems 16(2), 137–156 (1999)
122. Thomas, J.C., Baker, S.W.: Establishing an Agile Portfolio to Align IT Investments with Business Needs. In: Agile 2008, Toronto, pp. 252–258 (2008)
123. Bassellier, G., Benbasat, I.: Business Competence of Information Technology Professionals: Conceptual Development and Influence on IT-Business Partnerships. MIS Quarterly 28(4), 673–694 (2004)
124. Tanriverdi, H.S.: Information technology relatedness, knowledge management capability, and performance of multibusiness firms. MIS Quarterly 29(2), 311–334 (2005)
125. Tanriverdi, H.S.: Performance Effects of Information Technology Synergies in Multibusiness Firms. MIS Quarterly 30(1), 57–77 (2006)
126. Brown, C.V.: Horizontal Mechanisms under Differing IS Organizational Contexts. MIS Quarterly 23(3(3)), 421–454 (1999)
127. Podobnik, D., Dolinsek, S.: Competitiveness and Performance Development: An Integrated Management Model. Journal of Organizational Change Management 21(2), 213–229 (2008)
128. Kobelsky, K.W., et al.: Determinants and Consequences of Firm Information Technology Budgets. Accounting Review 83(4), 957–995 (2008)
129. Kohli, R., Devaraj, S.: Measuring Information Technology Payoff: A Meta-Analysis of Structural Variables in Firm-Level Empirical Research. Information Systems Research 14(2), 127–145 (2003)
130. Bharadwaj, A.S.: A Resource-Based Perspective on Information Technology Capability and Firm Performance: An Empirical Investigation. MIS Quarterly 24(1), 169–196 (2000)
131. Glass, R.L.: The Standish report: does it really describe a software crisis? Communications of the ACM 49(8), 15–16 (2006)
132. Glass, R.L.: IT Failure Rates: 70% or 10-15%? IEEE Software 22(3), 111–112 (2005)
133. Jørgensen, M., Moløkken-Østvold, K.: How large are software cost overruns? A review of the 1994 CHAOS report. Information and Software Technology 48(4), 297–301 (2006)

134. Molokken, K., Jorgensen, M.: A Review of Software Surveys on Software Effort Estimation. In: International Symposium on Empirical Software Engineering, ISESE 2003 (2003)
135. Krishnakumar, P., Sukumaran Nair, V.S.: A model for software development effort and cost estimation. IEEE Transactions on Software Engineering 23(8), 485–497 (1997)
136. Roepke, R., Agarwal, R., Ferratt, T.W.: Aligning the IT human resource with business vision: The leadership initiative at 3M. MIS Quarterly 24(2), 327–353 (2000)
137. Sambamurthy, V., Bharadwaj, A., Grover, V.: Shaping agility through digital options: Reconceptualizing the role of information technology in contemporary firms. MIS Quarterly 27(2), 237–263 (2003)
138. Ross, J.W., Beath, C.M., Goodhue, D.L.: Develop Long-Term Competitiveness through IT Assets. Sloan Management Review 38(1), 31–42 (1996)
139. Ambler, S.W.: Architecture and Design. Dr Dobb's Journal (2008)
140. Highsmith, J.: An Adaptive Performance Management System. Cutter Consortium Executive Summary (2006), http://www.infoq.com/resource/articles/Adaptive-Performance-Management/en/resources/apms0606.pdf (cited November 9, 2010)
141. Ostergren, K., Stensaker, I.: Management control without budgets: A field study of 'Beyond Budgeting' in practice. European Accounting Review 20(1), 149–181 (2011)
142. Lohan, G., Lang, M., Conboy, K.: A performance management model for agile information systems development teams. In: ISD 2012, Prato, Italy (2012)
143. Drucker, P.: The coming of the new organization. Harvard Business Review 66(1), 45–53 (1988)
144. Barley, S.R., Kunda, G.: Design and devotion: Surges of rational and normative ideologies of control in managerial discourse. Administrative Science Quarterly 37(3), 363–399 (1992)

Case Study in Responsive Web Design: Pragmatic Agile and Hero Team Approach - Time and Cost Savings with Quality Improvement

Maarit Laanti[1], Tommi Laitila[2], Mikko Mustakallio[3], and Jukka-Pekka Kääriäinen[4]

[1] Nitor Delta, Kalevankatu 3 A 45, Finland
maarit.laanti@nitorcreations.com
[2] Nitor Creations, Kalevankatu 3 A 45, Finland
tommi.laitila@nitorcreations.com
[3-4] Talent Base, Metsänneidonkuja 8, Finland
{mikko.mustakallio,jukka-pekka.kaariainen}@talentbase.fi,

Abstract. There has been a request to publish more research results on business impacts of agile adoption in software team. This is an empirical study done in one Fortune 500 company where agility was adopted while the team was working on in order to deliver a product consisting of responsive web design. The adoption resulted in Pragmatic Agile approach, where the agility and Hero team approach was found to result in significant savings in both efforts needed to make the product and quality of the product delivered.

Keywords: software engineering, agile software development, software processes, agile deployment.

1 Introduction

According to Forrester study [1], main reasons why organizations adopt agile practices (in priority order) are 1) Reduced time to market, 2) Increased quality 3) Reduced waste 4) Better predictability and 5) Better morale. Although these might be the reason why organizations seek to apply agile methods, according to Dingsøyr and Dybå [2] very few empirically validated studies support the claim that agile methods are effective and suitable for many situations and environments.

Often, the adoption of existing agile methods may require their radical modification to fit the operative context [3]. Thus, it is no surprise that several case studies report challenges in the adoption of agile software development methods [4]. It has been reported that agile adopters are often not aware of what agile adoption really means, and how broad a change is actually required [1].

Although there exists some reports how agile methods have been used to improve quality as number of lower amount of errors produced [5], or how adoption of certain agile practice, such as TDD, has improved quality [6] research is still lacking reports on radical improvements and how those were made. Sutherland's [7] report on hyper-performance teams still stands up as one of its kind.

B. Fitzgerald et al. (Eds.): LESS 2013, LNBIP 167, pp. 106–121, 2013.
© Springer-Verlag Berlin Heidelberg 2013

West [8] has reported another problem that adoption of Scrum typically faces in traditional organizations: the Scrum process is preceded by a waterfall-type specification phase. West calls these joint practices as Water-Scrum-Fall process, where the "Water" stands for specification phases following traditional methods, Scrum for implementation phase following Scrum model and Fall for gated releasing.

A hero-culture is often seen as controversial to agile development. Cockburn [9] for example state that it is much more interesting phenomena to observe ordinary people doing their work with sense of pride than looking heroes to save poorly run projects with overtime work. It's been said that the point in scrum is to make ordinary teams to perform better [7] although at the same time the agile culture has had emphasis on software craftsmanship [10, 11]. While there is a lot of critics towards hacking culture and hackers providing quick fixes, there is also a lot of respect towards the developers who can get the hard job done. Some agile researchers also think that one reason why extreme programming have failed in reaching the mainstream adoption while scrum has succeeded [12] might be due the fact that extreme programming requires more rigorous approach to development itself and only very capable developers can follow that process.

In this respect Sutherland's report on hyper-performing teams is also special, as it describes how a supposedly ordinary team can become a high-performance team by using Scrum. The origin of Scrum was different though – there has never been any question whether the Borland team where Scrum was originated from was formed of very capable individuals or not [13]; many sources emphasis the skills of these individuals as developers [14, 15] – but on the other hand, having too individualistic (but skilled) persons on Scrum team not willing to change their behavior can cause Scrum to fail [16].

In this paper we describe how an expert team was getting better in defining and developing software by adoption of scrum principles but also modified those principles to cover also the concepting phase that was necessary in order to figure out from business requirements what actually needed to be implemented. This eliminates the Water-phase from Water-Scrum-Fall development and changes it to behavior more suitable for co-operation with Scrum. Also the Fall-phase was eliminated; the Scrum team took care of the releasing and the "last mile". We give a measured impact of the improvement done, and describe the final process that was taken into use.

This paper is structured as follows: the next section provides background information of the responsive web designs as well as introduces the research setting. Section 3 discusses the agile adoption and introduces the selected Pragmatic Agile approach. Section 4 discusses Hero teams. Section 5 lists the measured results of the changed approach, limitations and items for future study with final remarks.

2   Background

In this section, the area of responsive web design is introduced. We also list the challenges that the project was facing and how we thought the approach of Practical Agility could be used to solve these problems.

2.1   Responsive Web Design

Internet pages can be accessed using many different means: desktop computers, laptops, handheld tablets or phones, each having different screen sizes and different methods for controlling the user interface. Content on internet pages can be also accessed using very different bandwidths. Quite typically, companies optimize their web site designs for desktop and laptop users and mobile devices are not really supported. When designing and implementing internet services only for fast internet connections and high performance desktop computers the lower-bandwidth mobile devices will usually freeze or content simply cannot be accessed. Mobile software manufactures have tried to solve this problem by making the browsers used in mobile devices smarter, and download only the static content of the web page.

A traditional solution to help the mobile users to access the web pages and content has been to prepare separate digital channels with custom designs and implementations optimized for different kinds of devices. In this approach separate mobile-optimized channels typically also have content managed separately from desktop site. Mobile-optimized channels usually cut available features of the page such as graphics and enlarge interface control elements to accommodate the "fat" finger problem.[1] However, these separate channels require much more attention, as they need to be separately designed, implemented and maintained. This causes extra costs to companies.

Responsive web designs (RWDs) are an approach to solve this problem. In responsive web design and technique, the same content can be scaled and optimized differently depending on the contacting device capabilities using single user interface implementation. For example in large displays there is more space available for presenting the content in more rich and visual way and when the same content is presented in small displays, content can be then presented using a different layout or even completely hiding something less important from the page.

See Figure 1 for more description. The benefit comes in smaller design, implementation and maintenance effort when comparing to multiple separately operated sites.

Fig. 1. Responsive web design on different screen sizes

---

[1] Finger is considered as a "fat" input mechanism compared to mouse pointer that allows more sophisticated interactions with active input elements.

2.2   Challenges

There were several challenges in how to organize and run the responsive web design project. The project at hand was seen as too large and too complex in order to follow a traditional waterfall model with big front-up design. Hence the project was already organized into an ostensibly agile Scrum-like mode but there were simply too many unanswered questions on how to make a practical and working solution considering the design of the system. Especially, due to a number of integrations to external systems developed by parties acting in a non-agile mode, made the project's dependencies complex. Also the project was facing high time pressures to deliver the new solution. We simply had to boost the way in which we were working, so we organized the work based on priorities and utilisation of self-organizing, empowered teams. See Table 1 for challenges faced and the selected approach.

Table 1. Challenges and how these were faced

Challenges	Solution under test	How this is supposed to help
Project is large and complex	Specifying the concepts in a dedicated design and prototyping cycle	Early feedback helps to figure out which of the proposed solutions are feasible
Making a delivery estimate for a complex large project	Delivery in increments	Future estimates are based on earlier deliveries
Time-to market pressure	Self-organizing, empowered teams	Eliminate the waste of waiting and not taking action
Agile methodology adoption failed	Introduce concrete Pragmatic Agile Toolbox for the teams	Ensure guidance, best practices, and accountability

2.3   Research Context

The organization under study is a large multinational Fortune 500 corporation. The project in question consisted of multiple teams that were co-located to one development site. Also the business representatives and the operational stakeholders, i.e. Product Owners, were physically present in the same premises as the development teams.

2.4   Research Methods and Data Collection

The figures that the comparison is based on have been collected from a stable mid-release sprint by organization under study executed before Pragmatic Agile approach was introduced into this project. Those figures were then compared to a similar sprint executed according to Pragmatic Agile model. The data was extracted by a member of the client organization. The backlog items or features have remained roughly of the same size although these are no absolute constants but rather ballpark figures of rough size.

3   Pragmatic Agile Approach

We started to call the approach that was taken as Pragmatic Agile. In Scrum, there exists no solution for concepting phase [17]. Figure 2 shows the elements that we needed to take into account when creating Pragmatic Agile model. The goal was to create a model that would allow a good Return of Investment (ROI) without a raise on product life-cycle costs.

3.1   Pragmatic Agile Toolbox for Teams

Pragmatic Agile development guidance provides set of tested practices to adopt agile in development teams. With the help of guidance the teams can then take product backlog items from planning to delivery with good quality and performance. The actual product backlog creation is excluded and it is covered in the definition cycle.

From Agile methodology point of view Pragmatic Agile covers sprint based and continuous development models.

The scope of the guidance documentation is:

- Examples how individual team can adopt agile covering key concepts like planning, development and day-to-day work
- Roles and responsibilities of individual team members
- Best practices in way of working
- Patterns for failure

Fig. 2. Elements of Pragmatic Agile Approach

- **Assumptions:** The basic assumptions that have to be made to have a successful agile team adoption
- **Terms and Concepts:** Quick overview of the commonly used terms and concepts. Can be used as quick reference card
- **Roles:** Roles in pragmatic agile development teams and projects
- **Wall:** Explanation of the wall and how it is used. Concrete and pragmatic examples included

- **Planning:** Section covers how content is planned and taken into team for development.
- **Common practices:** Lists practices that have been noticed to work well in teams e.g. daily standup, demo, retro etc.
- **Engineering Best Practices:** Explains some key best practices from engineering point of view that fits well with the agile team work
- **Patterns of Failure:** Common mistakes and patterns for failure - good point to check if your team's work is heading for disaster

3.2   Quality Input for Development Teams

Development cycle can be seen as function creating the ICT-system: the output quality is correlating with the quality of the input. There exist already many companies that have been able to improve the development cycle to some extent:

- Continuous integration machinery, version control systems etc. are in very good condition,
- Teams work well together and they are capable of measuring and evaluating their performance leading to predictability in operational level of the project,
- Teams have strong competence, so they are able to overcome and solve even difficult problems.

If these teams get their requirements as user stories why that then teams aren't capable of producing good quality releases? Agile Methods originate from software product development, where integration and production efforts can be standardized. Besides, the project team can know the future goals of the product well. In this kind of environment the software teams can be empowered to make right decisions.

When a new business environment is built using Agile Methods new kind of challenges will be encountered. There exist many things outside the project that the teams cannot directly influence:

- The joint projects and systems need to make their own preparations before end to end testing can take place
- Other external forces from projects point-of-view strongly guide the decision-making. These include decisions made in joined projects, solution- and enterprise architecture solutions that influence what kind of architecture solutions can be made in the project, etc.

In case any project just solely use their own viewpoint, and proceed empowered without any external guidance would it result as:

- Missing common Definition-of-Done between projects interlinking with each other; resulting end-to-end system integration problems
- Architectural decisions that would only support the project's interest, not organizational end-to-end optimization

The question is how to ensure that the input to a single project has good quality, i.e.

- A business case for each functionality is created according to which prioritization can be performed
- There is a solution concept outlining not only the solution itself as a set of features but also optimizing the post-deployment operational lifespan of the solution
- User stories get written
- The high-level architecture exists and is tested in practice
- The production environments and configurations needed are ordered on time

The aim is to build capabilities for development teams to continuously add functionality into existing system without interruptions. At the same time it needs to be ensured that the end product is produced according to organizations' generic guidelines.

3.3   Ensuring Architectural Integrity

Quite often the high-level preliminary system architecture is prepared a long time before the project team is even gathered together first time. Typically this is work done by a systems architect, who is also set responsible for the high-level solution. Without this guidance the roles and responsibilities what different parts of the system should do can get mixed, the result being a poorly maintainable messy system.

- For people who have never worked in a very large organization, "architect" may have left a bad taste in their mouth. However, it is not only a legitimate role but also a highly strategic one for companies.[2]
- When an application becomes so vast and complex that dealing with the overall technical vision and planning, and translating business needs into technical strategy becomes a full-time job that is an **application architect**. Application architects also often mentor and/or lead developers, and know the code of their responsible application(s) well.
- When an organization has so many applications and infrastructure inter-dependencies that it is a full-time job to ensure their alignment and strategy without being involved in the code of any of them, that is, a **solution architect**. Solution architect can sometimes be similar to an application architect, but over a suite of especially large applications that comprise a logical solution for a business.
- When an organization becomes so large that it becomes a full-time job to coordinate the high-level planning for the solution architects, and frame the terms of the business technology strategy, that role is an **enterprise architect**.

---

[2] There are also infrastructure architects, information architects, and a few others, but in terms of total numbers these comprise a smaller percentage than the "big three".

[3]Enterprise architects typically work at an executive level, advising the CxO office and its support functions as well as the business as a whole.

3.4   Pragmatic Agile Model

In the new Pragmatic Agile model the development team sprint is preceded by a concepting sprint that prepares bigger architectural decisions, solution concepting, prototyping, and operational optimization. The development work done is based on this work done in concepting sprint. Automation is widely used, and both concepting and development sprints reserve time for automation tasks.

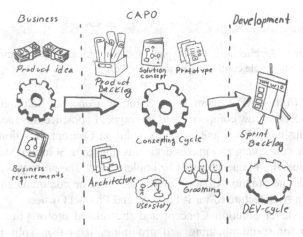

Fig. 3. Pragmatic Agile Model

4   Hero Team

The reason to try out CAPO and Hero Team approaches was to connect the concepting phase with implementation phase seamlessly.

4.1   CAPO Team

The idea in CAPO team was to cut the time previously used in Prototyping, Concepting, Architecture and Operational Process Design phases by melting these phases together as presented in Figure 4. The experienced benefits of this approach were:

- Small and efficient team means that no dedicated persons are needed to narrow strictly defined roles

---

[3] **Note**: numerous other answers have said there is "no standard" for these titles. That is not true. Go to any Fortune 1000 company's IT department and you will find these titles used consistently.

- Larger roles support wider understanding of the holistic product and problems when there is un-clarity what belongs under each of the roles responsibility
- Less interfaces between people and roles ensures seamless communication

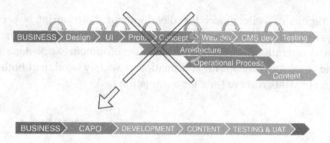

Fig. 4. Concepting, Architecture, Prototyping and Operational Optimization phases were melted together as one single continuous process (CAPO)

The output from CAPO team is a Solution Concept, Solution Architecture, Operational Model and new components to prototype. In practice this means that CAPO team takes in Business Needs and creates a Solution Concept. Solution Architect sits together with the concepting and makes decisions regarding Solution Architecture – i.e. where the functionality in question will be implemented. The prototype is continuously developed beside the Solution Concept and is used as one communication mechanism with the Solution Architecture towards business and Product Owners.

After Feature-level Solution Concept and the related prototyping are done it is taken to teams for sprint planning and grooming. It is then split into tasks and implemented in sprints.

The close co-operation between design offices, concept designers, solution architects and prototyping is an essential success factor - the essence of the CAPO phase is the insight that the quality of this input or initial guidance to the teams is one major reason why success may or may not follow the whole project. A wrong input in this phase could cause a penalty in the form of many implementation sprints, where the working solution would be iterated.

4.2   Hero Team

The reason why development team was called a "Hero Team" was to bring the attitude and ability to take responsibility and thus quality of what was being made into a new level. This was done in order to create an empowered team that also Scrum promotes. [17] Besides this, it was decided to use the automation to support the teams' effort as much as is possible, i.e. automating everything that could reasonably be automated.

A smaller, but empowered team resulted in:

- No dedicated persons with narrow roles
- Larger roles supporting understanding a developing "the whole"

- Less confusion what belongs to each person's role
- Less interfaces between people/ roles ensuring seamless communication

The prototype used as basis of development by Hero Team is located to same VCS as the final production code. Parts of the prototype end to production after Hero Team is finished with the complete solution. This includes e.g. adding business data.

Hero Team in fact receives a concept and a prototype reflecting the System level architecture solution, and does everything that is needed in order to finalize a full-fletched solution from it: plans the application architecture, implements the service and test automation, and sends to production using Continuous Deployment machinery that the team itself updates and maintains. All this requires a multi-talent team that is able to both implement the solutions but also support concepting, solving environment problems etc.

The Hero Team was working with these principles:

1. **Modeling solutions and architecture simultaneously:** Hero team has strong competences in solution creation and architecture co-located, in same team and same premises. It clarifies the business needs and prepares technical solutions, which are then put to product backlog for implementation. It optimizes the solutions as part of the solution creation process.
2. **From prototype to implementation**: HTML5-apprearance, CSS-style quides, Javascripts, and graphics are created in CAPO pre-sprint. Hero Team turns prototype implementation to real system implementation.
3. **Features implemented:** Hero Team implements directly deployable features from business requirements (Java-implementation + CMS-integration) with common responsibilities, and common tools.

These principles have led to:

1. Seamless cycles, i.e. from solution concepting via prototypes to operatively optimized ready system
2. Seamless functional quality. Concept designer is co-responsible with the developer for the product end-quality (sign-off before acceptance testing). Hero Team is responsible for test automation and code reviews.

With the ambitious attitude the Hero team has been able to take more responsibility, leading to reductions of the CAPO team size.

5   Results and Conclusions

The novel approach resulted into a new process where the customer was highly integrated to the process. Concepting, architectural guidance, prototyping and operational process optimization were made in pre-sprints that offered input to development sprint. New empowered multitalented Hero Teams were created. Acceptance test-driven development was applied from concepting phase to environments. Strong use of automation was utilized in prototyping, development, deployment, and testing.

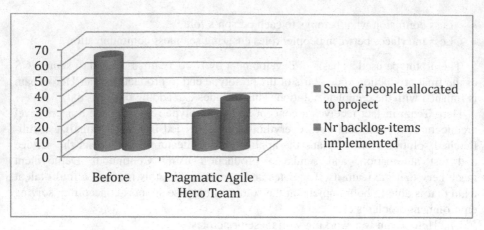

Fig. 5. Although the number of people in the project is only 1/3 of what is was before, the teams are capable of producing more functionality than before

Current project status is as follows:

1. Ability to develop bigger items with smaller group faster and with better quality (see Figure 5)
2. End-result is fully testable and design-debt is minimized (note – compare to traditional understanding of agile methods)
3. More even velocity and more accurate estimations
4. Business guidance of agile development is full-functional: business requirements in and working functionalities out
5. What is measured is visible to everybody via information radiators

Besides the time that the development team can spend on working towards the Sprint goals has increased (see Figure 6) and the time needed to complete one business feature has dropped (see Figure 7) because of improvement of the

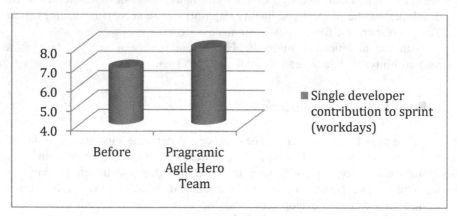

Fig. 6. Time that development team can contribute to sprint has increased 15%

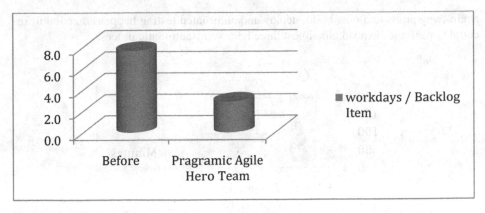

Fig. 7. Development team that works partly with Hero-team spend 60% less time with business case implementation than before

development environment. The improvement of the development environment is visible on Figure 8, showing how the build and integration times have dropped to one tenth of what it was previously and Figure 9 showing radical improvement on how fast the system is to set-up.

5.1 Automation for Productivity Increase

Analysis showed that building of complex application took so long time that development was slow and cumbersome. The target was set to make build and get it automatically unit tested in two minutes instead more than forty minutes like it was when the work started. The target was almost met already in the first sprint and was improved in the second. Efficiency increase was dramatic.

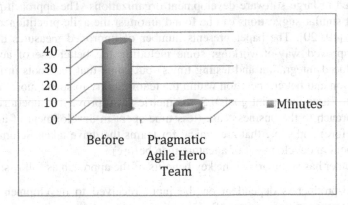

Fig. 8. Build and automatic test time is one tenth of what before

The other thing that was hindering the development was long deployment times on upper environments. The target was set to get build and deployment for integration test environment to the level that 'build on commit' was possible. To meet target took again two sprints and now build, deploy and automated testing happens on commit in couple of minutes instead old almost three hour semi-automatic process.

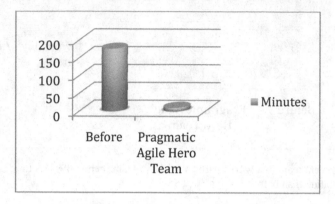

Fig. 9. Setting up the system is one twentieth of what before (enabling "build on commit")

One important improvement has been deployment automation for upper environments. Old labor intensive deploy process is replaced with fully automatized one. This automation along with hero team explains dramatic increase to productivity.

The summary of Pragmatic Agile Check-list that was created during the project is presented in Appendix A.

5.2   Discussion

The paper suggests a new Agile Method called Pragmatic Agile that is loosely based on Scrum and previous architectural, business modelling and concepting phase practices used in large software development organizations. The approach presented is novel, but similar suggestions can be found amongst the agile practitioners [18] or in literature [19, 20]. The paper presents number of improved measures that result from the improved way-of-working; some including the better use of automation (such as reduced integration and testing times) but some that has roots in improved communication and better operation within the team (ability to spend more work time in working towards the sprint goals). Some metrics also prove the superiority of the selected approach to the business case (less time spent in development of a business case than before) and some that are typical for teams that have taken Scrum into use (less time spent in development of a feature than before).

The customer has summarized the key benefits of the approach as follows:

- The end-product is dependent on the input received to development cycle – seamless co-operation ensures efficiency and quality
- Clear responsibilities with well-defined Definitions-of-done and seamless handoffs ensure that the development team is focusing on right things and their work is not interrupted in the middle of the sprint cycle

- The customers no longer need to buy large projects with several but narrow roles but can focus on generalists-type of persons with many competences who then can together create a working system from business requirements efficiently

References

1. Schwaber, K., Laganza, G., D'Silva, D.: The truth about agile processes: frank answers to frequently asked questions, Forrester Report (2007)
2. Dybå, T., Dingsøyr, T.: Empirical Studies of Agile Software Development: A Systematic Review. Information and Software Technology 50, 833–859 (2008)
3. Grenning, J.: Launching XP at a Process-Intensive Company. IEEE Software, 3–9 (November/December 2001)
4. Svensson, H., Höst, M.: Introducing an agile process in a software maintenance and evolution organization. In: Proceedings of 9th European Conference of Maintenance and Reengineering (2005)
5. Korhonen, K.: Supporting Agile Transformation with Defect Management in Large Distributed Software Development Organization. Dissertation, Tampere University of Technology, Publication 1032 (2012) ISBN 978-952-15-2790-6
6. Janzen, D.S.: An empirical evaluation of the impact of test-driven development on software quality. Diss. University of Kansas (1993)
7. Sutherland, J.: Future of Scrum: Parallel Pipelining of Sprints in Complex Projects. In: Agile Development Conference Proceedings (2005),
   http://doi.ieeecomputersociety.org/10.1109/ADC.2005.28,
   ISBN: 0-7695-2487-7
8. West, D.: Water-Scrum-Fall Is the Reality of Agile for Most Organizations Today (2011)
9. Cockburn, A.: Agile Software Development, the Cooperative Game, 2nd edn. Addison-Wesley (2007) ISBN: 0-321-48275-1
10. Martin, R.: Clean Code: A Handbook of Agile Software Craftsmanship, 1st edn., August 11. Prentice Hall (2008) ISBN-10: 0132350882, ISBN-13: 978-0132350884
11. Manifesto for software craftsmanship,
    http://manifesto.softwarecraftsmanship.org/
12. West, D., Grant, T.: Agile Development: Mainstream Adoption Has Changed Agility. Forrester Research (2010)
13. Sutherland, J., Schwaber, K.: The Scrum Papers: Nuts, Bolts and Origins of an Agile Process (2007), http://citeseerx.ist.psu.edu/viewdoc/
    summary?doi=10.1.1.108.814
14. Cockburn, A., Highsmith, J.: Agile software development, the people factor. Computer 34(11), 131–133 (2001)
15. Vriens, C.: Certifying for CMM Level 2 and ISO9001 with XP@ Scrum. In: Proceedings of the Agile Development Conference, ADC 2003. IEEE (2003)
16. Sutherland, J., Altman, I.: Organizational Transformation with Scrum: How a Venture Capital Group Gets Twice as Much Done with Half the Work. In: 2010 43rd Hawaii International Conference on System Sciences (HICSS). IEEE (2010)
17. Schwaber, K., Beedle, M.: Agile Software Development with Scrum. Prentice-Hall, Inc. (2002)
18. Clinton, K.: Agile for Game Development. Addison-Wesley,
    http://www.infoq.com/presentations/kanban-video-game-dev

19. Coplien, J., Børnevik, G.: Lean Architecture: for Agile Software Development. Wiley (2010) ISBN-10: 0470684208, ISBN-13: 978-0470684207
20. Leffingwell, D.: Agile Software Requirements. Lean Requirements Practices for Teams, Programs, and the Enterprise. Addison-Wesley (2011) ISBN-10: 0-321-63584-1, ISBN-13: 978-0-321-63584-6

Appendix A - Pragmatic Agile Checklist

A checklist for Pragmatic Agile practices:

Clearly defined product owner (PO)
- ☐ PO is dedicated to the project and easily available to the team
- ☐ PO is empowered and has knowledge to prioritize
- ☐ PO has direct contact with team
- ☐ PO has direct contact with stakeholders

PO maintains a product backlog (PBL)
- ☐ PBL is prioritized by business value
- ☐ PBL is visible to the team

Top PBL items are well understood and ready for development
- ☐ Grooming takes place before sprint planning
- ☐ Bizcases have been approved
- ☐ Architectural implications to other systems have been agreed
- ☐ Prototyping for new feature have been done an verified
- ☐ Items have been estimated by the team
- ☐ Items are small enough to fit in a sprint

Team understands architecture and goals of surrounding systems
- ☐ Team receives architectural guidance when needed
- ☐ Team can bring up architectural issues and proposals
- ☐ Issues and proposals are managed transparently

Team has sprint planning meetings
- ☐ PO brings an up-to-date PBL with well-understood items
- ☐ Whole team and PO participates
- ☐ Meeting is not longer than 4 hours
- ☐ Team decides what fits into the sprint
- ☐ Team has a visible sprint backlog and a burndown chart

Team has a release burndown chart
- ☐ Teams estimate in story points rather than hours
- ☐ Team velocity is measured and used for release planning

Daily scrum (max 15 minutes) takes places daily at the same time
☐ Whole team participates
☐ Impediments surface and are dealt with

☐ Clearly defined scrum master (SCM) who is not PO
☐ Team knows top impediments
☐ SCM works actively to solve impediments
☐ Escalated to mgmt. when team cannot solve

All code is automatically tested
☐ Continuous integration is used
☐ Unit tests are written and test coverage is followed
☐ Acceptance tests are automated and created based on user stories
☐ Demos are held after each sprint before the next one starts
☐ PO and the required stakeholders participate
☐ Useful feedback is received
☐ Retrospective takes place after each sprint
☐ The entire team including the PO participates
☐ Results in improvement proposals and some get implemented

Sprints of max 4 weeks
☐ Thee sprints always end on time
☐ Team usually finished most items
☐ Team is not disrupted by other tasks
☐ Team possesses all skills required for completing items

THIS IS WHAT COUNTS:

☐ Team delivers working, tested software after each iteration
☐ Team delivers what the business needs most
☐ Team is continuously improving its practices

POSITIVE INDICATORS:

☐ Team is having fun and is being trusted by stakeholders
☐ Work generally takes place within the limits of normal working hours
☐ The atmosphere is open for discussing, experimenting and criticizing

Success Factors in New Service Development - Digia Flowd Analysis

Raija Kuusela and Sari Vilminko

VTT Technical Research Centre of Finland,
Kaitoväylä 1, P.O. BOX 1100
FI-90571 Oulu, Finland
raija.kuusela@vtt.fi, sarivilminko@gmail.com

Abstract. Today, the importance of digital services with social aspects is increasing all the time. Many companies have been strong in new product development, but today they are moving to new service development. Customer value has become the strategic factor for contemporary companies when developing products and services for consumers; even so that companies are selling customer value instead of products or services. Customer orientation and customer involvement play important roles in service industries. This study describes how the case company entered to B-to-C digital service market and developed a new social network cloud service for music lovers. This theory testing case study discusses and reflects the success factors of new service development and the organization against the literature. Mostly the theory is confirmed, but also improvement of the theory is suggested. Finally, future research ideas are proposed.

Keywords: Cloud service, new service development, customer value, customer involvement.

1   Introduction

The ever-changing business environment requires companies to adapt to changes in order to survive or gain competitive advantage. Many companies have been skillful in new product development (NPD), but today they are moving to new service development (NSD). Many researches have concluded that NSD is an important competitive factor for companies in service industry [1].

Today, people talk ever more about services, digital services, e-services, web-services, and cloud services. Cloud computing has become a hype term, even though a clear definition is still missing [e.g. 2, 3, 4]. However, contemporary companies have started to utilize the opportunities created by the "cloud" by developing cloud services in order to maintain or gain competitive advantage over entrants. Today, there are already many B-to-B cloud services, but also B-to-C cloud services, still lots of opportunities related to cloud phenomenon are waiting to be explored and found.

When developing products and services targeted to consumers, customer value becomes a critical success factor. The customer value concept assesses the value a

B. Fitzgerald et al. (Eds.): LESS 2013, LNBIP 167, pp. 122–136, 2013.

product or service provides to a customer in terms of tangible and intangible features [5]. Today, there are lots of discussions and published articles related to customer value and all its aspects.

A major difference between NPD and NSD is in the involvement of customers in services, and thus, customer orientation plays an important role in service companies [6]. Matthing et al. [7] claim based on their research that consumers' service ideas are found to be more innovative than those of service developers. Posselt and Förstl [8] have reviewed literature of NSD success factors covering several industries including also high-technology service industry. The identified success factors are worthy arguments to be considered in any company developing new services.

The purpose of this paper is to examine how the case company developed a new cloud service targeted to consumer market. The focus is on the company's internal development process in creating the service with the intended customer value. The theoretical basis in the study is on new service development, cloud service, customer value, customer involvement, and success factors in NSD.

The research questions of this paper are: 1) How did the case company develop a new cloud service and 2) what are the success factors of the NSD process.

The paper is structured so that the theoretical background is explained first. Then, the research process and methods used in the study are described. The paper progresses by presenting the research results. Finally, discussion and proposed future work are presented.

2   Theoretical Basis

2.1   New Service Development

During the last decade the ever-changing business environment and considerably enhanced information technology (IT) have made companies to re-consider their business and offerings. Many companies have been strong in NPD, but today they are moving to NSD. Much research has concluded that NSD is an important competitive factor for service industry [1].

According to Matthing et al. [7] services are activities, deeds or processes and interactions where the customer plays the complex role of both contemporary consumer and producer. Riedl et al. [9] talk about electronic services or e-services saying that an increasing proportion of services are now electronic services delivered over the Internet. They define e-service as "a business activity of value exchange that is accessible through an electronic interface". Kirchmair [10] talks about digital services and claims that a digital service includes characteristics of both immaterial services and material products. He says (p. 18): "Although a digital service is based on software and, thus, constitutes a product with respect to design and development activities, it also shows inherent characteristics of a service when it comes to its commercialization and consumption."

Cloud computing has become a hype word, even though a universally accepted definition is still missing [4]. Cloud computing has been recognized as an important influencer in business and thus many companies have started to benefit from the opportunities the cloud offers. Many companies are developing or expanding their offerings to the commercial sector by giving businesses the opportunity to outsource elements of their IT infrastructure with access achieved via the Internet; this is also known as cloud-sourcing [11]. There are three main types of cloud-sourcing products, i.e. cloud storage, cloud platform, and cloud service [11].

In this paper, the research subject – "Flowd - Social network for music lovers" (in brief "Flowd") – qualifies all the previous concepts, i.e. Flowd is an e-service, a digital service, and a cloud service.

2.2   Customer Value

Today, customer value has become the strategic factor for Information and Communication Technology (ICT) companies when developing products and services for consumers. Companies are nowadays selling customer value instead of products or services [5]. Defining customer value is a topical issue today. Van der Haar et al. [5] say that the customer value concept assesses the value a product offers to a customer in terms of tangible and intangible features. They continue that customer value is a dynamic concept as it may change over time, and further they claim that customer value has to be defined at different abstraction levels.

2.3   Customer Involvement in NSD

When the user of the service is a consumer, the importance of user experience and customer value is highlighted. Kirchmair [10] says that development of successful products and services includes involvement of customers in the development process. Matthing et al. [7] argue that NSD relies on the task of understanding and anticipating latent customer needs.

Matthing et al. [7] have reviewed literature of customer involvement in product or service development and list concepts of customer involvement: lead user method, co-development, co-opting customer competence, user involvement, consumer involvement, and customer interaction. Based on the literature review of customer involvement they conducted a research of the subject and ended up arguing that customer involvement in NSD produces more innovative service ideas than those of service developers [7].

2.4   Success Factors in NSD

Posselt and Förstl [8] have reviewed literature of NSD success factors. The literature review covers several industries including also high-technology service industry. In their literature review, Posselt and Förstl [8] identified three categories of success factors: 1) antecedents of NSD success describing pre-conditions of an organization in service development, 2) NSD process success factors, and 3) service success factors. Figure 1 illustrates the identified categories of NSD success factors in relation to the service development process.

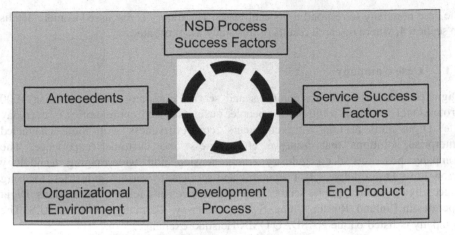

Fig. 1. NSD Success Factor Categories (modified from [8])

According to [8], antecedents of NSD success refer to general organizational aspects such as corporate culture, structure, and organizational capabilities. The most important antecedents of NSD success are: market orientation, technology, knowledge management, organizational culture, and strategic human resource management.

Posselt and Förstl [8] claim that NSD process success factors influence the effectiveness and efficiency with which the service success factors are implemented, and these factors have to be influenced during the development of the service. They list the most meaningful NSD process success factors as: employee involvement and employee expertise, appropriate level of process formalization, management measures, customer involvement, market orientation, the synergy between the development process and its environment, cross-functional involvement, and process quality.

Posselt and Förstl [8] continue that a service entails a unique experience between the service provider and service customer. It is important to be aware of certain elements which contribute most to the success of a service: unique or superior service, product synergy, and employee expertise.

3   Theory Testing Case Study Design

This study follows the principles of a case study [12]. The case study method is a suitable research approach for the overall study in which the researchers act as investigators rather than participants [13] and where the goal is to investigate a contemporary phenomenon in a real-life context. The case study is a suitable research methodology for software engineering research and it is descriptive and interpretive in nature, i.e. it aims at portraying a situation through the interviewees' interpretation of their context [14]. In this research, case study is used for theory testing [15]. The theory that is tested with this case study is the list of success factors in NSD created by Posselt and Förstl [8]. It was chosen as the theory to be tested, because it is topical and discusses the current, very turbulent business environment, which has made also the case company to respond to its challenges. The theory is discussed in more details in section 4, where research results of this study are presented.

3.1   Case Company

Digia is a Finnish software solutions and service company with more than 1000 professionals creating solutions for people, businesses and communities in everyday life. Digia aims at improving customers' competitiveness with multi channeled enterprise solutions that improve effectiveness and customer experience. The company possesses deep industry comprehension and wide-ranging technology know-how. Digia delivers ICT solutions and services to various industries, focusing especially on finance, public sector, trade and services and telecommunications. Digia operates in Finland, Russia, China, Sweden, Norway, Germany, and in the U.S. The company is listed on the NASDAQ OMX Helsinki exchange.

3.2   Research Subject Flowd – A New Cloud Service

Flowd – "Social network for music lovers" [16] is Digia's first cloud service targeted to consumer market. Flowd was created both for business and learning purposes. Through Flowd, Digia's research and development efforts are boosted in an environment with fresh business context. The main user groups are music artists/groups and their fans, but also club organizers and record labels. Flowd is music lovers' and artists' network. The business model of Flowd is to provide artists perfect tools for nourishing their fan relationships. This will lead to the sales of music and merchandise from which Flowd will receive an affiliate fee. The target was to create a service with the two most important differentiators compared to competing services: 1) a more appealing user experience, 2) communication tools for end users.

Development of Flowd started in late spring 2010. One reason for developing a new service was the fact that social media services had become common, and Digia wanted to go for social media services and more specifically to a service that was targeted to consumers; so far Digia had operated in B-to-B environment. The executive team of Digia was tasked with making the new service as successful as possible. Flowd team studied current trends such as social commerce, music, sports, entertainment, and location. The agile team wanted to find its way to success, which meant changing direction from time to time. At first, Flowd started with the focus on location like many other services; Foursquare and Gowalla (RIP) served as reference services. The first public beta version of Flowd was launched in June 2010; at that point of time, focus of Flowd was just in location, but later on, music was added to location. This addition was done, because Digia wanted to differentiate from others, and music is a global phenomenon and unlike many other entertainment phenomena with highly engaged fans (like football e.g.), music fans can be die-hard fans of many music artists and bands. Flowd team decided to integrate music artists, the ecosystem around the music artists, and their fans. In December 2010, Flowd - "The Music Lovers' Social Network" - was launched.

Some market analyses were done, but the target was not completely fixed in order to be able to react to market trends. Along the way, the target became clearer, along with iterations of Flowd. No formal surveys, only unofficial discussions, were conducted. Some musicians and labels were asked what they expected from the service; consumers were asked through conversations in social media. Roles involved in innovation process and creating the idea were marketing experts, technical experts, user experience specialists, developers and manager roles such as product manager and project manager.

A crucial thing for success of Flowd was good contacts from music industry, "really big names", as one interviewee said. They gave hints for the service. Another interviewee said: "Ideas don't matter. It's how you implement it, and the implementation itself is very often a series of ideas. And, I mean, any idea can be copied." ... "Somebody implements the right idea at the right time with the right product, and that turns into a success."

Customer value was considered very intensively during all development phases, even though the team did not have a precise definition for customer value. The team recognized that success comes from customer value, which however is different in B-to-B than in B-to-C environment. As well, the team discussed that people are temperamental; they value things differently in the course of time and experience, and they may change their minds. The team seemed to understand that what they as the developers of the service valued was not necessarily valued by the customers. The team was eagerly awaiting the customers' feedback from each release; the feedback was carefully analyzed and utilized in order to better respond to the customers' expectations.

During Flowd development, customers were involved all the time, more or less, depending on the development phase. The development process was iterative, which easily involved users. Both musicians and their fans were involved and they both benefited from their involvement. Some of them were contacted and asked how they would improve the service, and the feedback was considered when developing the service further. However in general, the feedback collection from customers was informally conducted. Customer feedback and new ideas were highly appreciated by the team. An interviewee describes: "As you look at any ... digital product, at the moment it's in, it's usually in constant evolvement. Usually you make gradual changes, you change this, and you change that and look at what happens. Especially for such a product, I think it's imperative to look at what your consumers are doing and looking at the effects of your development."

The team consisting of 12-13 members used agile development method (Scrum), which promotes a cross-functional team; developers, testers, user experience specialist, marketing manager, product manager and project manager The team favored lean practices, rapid development, fast and frequent (bi-weekly) releases, always trying to improve. Scrum was introduced in the beginning; however, later on the practices were modified to better respond the team's flexible working practices; the team tailored their own working practices (e.g. the team abandoned daily scrum-meetings, but had meetings when needed).

From developers' point of view information sharing was good. Development team received tasks (features) from management team, who had better understanding of customers' desires and better vision of the market needs. The concept of the service was initially created by the management team. User experience specialist drafted wire-frames to see how it could be integrated with all features, finalized graphics, made static images, and sent them to the developers for implementation. Flowd architecture was simple, which offered independency in the development work. Flowd integrates with other public external services, which have clearly defined interfaces.

Usability tests were conducted from the very beginning. Performance testing was conducted for ensuring reasonable response times and assuring scaling with large amount of users. Number of users was monitored; statistics of user amounts, errors and problems were recorded. In later phases of the development testing was more regular and planned due to test automation. Expert evaluations were conducted from time to time.

Flowd was launched via device manufacturers' web-pages (App Store, Marketplace, Nokia Store).

3.3   Research Method

This research aims at studying retrospectively the development of a new cloud service that was targeted to consumer market. The purpose was to find out how the team coped with NSD in order to transfer the learnings and experiences to future service development projects.

Semi-structured individual interviews, one workshop and one meeting were used as data collection methods. Seven persons of the case unit were interviewed. The senior project manager was the main contact person between the company and the research organization. She organized all the interviews (time and place). The interviews were conducted within one month in spring 2012. All data of about one hour interviews were recorded and transcribed by an external company. The interviewees' roles were senior project manager, graphic and interaction designer, marketing expert, web designer, server designer, IOS application designer, and Android application designer. The interviewees were located in two sites in Finland.

The interview questions covered the following topics:

- customer value (how the interviewees define it, how it is created in the development of the new service)
- customer involvement
- methods used to ensure the implementation of the designed customer value
- capabilities
- successes and failures in new service development.

The transcribed interview data was analyzed by the researcher. Firstly, the development process was described as a flow chart and the team members' activities were located in the process description in order to get an understanding of the work and information flows of the project. Secondly, the researcher combined each interviewee's sayings per each interview question in order to enrich the 'story'. Thirdly, the researcher studied all this data if Posselt's and Förstl's [8] NSD success factors were found. The researcher created material that included description of the development process, summary of the interviewees' responses to each interview question, and a list of NSD success factors complemented with descriptions of how they appeared in Flowd team. All this material was the input for the forthcoming workshop.

The three-hour workshop was organized in autumn 2012. All interviewees except for the senior project manager participated in the workshop, where all the above-mentioned material was discussed, clarified, corrected, complemented, and a few minor contradictions were sorted out together. Next, in the two-hour meeting with the senior project manager all the material was once more discussed and clarified aiming at ensuring the correctness of the research data.

The researcher acted as the interviewer, facilitator of the workshop and meeting, observer, and analyzer of the research data.

4   Research Results

This section presents the research results of the case study. As Flowd is the case company's first cloud service targeted to consumers, the overall experiences and the research results are extremely important for the whole company. In this theory testing case study, the case company's findings are reflected against Posselt's and Förstl's [8] NSD success factors.

4.1   Findings Discussed Against Theory

In their literature review, Posselt and Förstl [8] concluded three categories of success factors, i.e. category 1 - organizational environment aspect: antecedents of NSD success describing pre-conditions of an organization in service development; category 2 - development process aspect: NSD process success factors; and category 3 - end product aspect: service success factors (see Fig. 1). The main focus of this research stands in the category 2, i.e. success factors of the NSD process, but also some organizational success factors (category 1) were identified. The service success factors (category 3) would be the focus of future research.

Next, the most important success factors are discussed, how they become evident in the case company and in Flowd team, i.e. the theory is tested by the research findings.

Organizational Success Factors in NSD Process (Category 1). Posselt and Förstl [8] list 15 antecedents of NSD success; five most significant antecedents are: 1) market orientation, 2) technology, 3) knowledge management, 4) culture, and 5) strategic human research management (HRM). The organizational antecedents were not the main focus of this research. However, some antecedents came up. They are discussed next.

According to Posselt and Förstl [8] market orientation is the most prominent antecedent of successful NSD. Market orientation is important for the case company especially because it was the first time when entering consumer markets with a new service. In Flowd case, marketing experts were strongly involved in the team work, and Flowd provided an excellent opportunity for the company to increase knowledge of cloud services that are targeted to consumer market.

Technology was identified as an organizational success factor by Posselt and Förstl [8] as it appears as an enabler of developing and delivering new services. One of the strengths of the case company is its knowledge of many technologies and of different industries; this came evident in the interviews and workshops conducted during this research. However, they said that there is still room for learning of new technologies as well.

Knowledge management is about gathering and sharing useful information internally and externally [8]. In the case study, the interviewees said that they have a lot of knowledge in the company and in Flowd team. They say that the company has strong knowledge of technologies and technology platforms, and new knowledge is acquired continuously. Continuous learning and information sharing was emphasized by the team members. They said that information is shared well within the team. In Flowd team there is lot of tacit knowledge, which the team members identified both as strength and weakness.

Organizational culture and especially the learning culture, was recognized as a very strong factor in this research. The personnel of the company are committed to work and to continuous learning. One interviewee highlighted that continuous learning is a characteristic of an individual employee and the whole company. In the case company, organizational culture includes innovativeness, flexibility, agility, willingness and capability to develop.

The literature review of Posselt and Förstl [8] reveals also strategic HRM as an antecedent of NSD success. In this study it did not come up explicitly. It was only weakly touched.

Success Factors of the NSD Process (Category 2). Posselt and Förstl [8] list 25 NSD success factors; nine most significant success factors are: 1) employee involvement, 2) appropriate formalization, 3) management measures, 4) customer involvement, 5) market orientation, 6) synergy, 7) cross-functional collaboration, 8) employee expertise, and 9) process quality.

Employee involvement and employee expertise were clearly visible in the case unit. Flowd team showed very strong commitment and fruitful teamwork. The members are experts of their own fields and trust each other. All of them were enthusiastic about the service under development.

The literature review [8] indicates that NSD process needs to have an appropriate level of formalization of development processes. However, the review says that in turbulent environments it is more beneficial to implement non-formalized approaches. This was the case also with Flowd team. Mainly, the used processes were the same as in previous projects. However, they were tailored to be more flexible and suitable for the team. The team realized that when innovating and developing a brand new service it required also new abnormal ways of working; the team tailored their own working practices to support their agile way of working. The team had the freedom to tailor their own working practices to support the "get things done" attitude. The team appreciated flexibility and the possibility to use common sense, which motivated them and made working easier. The team favored rapid development with fast and frequent releases (bi-weekly), always trying to improve. They released frequently rather than trying to polish the service. Sometimes design and implementation took place in parallel to each other. It was also visible that the team abandoned heavy requirements management process and focused on implementing "fresh" features that were appreciated by consumers. One interviewee said: "...we are always looking for the core, the essence, what makes Flowd a truly invaluable application for users". As Flowd team worked independently at Digia, different types of production techniques and tools could be trialed as well.

Management measures promote the success of development projects in terms of support of innovation, risk-taking or innovation friendly attitude [8]. The Flowd case is an instance of management support in the case company; the project was started as a spearhead project. In Flowd project management support was evident as the team was allowed to work independently, freely and it was allowed to modify their working practices and processes. The independency of the team was felt as a key success factor by the team members. Management support was in evidence when product development decisions were made by the management team; the management team decided which features were to be implemented and the team received tasks (features) from the management team, who had better vision and understanding of customers' desires. Some further notices came up as well. Firstly, the interviewed team members mentioned that communication with the top management could have been more transparent. Secondly, they said that not enough resources were allocated for the project in order to have been able to conduct proper consumer interviews and surveys.

Customer involvement is said to have a positive impact especially in idea generation and in the development process, but even a negative impact on the radicalness of innovations [8]. Customer perspective was highly considered in Flowd team during the whole development process. The interviewees said that customers were involved in some phases and in some phases not, depending on what was on-going in the development. They disclosed that extent and way of involving should be considered case by case. However, the team claims that all customer feedback and new ideas were welcome. One interviewee considered that customers should be involved in all development phases; from the concept phase till the perfect product. In Flowd, both musicians and their fans are involved and they both benefit from their involvement. Both customer groups were also asked feedback. As the development of Flowd was an iterative process, customers were involved during the whole development process. The team members argued that good contacts from music industry were very important to Flowd development.

Market orientation concerns understanding consumers' desires and is especially important for the identification of market opportunities in idea evaluation and the test of developed concepts [8]. In the Flowd case, market orientation seemed to be one of the most critical topics. The team said that preparing to launch – how to launch, where to launch, when to launch - was crucial for the success of the service. It was also topical to consider, where to focus marketing. They also said that considering how much customer analyses, pre-phase studies, and interviews are reasonable to conduct. Some market analyses were done but the target was intentionally left slightly open in order to be able to respond to market trends. Along the way of Flowd development, the target became clearer. A crucial thing for Flowd development was good contacts from music industry, "really big names" as they say.

Synergy of internal and external environments determines the success of NSD [8]. Posselt and Förstl [8] say that "the project should respond to the demands of the marketplace, constituting a response to understanding and operationalizing actual changes in consumer needs". In Flowd development good contacts from music industry were very important as they helped the team to understand what consumers expected. The first launched beta version of Flowd was developed in only one month from the decision to build the service. This was done in order to get fast feedback from consumers about what they really expected from the service. From the organization's internal perspective, developing Flowd is seen a very good exercise, a spearhead project for learning and business purposes and to get knowledge of the "consumer cloud"; how to develop a cloud service, what kind of things to be considered when developing a new cloud service, how to create a network around the service, and how to activate actors in the network. From the business environment point of view Flowd taught how to act with other players in the market, and also from the technological point of view, e.g. how to connect to the interfaces of other services.

Cross-functional involvement is a success factor that has an impact during all development phases [8]. This is also the case with Flowd team. The team used Scrum (agile method) which fosters the idea of cross-functional team: developers, architect, user experience specialist, graphical designer, project manager, product manager, and marketing expert. Marketing expert was aware of the development status all the time and user experience specialist participated in the meetings when needed. The team consisted totally of 12-13 members. In the beginning of the project, Scrum method was used, but later on the practices were revised in order to support the team best, i.e. the team introduced Kanban method in parallel with Scrum and the team did not have regular planning sessions, but planning sessions were organized only when needed. In the cross-functional team communication was good, members were competent, committed, trusting each other, way of working was flexible, and the atmosphere was open encouraging to present new ideas and problems.

Process quality is determined by the emphasis put on the development phases and the way how actions are carried out [8]. This success factor was not very visible in the Flowd team. Nonetheless, one has to keep in mind that in turbulent environments it is beneficial to implement non-formalized approaches as was discussed above related to the success factor "appropriate level of formalization".

Service Success Factors (Category 3). Service success factors were not studied in this research.

4.2   Proposed New Theory

Most of the success factors of the NSD process were confirmed by this study, i.e. employee involvement, employee expertise, management measures, appropriate level of formalization, customer involvement, market orientation, synergy of internal and external environments, and cross-functional collaboration. As well, most organizational success factors were confirmed by this research, i.e. market orientation, technology, knowledge management, and organizational culture. Thus, this means that the theory is strong. However, we would like to propose some new aspects to the theory as follows.

Firstly, as shown above, the success factor of management measures was confirmed in this case study. Moreover, related to this success factor our research reveals that *organizational transparency* is an important element in contemporary ICT companies. We propose transparency as a new success factor both to organizational (category 1) and development process (category 2) success factors. Proper transparency throughout the whole organization helps it to improve information sharing, productivity, cooperation, resource allocation, and traceability of requirements among other things. Constant communication and mutual trust are the main antecedents towards transparency.

Secondly, on one hand, Posselt and Förstl [8] say that the process of NSD needs to have appropriate level of formalization, but they continue that this does not apply to all development projects. This deviation was confirmed by our study. On the other hand, Posselt and Förstl [8] argue that "the process quality is determined by the emphasis put on the development phases and the assiduousness with which actions within these phases are carried out". This was not very apparent in the Flowd-project, which was a spearhead project developing a brand new service at the company, and the team was allowed to tailor the processes to serve best the team's work. Consequently, we propose to replace the above mentioned two success factors ('appropriate level of formalization' and 'process quality') to *flexible and adaptable development processes*. This is necessary especially in contemporary business environment where turbulence seems to be a permanent state of affairs.

Organizational success factors were not in the focus of this research, even though some success factors were identified in the analysis phase. Therefore, we cannot claim that based on this study a new theory could be proposed related to organizational success factors. However, we can say that our initial findings related to them seem to support the theory. Further research is needed in this field.

4.3   Recommendations

In this research we reflected our findings against Posselt's and Förstl's [8] NSD success factors. As the result of the study we propose a revised set of the success factors as listed in Table 1. Our recommendation is that companies developing new services would consider the "Proposed NSD success factors" of Table 1.

Table 1. Revised NSD success factors

NSD success factors [8]	Proposed NSD success factors	Comments
Organizational success factors		
Market orientation	Market orientation	
Technology	Technology	
Knowledge management	Knowledge management	
Culture	Culture	
Strategic HRM	Strategic HRM	Not studied in this research
	Transparency	New success factor
NSD process success factors		

Table 1. (*continued*)

Employee involvement	Employee involvement	
Appropriate formalization		Replaced by the new success factor (x)
Management measures	Management measures	
Customer involvement	Customer involvement	
Market orientation	Market orientation	
Synergy	Synergy	
Cross-functional collaboration	Cross-functional collaboration	
Employee expertise	Employee expertise	
Process quality		Replaced by the new success factor (x)
	Flexible and adaptable development processes (x)	New success factor
	Transparency	New success factor
Service success factors		
Unique or superior service	Unique or superior service	Not studied in this research
Product synergy	Product synergy	Not studied in this research
Employee expertise	Employee expertise	Not studied in this research

5   Limitations and Validity of the Results

The single-case study chosen in this research raises a question if the results are generalizable. Additionally, in a single-case study there is a risk of misjudging and exaggerating the research data [15]. The primary goal of this study is to provide learning opportunity and information of how the case company succeeded in developing a new cloud service targeted to consumer market, where customer value emerges. The case study provides a possibility to learn about the development environment.

External validity of the results is achieved through the detailed description of the service development journey of the case company and by grounding the previous research to this study. Internal validity is achieved with different types of triangulation [14]. First, data triangulation was used in the data collection, as various data sources in terms of people with different roles and sites were interviewed. Second, methodological triangulation was used by combining different types of data collection methods, i.e. semi-structured interviews, a workshop, and a meeting. Third, investigator triangulation was used as several people with different backgrounds participated in the analysis; they included professionals of different competence areas from the company, and the researcher outside the company. Fourth, theory triangulation was used when utilizing different fields of research, i.e. new service development, customer value, customer involvement, and cloud computing.

6   Conclusions and Future Work

This paper reports experiences from a case study that explores how the case company succeeded in developing a new cloud service targeted to consumer market, where customer value emerges. The project is considered as a beneficial spearhead project in the case company. Its significance to the company is great as the experiences can be transferred to future projects. One interviewee said: "This is an experiment, experience, and they had set up, this ventures department, I think to develop this kind of products that they start almost as research and they can develop into real product". The new service, Flowd, can be considered as an internal start-up and a spin-off could be the final result.

The research findings were tested against theory, i.e. Posselt's and Förstl's [8] literature review of success factors in NSD. Organizational antecedents were not planned to be researched, however, they appeared in the run of the study and thus confirmed the theory. More importantly, most of the NSD process success factors were confirmed by this case study, i.e. employee involvement and expertise, appropriate level of formalization, management measures, customer involvement, market orientation, synergy of internal and external environments, and cross-functional collaboration. However, our research proposes two renewals to the theory: 1) transparency to be added as a success factor both to organizational and development process success factors, and 2) replacing 'appropriate level of formalization' and 'process quality' by 'flexible and adaptable development processes' in development process success factors.

Table 1 summarizes the success factors and recommendations based on this study. We recommend companies developing new services to consider the success factors discussed in this paper. This case study has shed light to NSD, but there is still room for further studies. Firstly, we propose to test again the success factors listed in Table 1, especially the proposed new and modified success factors. Secondly, further research in the case company is needed to test the success factors of the new service itself that was not studied at all in this research. Flowd and other new digital services targeted to consumers are very topical today, when the value experienced by the consumers has risen to the focal point of the current research.

Acknowledgments. This work was supported by TEKES as a part of the Cloud Software program of Tivit (Finnish Strategic Centre of Science, Technology and Innovation in the field of ICT).

References

1. Stevens, E., Dimitriadis, S.: Managing the new service development process: towards a systemic model. European Journal of Marketing 39(1/2), 175–198 (2005)
2. Vaquero, L., Rodero-Merino, L., Caceres, J., Lindner, M.: A Break in the Clouds: Towards a Cloud Definition. Computer Communication Review 39(1), 50–55 (2009)
3. Kim, W.: Cloud computing: Today and Tomorrow. Journal of Object Technology 8(1), 65–72 (2009)

4. Mircea, M., Ghilic-Micu, B., Stoica, M.: Combining Business Intelligence with Cloud Computing to delivery agility in actual economy. Journal of Economic Computation and Economic Cybernetics Studies 45(1) (2011)
5. Van der Haar, J.W., Kemp, R.G.M., Omta, O.: Creating value that cannot be copied. Industrial Marketing Management 30(8), 627–636 (2001)
6. Alam, L., Perry, C.: A customer-oriented new service development process. Journal of Services Marketing 16(6), 515–534 (2002)
7. Matthing, J., Sanden, B., Edvardsson, B.: New service development: learning from and with customers. International Journal of Service Industry Management 15(5), 479–498 (2004)
8. Posselt, T., Förstl, K.: Success Factors in New Service Development: a Literature Review. In: Ganz, W., Kicherer, F., Schletz, A. (eds.) Productivity of Services Next Gen - Beyond Output/Input. Fraunhofer Center for Applied Research and Supply Chain Service, Germany (2011)
9. Riedl, C., Leimeister, J.M., Krcmar, H.: New Service Development for Electronic Services – A Literature Review. In: Proceedings of the Fifteenth Americas Conference on Information Systems (AMCIS 2009). Citeseer (2009)
10. Kirchmair, B.: Outsourcing Innovation in Digital Service Creation: What Software Engineering Can Learn from Modern Product Development. In: Kern, E.-M., Hegering, H.-G., Brügge, B. (eds.) Managing Development and Application of Digital Technologies, pp. 17–37. Springer, Heidelberg (2006)
11. Joint, A., Baker, E., Eccles, E.: Hey, you, get off of that cloud? Computer Law & Security Review 25(3), 270–274 (2009)
12. Yin, R.K.: Case study research: design and methods. Sage Publications, Thousand Oaks (2003)
13. Benbasat, I., Goldstein, D.K., Mead, M.: The Case Research Strategy in Studies of Information Systems. MIS Quarterly, 369–386 (September 1987)
14. Runeson, P., Höst, M.: Guidelines for conducting and reporting case study research in software engineering. Empirical Software Engineering 14(2), 131–164 (2009)
15. Voss, C., Tsikriktsis, N., Frohlich, M.: Case research in operations management. International Journal of Operations & Production Management 22(2), 195–219 (2002)
16. Flowd – The Music Lovers' Social Networks, http://www.flowd.com

Creating Minimum Viable Products
in Industry-Academia Collaborations

Jürgen Münch[1], Fabian Fagerholm[1], Patrik Johnson[1], Janne Pirttilahti[2],
Juha Torkkel[2], and Janne Järvinen[2]

[1] Department of Computer Science, University of Helsinki,
P.O. Box 68, FI-00014 University of Helsinki, Finland
{juergen.muench,fabian.fagerholm,patrik.johnson}@cs.helsinki.fi
[2] F-Secure Corporation,
P.O. Box 24, 00181 Helsinki, Finland
{janne.pirttilahti,juha.torkkel,janne.jarvinen}@f-secure.com

Abstract. Customer value determines how products and services succeed in the marketplace. Early assessment of customer value is important
for software startups, spin-off companies, and new product development
in existing companies. Software technology often influences customer
value and typically defines the main competitive advantage in both entrepreneurial and intrapreneurial settings. Value-related feedback from
real customers is needed during software development and maintenance,
and decision-making should be increasingly based on empirical evidence
acquired through experiments. Getting such value-related feedback usually requires a so-called minimum viable product (MVP), i.e., an artefact
that may be incomplete in functionality or quality, but displays characteristics that allows determining its customer value. In this article we
report on a case study which used industry-academia collaboration for
creating such an MVP. Our goal was to identify strengths and weaknesses
of such an approach to creating MVPs while providing practical recommendations for improvement. The process followed in the case study was
found to be very suitable for creating MVPs, reducing company-specific
risks when testing customer-value, and advancing university education.

Keywords: Minimum viable product, prototyping, software start-ups,
entrepreneurship, intrapreneurship, Lean Startup, Software Factory, case
study.

1 Introduction

Software engineering experimentation aims at advancing the knowledge on how
software development processes and methods in specific environments impact
results [1]. According to Basili et al., experimentation is performed to help us
better evaluate, predict, understand, control, and improve the software development process and product [2]. As with any other experimental procedure,
experimentation in software engineering follows a cycle of building models for

B. Fitzgerald et al. (Eds.): LESS 2013, LNBIP 167, pp. 137–151, 2013.

development processes or products, defining and testing related hypotheses, and refining models and hypotheses based on experimental results.

Traditionally, the main focus of software engineering experimentation has been on the technical and managerial aspects; the developer and project manager perspectives have been emphasized. However, since software engineering is a field which is often associated with innovative high technology, a vibrant global community of entrepreneurs, and a customer base with increasing expectations, it should also take into account the customer-perceived value of its products and services. While customer value may be simply defined as "whatever the customer is willing to pay for", it is not simple to assess or measure this concept while designing a product or service. In software projects, multiple stakeholders may have several different needs that affect how they perceive the value of the end product [3]. Rather than attempting to fix a single assessment or measure of customer value, we emphasize the importance of a process of experimentation and learning which allows empirical discovery of customer value in a specific context, guided by analytically derived hypotheses.

This perspective is also important in software engineering education. Students are entering a field which demands not only programming skills, but also the ability to dynamically consider customer value. They should be equipped with suitable knowledge of how to participate in software projects where value considerations drive project activities. It is particularly important that students are exposed to realistic, current problem settings and learn to analyse and understand value-related experiments.

Developing innovative software technology requires early testing of customer-related hypotheses. To make this possible, experimental objects, such as product prototypes, need to be created. Prototyping is used heavily in Agile software development. For example, prototyping is a core technique in the Dynamic Systems Development Method (DSDM) [4]. DSDM recommends four categories of prototypes: business, usability, performance and capacity, and capability prototypes. Early in the development process, business prototypes provide opportunities to conceptualise and communicate the business processes being automated, while usability prototypes allow definition, refinement, and demonstration of the system from a user's perspective. These two types of prototypes are closest to the notion of prototyping used in this paper. However, DSDM does not explicitly consider prototypes as experimental objects for testing the business value of a product idea during development. In Lean Startup terminology, a value hypothesis and a minimum viable product (MVP) need to be developed. Following Ries [5], a value hypothesis "tests whether a product or service really delivers value to customers once they are using it". An example of a value hypothesis is that customers of a specific customer segment will choose to sign up for a service based on a given set of features being offered. An MVP is an experimental object that allows for empirical testing of value hypotheses. According to the Lean Startup method, it should be built with a minimum amount of effort and development time [5].

In this paper, we argue that industry-academia collaborations are especially well suited for developing such MVPs and thereby support the rapid understanding of customer value in software development. More specifically, we address the following research questions in the context of industry-academia collaborations:

RQ1: How should a product owner define a value hypothesis from which a minimum viable product is derived?

RQ2: How should an implementation team create a minimum viable product based on a value hypothesis?

RQ3: What are the main advantages and challenges for industry partners?

RQ4: What are the main advantages and challenges for academic partners?

The remainder of this paper is organised as follows. In Section 2, we describe work related to technology transfer and value-based software engineering. In Section 3, we describe our research and development infrastructure (i.e., the so-called Software Factory) for creating MVPs together with industry. In Section 4, we describe our case study, including the research design, method, and context, as well as the execution and results. In Section 5, we describe the limitations that apply when attempting to generalize the results. Finally, in Section 6, we summarize our findings and outline future directions for this work.

2   Related Work

As software is increasingly at the core of all kinds of innovations, the customer perspective comes more into focus. Rombach and Achatz [6] define innovation in software engineering as both invention and successful implementation. They present a 6-step generic process model for transferring an innovative technology from its creators to organizations which are able to make them a business success. There are many other similar technology transfer models proposed in the software engineering literature. Very often they are organized so that the technological invention comes first and the invention of a business case comes later. This is based on the implicit assumption that customers do perceive the invention as valuable or that the value can be identified later. In addition, it is often assumed that the link to business goals and strategies can be defined later or is obvious.

Although these assumptions might be true in some domains, they become questionable in domains of high uncertainty and highly competitive markets, such as start-up companies and companies entering new business segments. Here, business value is unclear or needs to be learned during the invention process. It is often more critical for business success to understand the perceived value for a real customer than to immediately bring an invention into technical perfection. Vice versa, perceived customer value might influence what innovative software technology is needed, i.e., the business drives the inventions. In such high-uncertainty environments, innovative software technologies and the understanding of their perceived customer value need to be integrated early in the software life cycle. Due to the fact that inventions often combine both innovative software technologies and innovative business models, it seems promising to analyse both experimentally. We argue that this approach is viable not only for new development, but also for evolution of existing software-based products and services. We also argue that the approach is viable both for new, entrepreneurial start-up companies as well as for existing companies which face a need for renewal through internal entrepreneurship, or intrapreneurship.

Several approaches exist that integrate the business and the product development functions of organizations. One prominent approach is the "Lean Startup" [5] that leverages experimentation on the business level by rapid prototyping, testing value hypotheses, and very early feedback for product development. Another approach that focuses on considering value during the software process is "Value-based Software Engineering" (VBSE) [7]. This approach provides different elements, such as techniques for determining value by analytical means, and methods for including value considerations into management activities [8,9]. Other related approaches exist, e.g. user-centered design [10], where design decisions are made based on empirical evidence gathered from user experiments and involvement. The approach presented in this article addresses the need to rapidly elicit and test value hypotheses through an empirical feedback cycle. The elements of VBSE and the experimental approaches in user-centered design can be seen as complementary to this approach.

3   Development and Usage of Minimum Viable Products in the Software Factory

Conducting experiments with customer value in the context of industry-academia collaborations requires a suitable infrastructure. The infrastructure we are using for this purpose is the co-called Software Factory. In this section, we sketch the concept of the Software Factory as an approach to MVP creation, outline some possible variations, and provide examples of how customer value can be operationalised and tested.

The Software Factory is a university laboratory that has been designed and implemented at the Department of Computer Science, University of Helsinki [11,12,13]. The main unique characteristics of the Software Factory are the integration of engineering- and business-level experimentation, a standardized laboratory infrastructure which supports conducting joint or comparative studies as well as the exchange of experience, the global network of Software Factories, which allows for running experiments in distributed settings, and the periodic conduction of projects several times a year, which allows efficient study set-up, rapid learning, and conducting longitudinal studies.

In the Software Factory laboratory, a company brings the vision about a new product or service and an initial value hypothesis. The company has the responsibility to test the value hypothesis whereas the Software Factory has the responsibility to create the MVP. The interaction between the Software Factory and the company can be seen as a learning cycle (Figure 1). The company provides an initial value hypothesis as input to a Software Factory project and acts as product owner. The Software Factory then creates an MVP that serves as an experimental object for testing the value hypothesis. During this development, the company provides feedback so that the MVP will be aligned with the value hypothesis. The MVP is used by the company to test the value hypothesis with real customers. Based on the results of this experiment, the company modifies the value hypothesis if necessary. Subsequently, the Software Factory develops a new version of the MVP that aims at testing the modified value hypothesis. The same applies for a set of multiple hypotheses to be tested simultaneously. One might consider this as a process consisting of developing first and testing afterwards, but actually the process is in the reverse order: the value hypothesis initially defines what needs to be developed in the Software Factory. Results from the evaluation guide further iterations of the MVP.

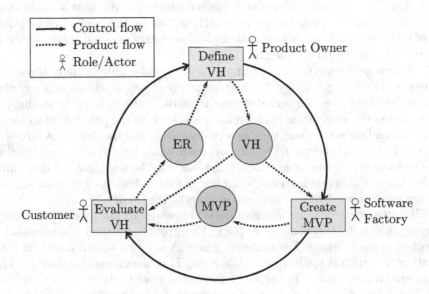

Fig. 1. Learning cycle: the Product Owner defines a Value Hypothesis (VH), which is used as input for the Software Factory to create a minimum viable product (MVP). The MVP is used to evaluate the VH in a customer test, resulting in an evaluation result (ER) that is fed back to refine or redefine the VH for the next cycle.

3.1 Variations in the Learning Cycle

The interaction between the company and the Software Factory is a crucial element of the experimental process, and there are several ways in which the interaction can occur. Depending on the context and constraints of the project, a company might replace testing the value hypothesis with qualitative expert feedback. This may occur especially in initial iterations when the customer is not ready to conduct potentially costly user experiments – but caution should be exercised here in order not to develop the product too far without empirical feedback. Another option could be to use the Software Factory project for the creation of the first MVP without testing the value hypothesis during this project. In this case, experimentation with customers would start after project completion. It could also be possible that the company needs to pivot and start again with a new value hypothesis and a new MVP in case the initial value hypothesis has been proven significantly wrong.

3.2 Techniques for Customer-Related Experiments

There are several techniques by which to perform customer-related experiments to validate value hypotheses of software-based products and services. Suitability of techniques depend on how far the software has been developed. Simpler techniques can yield coarse-grained insights quicker early on in the process, while more mature products and services can benefit from techniques which permit fine-grained analysis and linkage to business strategies. While this study does not cover the validation of the value hypothesis, we briefly explain three examples of techniques for conducting customer-related experiments: cohort analysis, A/B testing, and GQM+Strategies.

Cohort analysis refers to studies comparing groups of people on one or several attributes over time (e.g. [14,15]). A cohort is a group of people who share a common characteristic over a certain period of time. In medical research, cohort studies are used to assess the association between an event, such as the presence of a disease risk factor, and some outcome, such as actually developing the disease. Analysis of subgroups within a cohort can yield important insights that may confirm existing hypotheses or create new ones. Cohort analysis may be used, e.g., to determine whether users of different age groups signing up for a software service at a specific time are more or less likely to be frequent users of the service.

A/B testing is a technique where subjects are randomly assigned to two groups receiving different treatments (e.g. [15]). The groups are then compared with respect to some outcome. For example, group A may be shown a certain kind of feature in a mobile application, while group B is shown another feature. The groups are then compared to see which feature is more likely to attract the user to make a purchase decision. Such information can support the decision to focus implementation on one feature or the other.

For more elaborate needs, *GQM+Strategies* [16] is an approach to systematically break down business-level goals into sub-goals and strategies for implementing them, and to link these with software measurement. GQM+Strategies allows companies to streamline metrics collection to support business decisions. For customer-related experiments, GQM+Strategies allows companies to express the desired goal of measurement (e.g. to increase sales), construct strategies for reaching those goals, and devise metrics that determine how the actions taken are contributing to the realization of the goals.

Besides the mentioned techniques, many other techniques can be used for conducting customer-related experiments such as multivariate testing, big data technologies, live customer feedback analyses, etc. All of these methods require significant expertise to properly select and apply.

4   Industry Case

We use one of our projects in the Software Factory laboratory at the University of Helsinki to illustrate the experimental cycle. The main objective of the project was to validate a value hypothesis given by a customer. The project was initiated as a rapid-feedback development effort that would proceed from an initial value hypothesis to an initial MVP that could then be subjected to separate evaluation with real users. Consistently with the objective, there were no requirements to use any legacy code or perform potentially difficult integration into existing systems.

We focus here on the two first steps of the learning cycle shown in Figure 1 (definition of value hypotheses and creation of MVP). Intermediate versions of the MVP were subjected to expert evaluation and the value hypothesis and project priorities modified accordingly. The project completed two major cycles but did not include evaluation with specific customer experiments. We expect to study those separately.

4.1   Research Design and Method

This study can be characterized as a single-case study using multiple-researcher triangulation [17,18]. Case studies can be said to study "contemporary phenomena in their natural context" [19] and to "generalise from specific contexts" [18]. There are several types of case studies [17], some of which have been used and described specifically for software engineering [19]. However, case studies do not constitute a homogeneous class of studies, but display considerable variation. Since cases can vary arbitrarily, researchers must adapt their designs and methods to truthfully represent the case, while balancing considerations of generalisability.

In this study, we took an open-ended, participatory approach. Two persons from the Department of Computer Science, University of Helsinki, and one person from the case company, were present and participated to varying degrees in the project. Data sources included participatory and direct observation, notes taken during the course of the project, and analysis of project artefacts such as produced software, documentation, and other materials. In particular, the project coach kept a diary of project events and provided substantial input for this study. The other participating researcher organised meetings and performed open-ended, interview-like discussions with the project participants in the beginning, middle, and end of the project. The company representative was the project's product owner and interacted closely with the student team.

Our analysis method can be described as narrative and inductive. From the data and experiences gathered, we build a chronological story of the project, including different perspectives and considerations, and attempt to trace causal relationships that allow us to abstract from the case material to more general findings.

4.2   Goal and Context

The main goal of the project was to develop an MVP that could be used to test the end-user value of a cloud service. The MVP was a game that generated metadata regarding a set of objects in a cloud storage system as a by-product of playing. The overall value hypothesis was that the game would be satisfying to play and that users would consider the generated metadata to be valuable. To validate the overall value hypothesis, the customer wanted to find out i) whether users are motivated to use the software, ii) whether users perceive fun in using the software, iii) whether using the software creates valuable metadata, and more specifically, iv) whether the created metadata is usable for providing additional services. From an engineering perspective, the goal was to test v) if and how the game concept includes key elements of good game design. As a related goal, the execution of the project itself was expected to reveal valuable information regarding industry-academia collaboration. Finally, since the project team consisted of students, a separate goal of the project was to provide an educational experience.

The customer company was the Innovation and New Concepts division at F-Secure Corporation. The project team consisted of four students, with every student working 24-30 hours per week during the seven-week project. In addition to the students, a project coach was present with the team on a daily basis, and a customer representative in the product owner role was present at least once a week. The product owner was also available on demand over teleconference and email. The product owner was technically skilled, was one of the originators of the project idea, and was empowered to make all decisions regarding the project.

To determine which features would be implemented first to attempt to satisfy the value hypotheses, the product owner experimented with paper prototypes of the game. A question posed early in the project was whether to develop a single game with a tightly defined feature set, or to develop a configurable game platform. After some consideration, the team and product owner decided not to embark on the platform option, since it would lead to effort being spent on platform features which would not necessarily be needed for testing the value hypotheses. Instead, the decision was to make a game with a tightly defined feature set but with configuration options for testing the specific variations that the product owner had reason to believe would affect the playability of the game. These variations could then be exploited in subsequent testing of the value hypotheses.

The project team used Scrumban, a combination of Scrum and Kanban [20,21], to coordinate its work. The team was given a training session on the process during the first days of the project. Otherwise, no tightly controlled process was used, as the project was aimed to promote creativity and exploration. This is also in line with the process itself, as described by Kniberg [21], since it allows a team to develop and tune its own process.

4.3   Execution

The time-line shown in Figure 2 illustrates milestones and events during the project, and shows a classification of the overall focus of project activities. Since the development of the prototype had no initial technological restrictions, significant time was spent on deciding which technology the new prototype should use.

Aside from organization and initial training, most of the first two weeks of the project were spent evaluating technology choices. The team evaluated several options from multiple perspectives, including ease of use and speed of development, licensing, technological options, and prior experience of team members. The most promising alternatives were then further analysed by developing small proof of concept implementations of the product idea. During the second week, two platforms were developed in parallel until the final choice could be made with established knowledge and taking the whole project context into consideration. A modern HTML5-based browser platform was chosen, and the main implementation was made using JavaScript and HTML5 web technologies.

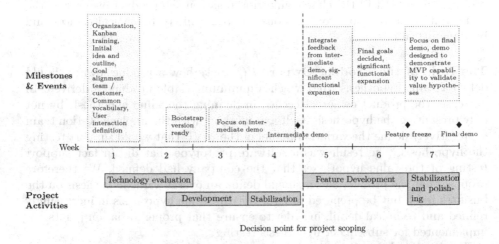

Fig. 2. Milestones, events, and activities per week

Throughout the project, there was a clear backlog of features generated by the team in conjunction with the product owner. Goals of both the product owner and development team were aligned, which aided discovery of new features that could potentially contribute to the value hypothesis. The product owner offered an opinion on how to prioritize high level features, but the final choice was left to the team, as well as breakdown of features into practical tasks.

Since the product owner was available on demand, the team was able to apply rapid prototyping of the MVP and validate first draft solutions close to the time of inception. This "fail fast" approach allowed the product owner to immediately influence the direction of the project based on tangible evidence from a product increment.

The initial MVP was delivered, and the first major learning cycle completed, approximately two and half weeks after the technology choice had been made. An intermediate demo was given at the customer's premises roughly half-way through the project. The fact that this demo was scheduled already at the start of the project gave the team a clear focus for its efforts. The project then proceeded in very iterative expansions of the functionality, which meant that the customer was provided with product variations that could be used for testing the value hypotheses. Code structure and architecture were expanded and developed iteratively, using several explorative solutions.

4.4   Results and Lessons Learned

In this section, we discuss the results of the study and list essential lessons learned from the project. We present each research question in turn, along with the lessons related to that particular question.

The most important lessons learned are concerned with i) the role of the product owner and ii) the close connection between the product owner and the team, but we also report some lessons regarding iii) technological choices and iv) demonstrations.

The Role of the Product Owner. *RQ1* asks how a product owner should define a value hypothesis from which a minimum viable product is derived. In our case, the product owner succeeded in defining the value hypothesis by not only presenting the hypothesis itself, but working with the implementation team to iteratively define the variation points in the MVP that would support testing the hypothesis. The result was a software prototype that did in fact support testing of the value hypotheses that the company had defined. We therefore propose that the product owner should define an overall value hypothesis on the business level, but be prepared to interpret the value hypothesis in increasingly refined and technical detail, in order to ensure that proper variation points are implemented for subsequent hypothesis testing.

We also found that being in close connection with the team allowed the product owner to correct misunderstandings and give further expansion on details that were not covered during active meeting time. This tight interaction with the team was essential for understanding and guidance, and therefore, the performance of the project. The product owner had both the technical and business-level skills to evaluate the product increments. The increments would not display stunning visual features immediately but would rather demonstrate some important behaviour in the software. The product owner's ability to see the essential characteristics of the feature under development was crucial. Being regularly present, the product owner facilitated continuous knowledge transfer, and no separate transfer process was required at the end of the project.

Technological Choices. *RQ2* asks how an implementation team should create a minimum viable product based on a value hypothesis. In our case, the team was able to interpret the value hypothesis and produce the desired MVP by efficient down-scoping of immediate next steps and by thoroughly experimenting with technology choices early in the project.

As previously noted, the team spent the first two weeks on evaluating technology choices. After the project, the team considered this appropriate, taking the project length into account. Also, the fact that the product owner knew the importance of making this choice helped the team to develop trust. The technology choice was not a simple feature list comparison, but was actually taken to the point where the candidate platforms were used to develop simple proof-of-concept programs. This ensured that the team and product owner made decisions based on a real evaluation for this particular case, not general information given by a third party.

The project had a critical dependency on the customer's cloud storage platform. This posed an unnecessary development risk for the project, since the objective was not integration into the platform but production of the MVP. Therefore, the team and product owner decided very early that the storage API would be abstracted using a mock implementation. This had multiple positive effects for the project: not only was the prototype development technically independent from the platform, but the project also depended only on the product owner. The customer provided an API specification with the same characteristics as the real platform, ensuring that integration would be possible later. Besides serving as an MVP, the prototype revealed potential improvement needs in the platform API.

The Team. The small size of the team ensured little or no communication overhead, since team members could develop individual relations with each other, the customer, and other stakeholders. Task generation was initially difficult for the team, but became easier later in the project when high level features could be split into concrete development tasks for each part of the product (front end, game logic, back end). Clearly visible tickets on the Kanban board allowed for interactive prioritisation by the team together with the product owner.

Together, the observations on technological choices and the team link research questions 1 and 2: while the responsibility of the product owner is the definition of the value hypothesis, and the responsibility of the team is the creation of the MVP, both need to approach each other in interpreting how the value hypothesis should be operationalised and turned into a technological artefact. We propose that both product owners and team members require both special knowledge and skills to be able to function effectively when developing an MVP from a value hypothesis.

Demonstrations. One way to facilitate the interpretation process between product owner and implementation team is to perform demonstrations. During the project, the team held weekly demonstrations for the product owner. In addition to this, an intermediate demo was scheduled for the middle of the project, and a final demo at the end. These were more comprehensive demonstrations held at the customer's premises and the audience included not only the product owner and team coach, but also experts from the customer organization.

The weekly demos provided clear intermediate deadlines for the team, and allowed it to focus on creating a tangible result. It also allowed the team to demonstrate functionality that had been defined during the development process in order to get feedback from the product owner. The demos made questions concrete and the product owner could base decisions on visible alternatives.

An interesting question arose after the intermediate demo: there was a trade-off between expanding the project scope and refining existing features (see Figure 2). For the customer, this decision highlighted the importance of defining what value was most important to test: whether the test should be more about comparing the viability of many features or about comparing the quality of a few features. The product owner chose to lean more towards comparing a larger set of features, since the concept was still in an early stage. In later stages, after the value proposition has been field-tested, the choice could lean more towards the details of a few promising features.

Advantages and Challenges. *RQ3* and *RQ4* ask what the main advantages and challenges of creating MVPs in industry-academia collaborations are for industry and academic partners, respectively. In our case, three particular advantages were clearly visible for industry partners. First, it is beneficial for industry partners to be able to conduct MVP creation in a relatively low-risk environment. Since the amount of company resources that are tied to the project is limited, the impact of project failure in terms of lost resources is also limited. Second, industry partners can benefit from the use of measurement experience that exists in academia. Researchers working in the Software Factory context are trained to design, conduct, and analyse experiments, and they can be utilised to assist in different stages of the project. Third, and more broadly, industry partners can utilise other kinds of research capabilities inherent in the academic environment. An MVP-creation project may be embedded in a larger research project, or it can be expanded into one.

For academia, we found a number of benefits. Collaboration projects can provide real cases for research, as is evident in this article. Also, the benefit for students in the form of valuable learning experiences was clearly visible. As an example, one student who worked as a software developer remarked after the project that "I now understand much better what I'm doing at work". We also found that the project brought contemporary realism into the world of academia, and we were challenged to keep up to date with relevant problems from practice.

Based on our experience, a number of challenges apply when creating MVPs in industry-academia collaboration projects. A first challenge relates to synchronisation of schedules. University course calendars, in our case especially the Software Factory project schedule, needs to be positioned in an appropriate time window where a partner company has the willingness and available resources to test innovations. Second, technological infrastructure presents a challenge: MVPs must be deployable on either existing platforms, which may include legacy components, or on new platforms, which may be under development. In some cases, the MVP may need to be deployed on end-user systems, which requires careful consideration of platform compatibility and data security. Finally, properly conducting value-based experiments requires measurement competence. Appropriate training and competence is needed when defining value hypotheses, design appropriate experiments, derive necessary measures, conduct experiments, and reason from analysis results. Especially the customer should have adequate competences in defining value hypotheses and be able to draw conclusions from analysis results.

5   Limitations

Despite the case project having many realistic features, this study has a number of limitations. First, the produced MVP was not subject to field evaluation with real users. Therefore, lessons learned with respect to appropriate experimental instruments for customer validation are missing. On the other hand, this was precisely the intended scope of the project: to demonstrate how a concept idea can be developed into a prototype implementation for subsequent evaluation. We expect to evaluate the end result separately.

Second, since the project team consisted of students, the results may not be applicable to professional software development. Furthermore, the team was new, and with repeated cycles of execution, they may change their approach. Also, another team may have done things differently. However, we argue that these limitations are not as severe as they may first appear. It is well known that the programmer productivity can vary considerably [22]. The fact that this programming team was able to implement the prototype with unfamiliar technology in the given time-frame indicates that a professional team should be able to do the same in a similar amount of time, with the limitation imposed by varying individual degrees of productivity. In the formation of the team, a simple, single-task programming test was administered before team members were admitted to the project. There were no indications that the team members would all have been unusually skilled. In addition, the goal of of an MVP is to test value hypotheses. Therefore, the main criterion is that the MVP is suited for such testing, regardless of who has developed it. A more experienced team may have reached better results, but even at this baseline, the result was acceptable.

A final limitation relates to rapid prototyping. Many technologies are ill-suited to rapid prototyping and thus the proposed approach may not be applicable when using such technologies. However, it may be possible to set aside the less flexible tools and prototype with other technologies only for the purpose of testing a value hypothesis. Once the value has been determined, a production version can be implemented with another technology, thus avoiding potentially long and costly implementation projects when the value is uncertain. As demonstrated in this project, it is often possible to abstract away parts of the system that are not relevant for testing the value proposition, and address them at a later stage. A potential risk with this approach is that the technology to be used in the production version can cause significantly different cost of implementation than the prototyping technology for the chosen feature set. However, this question is different from the question of customer value. Also, the prototyping itself is likely to reveal important requirements for implementation technology.

6   Summary and Future Work

This paper presents experience with creating an MVP in the context of an industry-academia collaboration. The experience is based on a concrete case study. In summary, rapid prototyping for getting value-related feedback can be systematically conducted using a simple framework process, in which the implementation team is given freedom to explore the concept design space in short, incremental cycles in close cooperation with the customer. Factors critical for success are i) the role of the product owner, who should come from the customer organization, have enough technical and domain knowledge to make correct design decisions, and be empowered to make those decisions, ii) taking the proper time to investigate technology options with the goal of selecting an implementation technology that supports rapid prototyping, iii) abstracting away parts of the target platform to keep the project focused on testing the value proposition, not the integration into the platform, iv) systematically employing a light-weight process in which the implementation team and the product owner can prioritize high-levels features and the team has autonomy to decide on feature decomposition into tasks, and v) having frequent demonstrations, including demonstrations with an audience that is not directly taking part in the project.

Our study provided several insights on how the development of MVPs with value-related feedback can be organized in short iteration cycles. The following questions illustrate some interesting future directions. First, testing value hypotheses in the field requires a suitable experimental infrastructure. What are the requirements for such an infrastructure in different contexts? How can software products and services be integrated into such an infrastructure? These questions are also relevant for supporting design decisions on how to evolve existing products or services. Second, an open question is how to integrate experimentation on the business level with experimentation on the technical level. Sustainable innovations require technological advantages that also need to be evaluated by experimental means. This warrants further research. Third, can experiment-based software development be aligned with organizational and legal constraints? For example, contractual issues may need special consideration in experiment-based software development. Finally, how should customer value be evaluated in cases where the value creation is part of an ecosystem? For example, the value could come from the number and type of apps available in an ecosystem.

Both start-up companies and innovative intrapreneurial divisions in established companies can benefit from insights into these questions. We expect more systematic experimentation with customer value in software development and evolution to significantly speed up the pace of innovation and help release more disruptive software-based solutions. Through industry-academia collaboration, companies can reduce the barriers to experimenting with MVP creation.

References

1. Wohlin, C., Runeson, P., Höst, M., Ohlsson, M., Regnell, B., Wesslén, A.: Experimentation in software engineering. Springer (2012)
2. Basili, V.R., Selby, R.W., Hutchens, D.H.: Experimentation in software engineering. IEEE Trans. Softw. Eng. 12(7), 733–743 (1986)
3. Boehm, B., Jain, A.: Developing a process framework using principles of value-based software engineering. Software Process: Improvement and Practice 12(5), 377–385 (2007)

4. Howard, A.: A new RAD-based approach to commercial information systems development: the dynamic system development method. Industrial Management + Data Systems 97(5), 175–177 (1997)
5. Ries, E.: The Lean Startup: How Today's Entrepreneurs Use Continuous Innovation to Create Radically Successful Businesses. Crown Publishing Group (2011)
6. Rombach, D., Achatz, R.: Research Collaborations between Academia and Industry. In: 2007 Future of Software Engineering, FOSE 2007, pp. 29–36. IEEE Computer Society, Washington, DC (2007)
7. Boehm, B.: Value-based software engineering. ACM SIGSOFT Software Engineering Notes 28(2), 4 (2003)
8. Rönkkö, M., Frühwirth, C., Biffl, S.: Integrating value and utility concepts into a value decomposition model for value-based software engineering. In: Bomarius, F., Oivo, M., Jaring, P., Abrahamsson, P. (eds.) PROFES 2009. LNBIP, vol. 32, pp. 362–374. Springer, Heidelberg (2009)
9. Raffo, D., Mehta, M., Anderson, D., Harmon, R.: Integrating Lean principles with value based software engineering. In: 2010 Proceedings of Technology Management for Global Economic Growth (PICMET 2010), pp. 1–10 (2010)
10. Greenbaum, J., Kyng, M.: Design at work: cooperative design of computer systems. Lawrence Erlbaum Associates, Inc. (1991)
11. Fagerholm, F., Oza, N., Münch, J.: A Platform for Teaching Applied Distributed Software Development: The Ongoing Journey of the Helsinki Software Factory. In: Collaborative Teaching of Globally Distributed Software Development Workshop (CTGDSD) (2013)
12. Software Factory: Software Factory Web Site, http://www.softwarefactory.cc/ (last visited: April 12, 2013)
13. Abrahamsson, P., Fagerholm, F., Kettunen, P.: The Set-Up of a Valuable Software Engineering Research Infrastructure of the 2010s. In: The 11th International Conference on Product Focused Software Development and Process Improvement (PROFES 2010)/Workshop on Valuable Software Products (VASOP 2010) (11) (2010)
14. Porta, M. (ed.): A Dictionary of Epidemiology. Oxford University Press, New York (2008)
15. Croll, A., Yoskovitz, B.: Lean Analytics: Use Data to Build a Better Startup Faster. O'Reilly Media, Inc., Sebastopol (2013)
16. Basili, V., Heidrich, J., Lindvall, M., Münch, J., Regardie, M., Trendowicz, A.: GQM+Strategies – Aligning business strategies with software measurement. In: Proceedings of the 1st International Symposium on Empirical Software Engineering and Measurement, ESEM 2007, pp. 488–490 (2007)
17. Yin, R.: Case study research: design and methods, 4th edn. SAGE Publications, Inc. (2009)
18. Eisenhardt, K.M.: Building Theories from Case Study Research. The Academy of Management Review 14(4), 532–550 (1989)
19. Runeson, P., Höst, M.: Guidelines for conducting and reporting case study research in software engineering. Empirical Software Engineering 14(2), 131–164 (2009)
20. Ladas, C.: Scrumban – Essays on Kanban Systems for Lean Software Development. Modus Cooperandi Press (2009)
21. Kniberg, H., Skarin, M.: Kanban and Scrum – making the most of both. C4media (2010)
22. Endres, A., Rombach, D.: A Handbook of Software and Systems Engineering. Empirical Observations, Laws and Theories. The Fraunhofer IESE Series on Software Engineering. Addison Wesley (2003)

Towards Data-Driven Product Development: A Multiple Case Study on Post-deployment Data Usage in Software-Intensive Embedded Systems

Helena Holmström Olsson[1] and Jan Bosch[2]

[1] Department of Computer Science, Malmö University, Malmö, Sweden
`helena.holmstrom.olsson@mah.se`
[2] Department of Computer Science and Engineering, Chalmers University of Technology,
Gothenburg, Sweden
`jan.bosch@chalmers.se`

Abstract. Today, products within telecommunication, transportation, consumer electronics, home automation, security etc. involve an increasing amount of software. As a result, organizations that have a tradition within hardware development are transforming to become software-intensive organizations. This implies products where software constitutes the majority of functionality, costs, future investments, and potential. While this shift poses a number of challenges, it brings with it opportunities as well. One of these opportunities is to collect product data in order to learn about product use, to inform product management decisions, and for improving already deployed products. In this paper, we focus on the opportunity to use post-deployment data, i.e. data that is generated while products are used, as a basis for product improvement and new product development. We do so by studying three software development companies involved in large-scale development of embedded software. In our study, we highlight limitations in post-deployment data usage and we conclude that post-deployment data remains an untapped resource for most companies. The contribution of the paper is two-fold. First, we present key opportunities for more effective product development based on post-deployment data usage. Second, we propose a framework for organizations interested in advancing their use of post-deployment product data.

Keywords: Post-deployment data collection, product data, software-intensive systems, embedded systems.

1 Introduction

The evolution of software, and the variety of domains in which it is used, is impressive. From being considered a configuration mechanism for electronic systems, software has become the core of most modern systems supporting individuals, companies and societies [1]. As a result, more and more organizations are realizing that while their main business may be in areas such as hardware development,

B. Fitzgerald et al. (Eds.): LESS 2013, LNBIP 167, pp. 152–164, 2013.

telecommunication, transportation, home automation or finance, the software part of their products is responsible for a majority of the functionality, as well as for a majority of the development costs and investments. In this transition, the ability to learn about customers, and especially the way in which customers use software functionality, becomes increasingly important. Hence, agile software development practices that are flexible, responsive and adaptive to customers [2, 3] are gaining momentum. In advocating customer collaboration and the importance of test-driven development practices [4], agile practices have attracted not only small software development companies, but also companies involved in large-scale development of software-intensive embedded systems.

However, while many companies have succeeded in applying agile practices and, as a result, leveraged the benefits of close customer collaboration and continuous validation of functionality in pre-deployment phases, there are few examples of companies that have succeeded in maintaining this close relationship to customers also after product deployment. One technique that has emerged due to the online nature of most software-intense systems today is the opportunity to continuously collect post-deployment data, i.e. data generated by the product after commercial deployment. This data can be operational data reflecting product performance, it can be diagnostic data recording product behavior, and it can be data indicating feature usage. For online technologies such as Web 2.0 software, software-as-a-service (SaaS) systems, and cloud computing services, the collection of post-deployment data is a well-established technique used for continuous collection of information about product usage. In this domain, companies like Microsoft [5] and Intuit [6] successfully collect post-deployment product data and use this as a basis for continuous improvement of existing products, as well as for input to innovation and new product development.

Interestingly, the opportunity to collect post-deployment data extends also to software-intensive embedded systems. Today, these systems are increasingly connected, bringing with it the opportunity to collect data from real-time usage of these systems. For example, companies developing systems within the telecom and automotive industry, i.e. mobile phones and cars, are starting to explore the advantages of collecting product data from their systems in the field. However, while this trend is discernible, research in this domain is still scarce, resulting in companies investing significantly in development efforts without having an accurate way of continuously validating whether the functionality they develop is of value to their customers.

In this paper, we present a multiple case study on three companies developing software-intensive embedded systems. While in different domains, all companies develop products consisting of an increasing amount of software, and they all collect large amounts of data from the products they release. In our study, we explore *what* data they collect, and especially, *how* this data is *used* for increasing their understanding of how their products are used by customers. The contribution of the paper is two-fold. First, we present key opportunities for more effective product development based on post-deployment data usage. These key opportunities were identified by key stakeholders within the companies, and work as drivers for increasing the use of post-deployment data. In our discussion, we refer to 'effective' as the ability to confirm that the functionality that is developed is used and appreciated by customers, i.e. the ability to continuously evaluate development investments and efforts. Second, we propose a framework for organizations interested in advancing their usage of post-deployment product data. Our framework reflects the different levels of post-deployment data usage, as well as the mechanisms needed for improving post-deployment data usage.

2   Background

2.1   Pre-deployment Data Collection

Typically, feedback on a software system is collected during pre-deployment phases, i.e. before and during development. Most often, this is done by applying techniques that allow customers to engage in problem definition, requirements engineering and system evaluation and validation. To involve customers in the development process is not a new phenomenon and it is well elaborated upon in user-centered development approaches such as participatory design [7], cooperative design [8], and joint-application design [9]. In these approaches, techniques such as use cases, scenarios, prototyping, stakeholder interviews, joint requirements sessions, joint application design sessions etc. are common. Likewise, alpha- and beta testing, observations, expert reviews, and prototyping are efficiently used before and during development in order to continuously validate that the functionality that is developed is of value to customers. Also, and as can be seen in research on agile methods [4, 10, 11, 12], and requirements engineering [13, 14], these techniques are efficient for capturing generic needs for mass-market products [15]. Likewise, large-scale software development organizations often use product management as a proxy for communicating customer feedback before and during development of the product [16].

2.2   Post-deployment Data Collection

System use evolve over time and hence, system characteristics need to be adjusted, adapted and updated according to emerging customer requirements and needs. This implies that mechanisms for post-deployment customer collaboration are as important as those used during pre-development and development phases of a system. With regard to post-deployment data collection, the concept of 'lead users' is often used to reflect close collaboration with innovative customers in order to use their feedback for improvement and innovation of products [17]. In similar, the 'software ecosystem' approach is referred to as a way for companies to involve customers in improvement activities that start after product delivery. As can be seen in research within this field, many software development companies have realized the economic and strategic potential of establishing collaborative communities of third-party organizations, customer organizations and individual developers who contribute to the product development process [18]. According to Jansen et al [19], a software ecosystem is described as a set of actors functioning as a unit and interacting with a shared market for software and services, together with the relationships among them. While the definitions of a software ecosystem are numerous, they all involve the notion of interactions, relationships and co-evolvement among stakeholders such as development organizations, suppliers and customers.

However, with the more recent introduction of Web 2.0 systems, cloud computing, and online Software-as-a-Service (SaaS) technologies, the opportunity to collect post-deployment data from the product itself has significantly increased. Due to the online nature of these systems, data is generated and hence, can be collected, as soon as customers use the systems, and the advantage is that the cost of collecting data from, and about, the customer is low [20]. Examples include the amount of time a user spends using a feature, the frequency of feature selection, the path that a customer takes through product functionality, etc. If continuously collected and analyzed, product data can be used as efficient input for improvement of the existing product, and as a basis for new product development and innovation. As a result, these online systems allow for an approach where instead of freezing the requirements before development starts, requirements evolve in real-time based on data collected from the products.

Interestingly, and as the focus of this paper, these benefits extend also to software-intensive embedded systems. Today, companies developing connected embedded systems, from mobile phones to cars, are starting to exploit the advantages of continuous collection of product data. For example, connected cars can collect diagnostic data such as fuel efficiency and energy consumption data, whereas telecom equipment can collect performance data such as real-time bandwidth, restarts, outages and upgrade success rate etc. Therefore, although the first area of post-deployment data collection can be found in online services such as SaaS and cloud computing, the techniques can be applied to any product that is able to collect and provide data about its usage and performance, and that can be connected to the Internet for data access and retrieval. This includes software-intensive embedded systems intended for a mass-market from which evolving needs might be difficult to capture during pre-deployment phases, and where post-deployment customer involvement might be difficult to maintain.

3   Research Site and Method

3.1   Research Site

This paper presents on-going research based on a multiple case study conducted at three software development companies. Today, all the companies are collecting large amounts of data from the products they release to customers.

Company A is a provider of telecommunication systems and equipment, communications networks and multimedia solutions for mobile and fixed network operators. The company has a number of post-deployment data collection mechanisms in place, and is currently collecting data related to system operation and performance. For the purpose of this study, we met with key stakeholders at two different company sites in two different countries:

- *Site 1:* The first site is involved in the development and maintenance of nodes within the 3G networks. At this site, we met with a group of four people involving the head of system and architecture, two system managers and a deputy manager. During this meeting, a high level discussion on the topic was held, and we decided on what people that would be of relevance for a more focused group interview related to our research questions. As a second step, we conducted a group interview with people identified as key stakeholders within the organization. In total, we met with 15 people during the group interview, including product managers, project managers, support managers, product specialists and integration leaders. Finally, a workshop was held in which we met with all involved in the project, i.e. people from the initial meeting as well as people from the group interview, as well as a few additionally invited managers, to discuss and confirm our findings.

- *Site 2:* The second site is involved in the development, supply and support of media gateways for mobile networks. At this site, we conducted a group interview in which we met with a group of six people involving two department managers, a support manager, a senior specialist, a product manager and an integration leader.

Company B is a manufacturer and supplier of transport solutions for commercial use. The company has a number of sophisticated data collection mechanisms implemented in their products, and the majority of the data that is collected is related to diagnostics of the vehicles. The products consist of a huge number of microprocessors and sensors with the potential to collect data for more advanced purposes. For the purpose of this study we met with two attribute leaders, two developers, and one software expert focusing on software process improvement. In addition, we met with a group of managers and developers focusing on the human machine interface of the vehicles, and with significant experience on user interface design and different collaboration techniques for this.

Company C is world leading in network video and offers products such as network cameras, video encoders, video management software and camera applications for professional IP video surveillance. The company has a number of post-deployment data collection mechanisms in place in their products. The data they collect is primarily performance data related to the operational use of the products. For the purpose of this study we met with a group of seven people involving the company CTO, two team leaders, a test manager and two software architects. During this meeting, a high level discussion on the topic was held, and we decided on what people that would be of relevance for more focused group interviews. As a second step, we conducted five group interviews in which we met with developers, testers, system architects, product owners, project managers and product specialists. In total, we met with 5 groups and a total of 44 people.

3.2   Research Method

Our paper reports on a multiple case study [21] involving three companies involved in large-scale development of embedded software products. The main data collection method used was semi-structured group interviews with open-ended questions [22]. In total, eight group interviews were conducted. All group interviews were conducted in

English and lasted for two hours. During the interviews in company A (site 1) and B, we were two researchers sharing the responsibility of asking questions and facilitating the group discussion. Notes were taken and after each interview these notes were shared among the researchers. The interviews in company A (site 2) and company C were conducted by one of the researchers. These interviews were also recorded, and notes were taken to summarize the discussions. The recordings, as well as the summarizing notes, were shared between the two researchers to allow for a discussion and interpretation of the interview findings. In total, we had 18 hours of recorded interviews and 58 pages of summarizing notes. During analysis, the summary notes were used when coding the data, and as soon as any questions or potential misunderstandings occurred, the recordings were used to replay the discussion and capture all interview details.

In terms of data analysis, a qualitative grounded theory approach was adopted [23]. In this process, the empirical data was coded using open coding principles, and clusters and categories emerged as a result of reading the transcribed data with the intention to identify similarities in the respondents' experiences. A problem that has been identified in relation to qualitative research is that different individuals may interpret the same data in different ways [24]. This problem was addressed in two ways. First, the coding processes prescribed by grounded theory provide an audit trail of the process by which conclusions are reached. Second, we used a 'venting' method, i.e. a process whereby interpretations are discussed with professional colleagues [25]. By sharing notes, and by discussing the results of each group interview, we could develop an accurate understanding of the different contexts and hence, explore the research questions guiding this study: (1) *What* post-deployment product data do the software development companies involved in our study collect? (2) *How, and for what purposes,* is this data *used* for increasing their understanding of how their products are used?

4   Findings

In this section, we present our interview findings. Also, we present key opportunities for more effective product development. The key opportunities were identified during our study and expressed as important by our interviewees when reflecting on ways in which post-deployment data collection can help advance their development practices.

4.1   Post-deployment Data Collection

Our interviews reveal a wide range of data that is collected after product release. All companies have mechanisms in place for collecting data from their products, and all agree that post-deployment product data constitutes an important asset for product improvement and innovation. In company A, huge amounts of post-deployment data are collected in relation to system operation and performance. Information on re-starts, system outage, faults, card re-booting and upgrade success rate is continuously collected and used for assessing system performance and behavior. In addition, dimensioning data such as CPU load, licenses sold etc. serve as important input for system configuration and capacity, as well as for producing sale statistics and market assessments. Most often, post-deployment data becomes useful when a trouble report or a customer request is reported. As a way of answering to a query, company A uses this data to track system behavior, identify a problem, and compare system performance before and after an intervention with the system. As mechanisms for collecting this data, company A reports on a number of support logs and counters, monitoring systems such as the 'Event Based Monitoring System', customer satisfaction indexes based on Key Performance Indicators (KPI's), and tools for collecting and storing trouble reports, trouble tickets and customer requests. While all respondents agree that post-deployment data is important, they experience difficulties when it comes to getting an overview on what is collected and for what purpose. One of the respondents touch upon this when saying that: *"We have all the mechanisms we need for collecting data from our products...we only have to agree on what to collect and why..."*

In company B, post-deployment data is continuously collected in order to assess system behavior of the vehicle. For evaluation purposes and development investments, performance data such as speed, fuel efficiency, energy consumption, acceleration, road conditions etc. is collected. In addition, diagnostic data such as trouble codes, failure reports etc., is continuously collected by the electronic nodes in the vehicle in order to help trouble shoot a problem whenever the vehicle is handed in for service at a garage. After having read the data from the different electronic nodes, the mechanics send this data to a central database in which all diagnostic data is stored. Finally, data is collected in order to fulfill legislation purposes since company B is involved in development of products where safety regulations are immense. Besides the electronic nodes that collect data, there is also ways in which 'flight recorders' collect important data. A 'flight recorder' is an instrument that is put in vehicles to track system performance while driving. The recorders are put in a limited number of test vehicles and only used within restricted areas, and serve as important input in assessing system performance when the product has been taken into use. In similar with company A, the respondents at company B agree that they have sophisticated mechanisms in place to collect post-deployment data, and that the challenge is to make it useful within the organization: *"For the diagnostic data we depend on the mechanics reporting it to us. Once we get it we store it in a database that is hosted centrally. What I don't know is how widely it is used for purposes other than those of the mechanics..."*

In company C, post-deployment data is collected on a continuous basis, and primarily for observing and assessing system performance. Here, data on frames per second, stability and usage hours is important as well as configuration data on camera models and number of sites. In similar with company A and B, the interviewees at company C find post-deployment data useful for answering to customer requests and for supporting the system.

4.2   Post-deployment Data Usage

Based on our interview findings, we see that collection of post-deployment product data is common practice at the companies involved in our study.

However, usage of this data is still scarce. In company A, both sites report on system operation and performance as types of product data being continuously collected. Also, bug report data is collected in order to learn about system behavior and use. Based on this data, statistical analysis and trend analysis is done and there is the opportunity to learn about current system operation and future dimensioning needs. However, while performance data, such as upgrade success and downtime reports, is collected, company A report on difficulties to use the data. As it seems, customer data is used for troubleshooting and for maintaining the current version of the product, but very seldom for improving functionality or as a base for developing new functionality. Managers at both sites describe a situation in which data is collected but not used, and they find it difficult to analyze the data to, for instance, learn about what features that are used and what features that are "waste". This is reflected upon by one of the developers when saying: *"We have an idea on what functionality is used...based on sales statistics... but we don't really know"*.

In company B, diagnostic data is collected when the vehicle attends service at an authorized garage. Based on this data, data mining techniques are used to learn about system performance. However, while this data is useful for the next iteration of development, i.e. for the next version of the product family, it is collected with very long intervals and is not used for improving the current version of the product. Also, to integrate and to visualize the data is regarded difficult. One of the software architects emphasizes this when saying: *"We use the data only for troubleshooting purposes – when something is already a problem for the customer. What we would like to do is to find ways in which we could make more efficient use of the data..."*

In company C, there are no established techniques for post-deployment data usage. While large amounts of data are generated in the systems, these are not used to systematically improve current versions of the systems. As a result, interviewees feel that they have only limited knowledge on what features of their product that are used, and they feel that whenever post-deployment data is used it is for troubleshooting and support of problems that have already occurred. One of the project managers reflects on this when saying: *"We get feedback only on things that don't work...things that are problematic. This is not necessarily an indication on what is used the most..."*

In summary, our study shows that product data constitutes an enormous asset for understanding product use, for informing product management and for improving deployed products. However, post-deployment data usage is scarce, and while all companies report on this data as useful for troubleshooting and support, they recognize that mechanisms for continuous improvement of existing products, as well as for innovation of new products, are not in place.

4.3   Key Opportunities

While still in the process of establishing techniques for post-deployment data usage, all companies view this activity as critical for continuous validation of their development efforts. In our interviews, we asked the interviewees to share with us why they consider post-deployment data collection important, and for what purposes this data could be used in their organization. From the interviews, we learnt that there are a number of key opportunities associated with post-deployment data collection and usage:

- To continuously validate what functionality customers value.
- To improve requirements prioritization.
- To optimize customers' use of the product.
- To increase the ability to anticipate future customer needs.
- To increase delivery frequency of functionality.

As can be seen, the interviewees consider post-deployment data critical for improving validation, prioritization, optimization, anticipation and delivery frequency of functionality. As a driver for these processes, post-deployment data collection and usage is viewed as an area of great potential and with a number of opportunities associated to it.

5   Discussion

Everyone involved in development of a software product has ideas on how to make it better. Typically, these ideas are collected and prioritized during the road mapping and requirements engineering process as part of the yearly release cycle and before any development starts. Often, the selection and prioritization of ideas are based on expert opinions originating from previous experience, and predictions by product management [6]. These opinions form the basis of hundreds or dozens of person years of development effort, and the confirmation of the correctness of these opinions usually takes place after the product has been released to its customers.

However, with the introduction of Web 2.0 systems, cloud computing, and online Software-as-a-Service (SaaS) technologies, the opportunity to collect post-deployment data from the product itself has significantly increased and brought with it interesting opportunities related to increasing the understanding for how customers use a product. Due to the online nature of these systems, data can be collected as soon as customers use the systems, and the cost of collecting data from, and about, the customer is low [20]. These benefits extend also to software-intensive embedded systems such as telecom equipment and vehicles. With the majority of functionality being software, and with the opportunity to be connected to the Internet, these systems are now increasingly interesting from a data collection perspective. Therefore, although the first area of post-deployment data collection can be found in online services, the techniques can be easily transferred to any product that is able to collect and provide data about its real-time usage and performance. From a product development perspective this is interesting as it opens up for continuous improvement of existing systems, i.e. companies do not need to wait until the next version of a system before they can improve it. Instead, they can deploy new functionality to the current version of the system and to customers already using the system.

5.1   Post-deployment Data as Pre-development Input

In our study, we explore post-deployment data usage in three companies involved in development of software-intensive embedded systems. On the basis of qualitative interviews we see that all companies collect huge amounts of product data. However, even though the companies have data collection mechanisms in place, they find it difficult to integrate, communicate and visualize the data so that it becomes accessible for people in their organization. As a result, post-deployment product data is used primarily as input to the next pre-development phase, i.e. as input for the next version of the system but not for improving the current version, or for innovation of new functionality. This shortcoming is recognized in previous research in which concepts such as 'online experiments' [5], 'test-and-learn' mind-set [6], and 'innovation experiment systems' [6] are used to denote techniques that allow for real-time use of post-deployment product data.

5.2   Post-deployment Data as Troubleshooting Input

While our study conveys a number of opportunities for efficient use of post-deployment product data, our interviews show that this data is currently used only for troubleshooting, for product support and maintenance, and for bug fixing purposes. Hence, our interviewees confirm previous research [1, 6] in that even though collection of post-deployment data is increasing, there is a range of opportunities still to explore for companies involved in software-intensive embedded systems development. In all companies involved in our study, people have a good understanding for system-level operations and system-level performance, but they lack insight in individual feature usage and user patterns related to specific system functionality. Hence, we see that while the data is used for troubleshooting purposes, it is not used for more advanced purposes such as improvement of existing functionality or innovation of new products.

5.3   Post-deployment Data Usage Framework

As a result of our study, and the insights provided by our interviewees with regard to how post-deployment data is used, we propose a framework that supports companies interested in advancing their usage of post-deployment product data (figure 1).

In the framework, we outline the different levels of post-deployment data usage, i.e. different purposes for which this data is used. At the first level, operational data represents data that helps companies understand how the system performs, i.e. data generated during real-time use and that is collected in order for companies to get a system understanding. However, at most companies, operational data is collected without a clear purpose of how to analyze and use it and therefore, primarily a high-level understanding of the system is obtained. At the second level, diagnostic data represents data that is collected with the specific purpose of troubleshooting activities. Here, data is collected in order to support bug fixing and error correction, and to provide input for system maintenance. At this level, a more systematic collection of data is required and companies make use of effective data storage in order to document and trace troubleshooting and maintenance processes. The third level, i.e. feature usage, represents a level at with companies collect data that helps them understand usage (or non-usage) of individual features. In comparison to the high-level system understanding that is provided by collection of operational data, this level requires mechanisms and tools that allow for a more sophisticated data analysis in which usage patterns of specific features can be discerned. At the two most advanced levels, i.e. feature improvement and new feature development, data is collected in order to support continuous improvement of current functionality, as well as for innovation and development of new features. To achieve these levels, advanced development practices that allow for new software functionality to be easily tested and integrated are required.

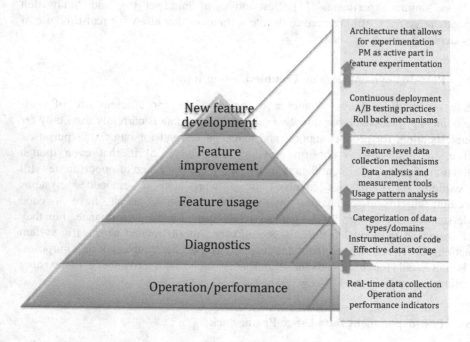

Fig. 1. Post-Deployment Data Usage Framework

Based on insights acquired during our interview study, as well as on our previous work on how to advance beyond agile development practices [26], our framework suggests mechanisms (see the boxes to the right in the figure) that are needed for climbing these levels and move towards more advanced use of post-deployment product data. These mechanisms are related to organizational processes and development practices that will allow a company to not only collect post-deployment data for operational and diagnostic purposes, but to use this data for more advanced purposes such as a detailed understanding of features, improvement of features and innovation of new features.

6   Conclusions

In this paper, we explore collection and usage of post-deployment product data. We highlight the existing limitations in post-deployment data usage, and the untapped resource that post-deployment product data remains. Based on a multiple case study at three software development companies, we present the following findings:

– Post-deployment product data is used primarily as input to the next pre-development phase, i.e. as input for the next version of the product, but *not* for improving the current version of the product, or for innovation of new functionality.
– Post-deployment product data is used for diagnostic purposes, i.e. troubleshooting and maintenance activities, and provide a good system-level understanding of operation and performance, but does *not* provide insight in individual feature usage and user patterns related to specific system functionality.
– There are a number of *key opportunities* that work as drivers for advancing the practices related to the collection and usage of post-deployment product data. These key opportunities are related to organizational processes and development practices that allow for more effective product development.

Finally, we propose a framework for post-deployment data usage in which we outline what development practices and organizational mechanisms that need to be in place for advancing the usage of post-deployment product data and hence, advance the development of software-intensive embedded systems.

Acknowledgements. This study was funded by Malmö University as part of a research collaboration between Malmö University and the Software Center at Chalmers University of Technology and University of Gothenburg, Sweden. We would like to thank the three companies involved in the study for the time and engagement allocated by all interviewees at these companies.

References

1. Bosch, J., Eklund, U.: Eternal embedded software: Towards innovation experiment systems. In: Margaria, T., Steffen, B. (eds.) ISoLA 2012, Part I. LNCS, vol. 7609, pp. 19–31. Springer, Heidelberg (2012)
2. Desouza, K., Awazu, Y., Jha, S., Dombrowski, C., Papagari, S., Baloh, P., Kim, J.Y.: Customer-Driven Innovation. Research Technology Management, 35–44 (May-June 2008)
3. Fogelström, N.D., Gorschek, T., Svahnberg, M., Olsson, P.: The Impact of Agile Principles on Market-Driven Software Product Development. Journal of Software Maintenance and Evolution: Research and Practice 22, 53–80 (2010)
4. Highsmith, J., Cockburn, A.: Agile Software Development: The business of innovation. Software Management, 120–122 (September 2001)
5. Kohavi, R., Longbotham, R., Sommerfield, D., Henne, R.M.: Controlled experiments on the web: survey and practice guide. Data Mining and Knowledge Discovery 18(1), 140–181 (2009)

6. Bosch, J.: Building Products as Innovation Experiment Systems. In: Cusumano, M.A., Iyer, B., Venkatraman, N. (eds.) ICSOB 2012. LNBIP, vol. 114, pp. 27–39. Springer, Heidelberg (2012)
7. Schuler, D., Namioka, A.: Participatory design: Principles and practices. Erlbaum, Hillsdale (1993)
8. Grønbæk, K., Kyng, M., Mogensen, P.: CSCW challenges: cooperative design in engineering projects. Communications of the ACM 36(6), 67–77 (1993)
9. Wood, J., Silver, D.: Joint application development. John Wiley & Sons, New York (1995)
10. Abrahamsson, P., Conboy, K., Wang, X.: 'Lots done, more to do': the current state of agile systems development research. European Journal of Information Systems 18(4), 281–284 (2009)
11. Beck, K.: Embracing Change with Extreme Programming. Computer 32(10), 70–77 (1999)
12. Larman, C.: Agile and Iterative Development: A Manager's Guide. Addison-Wesley (2004)
13. Nuseibeh, B., Easterbrook, S.: Requirements engineering: A roadmap. In: Proceedings of the 22nd International Conference on Software Engineering (ICSE), Limerick, Ireland, June 4-11 (2000)
14. Bennett, K.H., Rajlish, V.T.: Software maintenance and evolution. In: Proceedings of the 22nd International Conference on Software Engineering (ICSE), Limerick, Ireland, June 4-11 (2000)
15. Sommerville, I.: Software engineering, 9th edn. Addison-Wesley, Boston (2010)
16. Larman, C., Vodde, B.: Scaling lean & agile development: Thinking and organizational tools for large-scale scrum. Addison-Wesley (2008)
17. Von Hippel, E.: Democratizing Innovation: The evolving phenomenon of user innovation. Journal für Betriebswirschaft 55, 63–78 (2005)
18. Iansiti, M., Levien, R.: Strategy as ecology. Harvard Business Review 82, 68–78 (2004)
19. Jansen, S., Brinkkemper, S., Cusumano, M.: Software Ecosystems: Analyzing and Managing Business Networks in the Software Industry. Edward Elgar
20. Bosch, J.: Building products as innovation experiment systems. In: Cusumano, M.A., Iyer, B., Venkatraman, N. (eds.) ICSOB 2012. LNBIP, vol. 114, pp. 27–39. Springer, Heidelberg (2012)
21. Walsham, G.: Interpretive case studies in IS research: Nature and method. European Journal of Information Systems 4, 74–81 (1995)
22. Runesson, P., Höst, M.: Guidelines for conducting and reporting case study research in software engineering. Empirical Software Engineering 14 (2009)
23. Corbin, J., Strauss, A.: Basics of Qualitative Research: Grounded Theory Procedures and Techniques. Sage, California (1990)
24. Kaplan, B., Duchon, D.: Combining qualitative and quantitative methods in IS research: A case study. MIS Quarterly 12(4), 571–587 (1988)
25. Goetz, J., LeCompte, D.: Ethnography and Qualitative Design in Educational Research. Academic Press, Orlando (1984)
26. Olsson, H.H., Alahyari, H., Bosch, J.: Climbing the Stairway to Heaven. In: Proceedings of the 38th Euromicro Software Engineering Advanced Applications (SEAA) Conference, Cesme, Turkey, September 5-7 (2012)

Feature Prioritization Based on Mock-Purchase: A Mobile Case Study

Alexander-Derek Rein[1] and Jürgen Münch[2]

[1] Technical University of Munich, 85748 Garching, Germany
alexander-derek.rein@in.tum.de
[2] University of Helsinki, Software Systems Engineering Research Group,
00014 Helsinki, Finland
juergen.muench@cs.helsinki.fi
http://www.sserg.org

Abstract. As development teams' resources are limited, selecting the right features is of utmost importance. Often, features are considered right if they result in increased business value at acceptable implementation cost. Predicting implementation cost and prioritizing features is well documented in literature. However, there has only been little work on the prediction of business value. This article presents an approach for feature proioritization that is based on mock-purchases. Considering several limitations, the approach allows key stakeholders to depict the real business value of a feature without having to implement it. Hence, the approach allows feature prioritization based on facts rather than on predictions. The approach was evaluated with a smartphone application. The business value of two features which were subjectively considered to be equally important was investigated. Moreover, the users were assigned different price categories for the features. Combined with live customer feedback, the approach allows us to identify an adequate pricing for the features. The study yielded insightful results as it showed which of the features incorporates higher revenue as well as how users react to the approach. It contributes to the body of knowledge in requirements engineering and software engineering as it enables practitioners to select features based on facts rather than predictions and to find ideal price points.

Keywords: feature prioritization, requirements prioritization, live customer feedback.

1 Introduction

As practitioners as well as academics agree upon, feature prioritization is crucial for software development as it helps to deliver value to customers sooner. Specifically small development teams need to make sound judgements about the features they develop as they are limited to developing a narrow set of features. When investigating requirements prioritization in practice, Bakalova et al. [1] found that the key prioritization criteria is business value, e.g., revenue. Further

B. Fitzgerald et al. (Eds.): LESS 2013, LNBIP 167, pp. 165–179, 2013.

important criteria are any risks and dependencies associated with the features.

The most common prioritization techniques such as the Kano Model of Customer Satisfaction or the Relative Weighing Model are mainly based on individual stakeholders' assessments on the business value of features.

However, it is undisputed that stakeholders' predications are affected by contextual biases[1]. Empirical work has shown that such biases can affect the estimates significantly [2]. On top of that, decision-making literature reports how a set of general biases can affect judgments. Such biases have shown to apply to the software domain as well [3].

Several approaches seek to address these issues by leveraging end-user feedback. Usually, end-users are surveyed in order to find out which features entice users to purchase, cause users to upgrade, or increase the business value in a different way. However, such approaches assume that end-users have clearly defined product priorities. Hence, these methods suffer from contextual biases as well. The reasons why end-users' feedback suffers from a lack of liability are manifold:

- A user who answers the question Would you buy this feature? in the affirmative does not necessarily really purchase the feature when it is available.
- Most users do not have clearly defined product priorities. Hence, they might say "I want them all" when presented with a set of features [4].
- Users might favour a particular feature over other features and therefore downgrade the other features on purpose.

As a step towards overcoming such deficiencies, we present an approach which aims at eliminating such biases. The key idea behind the approach is to have users mock-purchase features which are actually not yet implemented. Mock-purchase means that the purchase processes of the users' smartphones are emulated to resemble an organic purchase process. In the context of a smartphone application, this means emulating the In-App Purchase (IAP)[2] construct. Hence, users consider the features as actual IAPs prior to mock-purchasing them. As a result, there is no contextual bias. After the purchase, users are made aware about the methodology and informed that they were not charged any money. Moreover, their feelings towards the approach are surveyed, e.g. with the question *Are you okay with the approach?*. Personal feedback can be provided as well.

If users show interest in a feature, e.g., by loading the feature's price but do not purchase the feature, they are surveyed as well. Thereby, the approach allows us to find out whether the feature's pricing is too high.

In order to evaluate the approach, it was implemented in a smartphone application. Prior to that, two features which were considered equally important by the app author were derived from feature requests users had made.

---

[1] *Contextual Bias* occurs when a decision is influenced by specific knowledge about the case and applies this knowledge in order to influence the prioritization outcome.

[2] In-App Purchases are features or add-ons to a smartphone application that can be bought with real money. In-App Purchases are very convenient to use as smartphone users can pay for the features simply by pressing a button as their payment information is already stored on their phone.

The case study is structured as follows. Section 2 reviews related work, Section 3 describes the research method, Section 4 highlights study execution details, Section 5 presents the study results, Section 6 discusses validity issues, and finally Section 7 concludes and introduces directions for future work.

2   Related Work

Feature prioritization is an interdisciplinary problem. Therefore, there exist many approaches in other disciplines such as market research which might also be relevant for software engineering.

Several feature prioritization approaches are based on the Kano Model of Customer Satisfaction (Kano). Kano is a questionnaire-based approach that was originally developed in order to investigate customer satisfaction [5]. However, it is also commonly used in order to prioritize features in the context of requirements engineering [4]. As such, it surveys end-users with both functional and dysfunctional questions. The results can be assigned to a ranking scheme which allows to distinguish between essential and differentiating attributes. The question *How would you feel if this smartphone had GPS capabilities?* is an example of a functional question whereas *How would you feel if this smartphone would not have GPS capabilities?* is an example of a dysfunctional question. However, such questions provoke contextual bias, as only few users would dislike having GPS capabilities on their phones. As a result, it is hard to differentiate between features.

As feature prioritization is a cross-discipline problem, there have been efforts to solve the problem outside the software engineering world as well. Hohmann's Innovation Games are popular in primary market research. The game Buy a Feature as an example seeks to eliminate contextual biases by assigning a price to each feature. Users are then provided with play money to buy the features. However, Buy a Feature does not eliminate contextual biases, either, as users pay with play money rather than real money. As a result, users are more willing to spend money and are very likely to spend all their play money whereas in real conditions many users do not want to pay at all and will most certainly not spend all their money.

Carrenño and Winbladh suggest *ASUM*, an approach that allows us to automatically derive feature requests from mobile application comments. Their approach is helpful as it decreases the time required to extract features from the topics as well as finding out how often those were requested [6].

An approach that seeks to prioritize features not only based on user input but also on stakeholder judgements is Karl Wiegers Relative Weighting [7]. The approach allows finding out about which features to implement and what priority order. In Relative Weighting, weights are assigned to the relative benefits, relative penalties, relative costs, and relative risks of features by the developers and product owners. Subsequently, users are asked to weight the features. In fact, assessing benefits and penalties is similar to functional and dysfunctional questions in Kano. Based on the resulting numbers the priority per feature can be calculated.

Besides, finding out about a feature's priority, Relative Weighting provides ground for discussions as benefits, penalties, costs, and risks assigned to features were objectively assigned.

3   Research Method

The research method is based on the guidelines for conducting case studies by Runeson et al [8].

3.1   Rationale and Objective of the Study

The rationale behind the case study is to find out whether the approach can contribute to the body of knowledge by eliminating contextual bias and thereby enabling feature selection based on facts rather than predictions. Moreover, whether the approach allows us to find out about how to set the price of features is under investigation.

The objective of the study design is threefold:

- Eliminate contextual bias by having users mock-purchase features.
- Randomly assign users different prices for the features in order to find out adequate price points. At the same time, collect information on how the users react to the pricing in order not to resent users.
- Collect information on why generally interested users decide not to purchase the feature (e.g., too expensive) in order to gain more insight.

As not all features qualify for being implemented as mock-purchases, such features need to be identified in the product backlog and treated with other methods.

3.2   Study Context

The context of the case study is a smartphone application called Track My Life (TML) which is developed by the study author. TML is a GPS tracker[3], which collects the users' location information automatically in the background. Upon starting the application, algorithms analyze the collected data and visualize the results using a map.

Moreover, the app provides its users with statistics on how many kilometers they have travelled as well as at which places, on which journeys, or in which countries they have spent most of their time.

On top of that, the app provides its users with multiple possibilities to provide feedback to the developer: (1) application reviews, (2) a Zendesk[4] client to create tickets from within the app or the apps' website, (3) a Jira[5] client which allows

---

[3] Application that periodically samples the user's GPS coordinate in order to fulfil a task such as collecting data on the user's jogging behaviour.

[4] Zendesk is a SaaS ticket system.

[5] Jira is a defect and issue tracking system.

to comment on and create issues and private emails. At the time of the study, the app had received more than 3000 records of such feedback. Track My Life is available on Android, iOS, and Windows Phone.

3.3   Study Design

As the approach is only eligible for features that can be implemented as some sort of IAPs, the study design requires eliminating non-eligible features first. Features which meet any of the following criteria need to be eliminated from the backlog: (1) bugs, (2) improvements, (3) features with ethical issues, (4) features which do not qualify as IAPs.

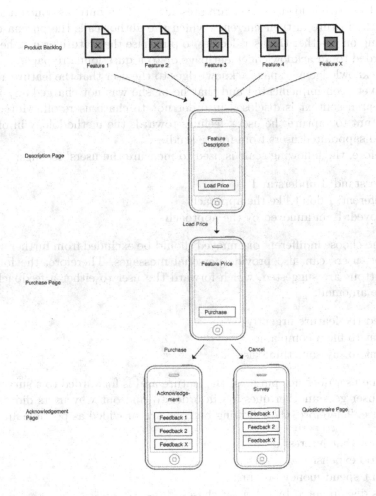

Fig. 1. Approach

Figure 1 depicts the different steps of the approach. At first, the product backlog may contain one or more features that are eligible for the approach. Upon starting the app, each user is assigned to only one of the features. Thereby, each user tests only one feature. For each feature, an individual description page has to be designed. The page contains a button that invokes the price-loading routine, as well. From loading the price, the author deduces that the user is interested in the feature. A click on the Load Price button invokes the price to be loaded. In case the software is just available in one currency, the price can directly be displayed. If the software is distributed internationally, the price needs to be converted. After conversion, the price needs to be rounded to realistic values. As an example, after conversion a price might be $1.73 which is an uncommon price. Hence, users might doubt the validity. Therefore, rounding the price to $2.00 is more convenient.

After the price is loaded, users are presented with a purchase button and the price of the feature in their currency which the author calls the purchase page. Depending on whether the user decides to purchase the feature or not, he or she is forwarded to an acknowledgement page or to a questionnaire page.

The acknowledgement page acknowledges to the user that the feature actually has not yet been implemented and that he or she was not charged any money. The research context is disclosed in order not to chase users off. Moreover, it is important to capture the users' feelings towards the methodology in order to exclude disappointed users from future studies.

Therefore, the following scale is used to measure the users' feelings:

- Understand: I understand
- Indifferent: I don't like the approach
- Annoyed: I am annoyed by the approach

Users who choose indifferent or annoyed should be excluded from further studies. Moreover, users can also provide personal messages. Therefore, the following three buttons are suggested, which forward the user to either a feedback form or invoke an email:

- I need the feature urgently
- I want to file a complaint
- I want to say something else

In case the user does not purchase the feature and is forwarded to a survey page (4), the user gets another question in order to find out why users did not buy the feature. Therefore, the following buttons are provided as possible answers:

- It's not that interesting
- It's too expensive
- I don't spend money on apps
- I was disappointed by other purchases
- Write down custom reason

The question on the pricing is especially interesting as it might reveal that there are people willing to purchase the feature at a lower price point.

3.4   Data Collection

The data collection cares about metrics regarding conversion rate and adequate pricing and differences of the features, feedback concerning the research methodology, and the data on why users did not purchase the features.

The following measures were derived for data collection:

Total Number of Purchases per Feature and Price
  The number of purchases that were made per feature and per price. As an example, it is of high interest how many users purchased feature A at price X.

Hypothetical Revenue
  The amount of money that would have been generated in case the feature was a real IAP.

Feelings After Purchase
  How the users reacted after purchasing the feature.

Reasons for Cancellation
  The reasons for which users decided not to purchase the feature.

Organic Feedback
  Whether the approach affects the reviews or other types of feedback that is provided to the app's developer.

3.5   Data Analysis

In order to find the right feature as well as the right price for the feature, the analysis focuses on with which feature at what price revenue can be maximized. Since users who cancelled a purchase are asked whether they cancelled because of the high price of the feature, the author assumes that those users would have purchased the feature at a lower price point.

Moreover, the analysis focuses on how many users are scared off due to the somewhat unethical approach as well. Therefore, the amount of users who understand the approach are opposed to the users who resent the approach.

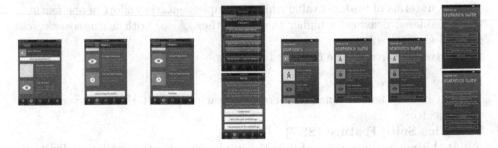

Fig. 2. Implementation on iOS and Windows Phone

4 Study Execution

This section focuses on how the author selected the features which were implemented, as well, on the implementation effort related to the approach. Moreover, the course of the study is outlined.

4.1 Feature Selection

As not all features in the backlog are eligible for the approach, the product backlog needs to be filtered. The following characteristics disqualify features: bugs, improvements, features with ethical issues, features which do not qualify as IAPs e.g. internationalisation.

Table 1. Results of the feature selection

Selection Step	# Features	# Requested
Beginning	40	2127
Bugs Eliminated	25	485
Improvements Eliminated	15	194
Non-IAPs Eliminated	4	41

Table 1 depicts how the features were selected. At the beginning of the study, the product backlog contained 40 elements which were requested 2127 times. The backlog was established by the analysis of different feedback sources such as application reviews, issues which were created by users in the issue tracker, emails by users, or personal messages via the ticket system.

The elimination of bugs from the list decreased the amount of features to 25. After improvements were removed 15 features were left. At the last step, feature requests which are not eligible as IAPs were removed. At the end, four feature requests remained which were requested 41 times.

Out of the four feature requests, two were selected to be implemented. The selection criterion was that the developer considered both features equally important in terms of business value while the implementation effort of one feature was considered drastically higher than the other. Also, both features were requested similarly often.

The two features can be described as follows:

History Feature (HF)
  The history feature enables users to retrace and edit the history of their trajectory.
Statistics Suite Feature (SSF)
  At this point, the amount of statistics implemented in the app is very limited. The statistics suite feature promises to provide users with more statistics.

4.2   Implementation

Figure 2 depicts the implementation of the approach on iOS and Windows Phone. The approach was not implemented in the Android version of the application due to the low amount of users.

The implementation resembles the approach described in 3.3. In order to draw the users' attention to the new feature, a note on the new feature is presented on a very popular page of the app.

Moreover, a mechanism to enable and disable the approach remotely was needed in case the study would result in scaring away many users. Hence, the application makes an http request to a server in order to find out whether the experiment is live or not. Another challenge of the implementation was the currency conversion and adaption of the result to common price application prices in various countries.

4.3   Implementation Effort

The implementation of the approach demanded about one and a half man-days per platform. Implementing the approach itself (i.e. functionality to mock-purchase features as well as the feedback mechanism) consumed most of the time. Adjusting the user analytics in order to derive the required data as specified in section 3.4 was time-consuming as well. Establishing the client-server connection in order to be able to remotely switch the approach on and off did require implementation effort as well. Lastly, packaging the application for release required testing and the usual packaging effort e.g. updating the application description, as well.

4.4   Course of the Study

The study started on April 5 on the Windows Phone platform and on April 7 on iOS. Figure 3 depicts the number of daily new users. The number is composed of new users downloading the app on a given day as well as existing users updating

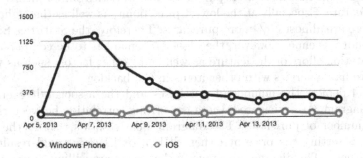

Fig. 3. Course of the Study

the app to the current version. The study ended on both platforms on April 23. In total, 9426 users participated in the study.

5 Results

The content of this section is twofold: at first the results regarding the feature selection and feature pricing is revealed. Then the data collected regarding the approach is presented.

5.1 Participants

In total, 9426 users have participated in the study. 8501 of those were using the app with Windows Phone, 925 on iOS. 2664 users clicked on the *Check the new Feature Out* button on TML's Statistics Page as shown in figure 2. 1493 showed interest in the feature by loading its price. In total, 294 users did a mock-purchase.

Table 2. Number of purchases and revenue

Purchases	SSF1	SSF3	SSF5	HF1	HF3	HF5
# Purchases	93	45	33	63	47	22
# Purchases	Statistics Suite: **171**			History Feature: **132**		
in Euro	93	136	**166**	63	142	108
in Euro	Statistics Suite: **395**			History Feature: **313**		

5.2 Purchases

Table 2 depicts the number of purchases in each of the categories as well as the revenue the mock-purchases would have generated. The letters in the columns depict the type of feature, SSF represents the Statistics Suite Feature and HF depicts the History Feature. The number depicts the price point in Euros. Hence, SSF3 depicts the Statistics Suite Feature at EUR 3.

Table 2 depicts that more users purchased the Statistics Suite Feature than the History Feature. Especially at the lowest price point, as well as the highest price point, there are almost 50% more purchases. Therefore, the Statistics Suite can produce more revenue. However, the higher revenue has to be compared to the implementation effort of the feature as well as to other factors such as whether the feature has synergies with other items in the backlog.

Figure 4 depicts the number of purchases and the associated revenue in a column diagram. As anticipated, there is a strong correlation between the price and the number of purchases. The diagram clearly shows that in the case of my features setting the price at either EUR 3 or EUR 5 would result in the highest revenue. The diagram also reveals that users are willing to pay more for the Statistics Suite Feature than for the History Feature. Therefore, the most

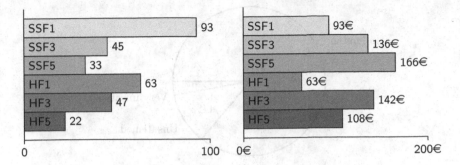

Fig. 4. Number of purchases and revenue

Table 3. Reasons for which the users cancelled the purchase

Feature	SSF1	SSF3	SSF5	HF1	HF3	HF5
Other reason	**38%**	15%	15%	**29%**	20%	14%
Not interested	12%	10%	4%	**16%**	14%	7%
Do not spend money	19%	22%	15%	**23%**	19%	10%
Disappointed	**6%**	1%	2%	4%	2%	1%
Too expensive	25%	51%	64%	28%	45%	**68%**

revenue might be achieved at an even higher price point such as EUR 5 for the Statistics Suite Feature. The adequate price of the History Feature is clearly between EUR 1 and EUR 5.

Table 3 depicts the reasons why users cancelled the purchase per category. Most users cancelled the purchase because they considered the feature too expensive. Other than that, many users stated that they do not spend money on apps in general. Very interesting is that only 10% of the users said that they are not interested in the feature. As the number is higher for the History Feature, we can predict that users are more interested in the Statistics Suite Feature. Also very interesting is that 20% cancelled for another reason. However, they were forwarded to a feedback page. Only 0.9% of the users actually submitted feedback. It is also interesting to see, that a small number of users said they did not purchase the feature because they were disappointed with other features they had purchased previously in the app.

Figure 5 depicts the feedback that was collected from users who mock-purchased a feature directly after the purchase. The majority of users understood the methodology. 11% disliked the methodology and 3% were very annoyed by the methodology. Only one user selected I need the feature urgently. However, this user was forwarded to a custom message form which he or she did not fill out. No user chose either I want to file a complaint or I want to say something else.

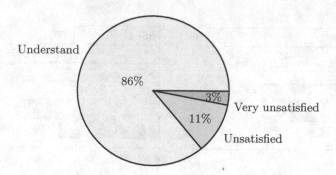

Fig. 5. Feedback after purchasing

Apparently, some of the very annoyed users were extremely annoyed. Hence, they gave bad reviews. Moreover, the author was approached a few times by users who were exceptionally aggressive. In fact, he was insulted both personally and professionally. For privacy reasons, the letters are not included in this paper.

There were also several reviews by users who obviously did not mock-purchase one of the features but loaded the price. As a result, they wrote bad reviews because of the too high pricing. As an example, one user commented:

> So close to being worthwhile, yet just sad not fulfilling in its potential, and 6 bucks for the good stuff?? Insanity

As user comments are essentially important for smartphone applications, choosing a price which does not achieve the maximum revenue but balances the trade-off between happy users and feature price in a more convenient way might be a good choice. In order to minimize the number of users who dislike the approach or are very annoyed by it, there should be some benefits for users who participated in the approach. As an example, a price reduction once the feature is finally released. On top of that, users who dislike the approach or are annoyed should be excluded from further studies.

5.3   Interpretation

In order to balance between highest revenue and customer satisfaction, the author of the app considers the EUR 3 price point to be the most adequate price for both the Statistics Suite Feature and the History Feature.
Moreover, the author would implement the Statistics Suite Feature as it obviously results in higher revenue and meets the app's general roadmap better than the History Feature although the implementation effort is higher.

The results also match the demand for SSF that was identified during the feature selection process as SSF was requested more frequently than HF.

Specifically with smartphone applications, users are not accustomed to purchasing IAPs for EUR 5. However, in different contexts such as desktop applications, higher prices are usual. Therefore, users might not leave bad comments due to high pricing in desktop applications.

6   Discussion

The results have shown that the approach allows testing the business value of different features as well as how often they are purchased at various price points. However, the test comes at the price of potential customer dissatisfaction and other interaction effects (such as implications on customer ratings that might influence future buying decisions). The essential limitations are the following:

6.1   Applicability

The approach is only applicable for features that can be implemented as IAPs. In the presented case, most requirements that were extracted from user feedback were either bugs, improvements, or other non-IAP-eligible requirements.

6.2   Validity for Larger Development Teams

The context of the study is an app that is developed by a single developer. Hence, prioritization issues that are common in larger development teams such as disagreements between team members did not occur in the execution of this study. Therefore, the results may vary in larger development teams.

However, we assume that the core of the presented prioritization approach applies in larger teams as well.

6.3   Validity of the Identified Ideal Price Points

In the context of this study, a price is considered *ideal* in case it yields the highest revenue at the fewest concerns regarding customer satisfaction, app reviews, and user retention. However, these criteria are very smartphone app-specific. Hence, the criteria for an *ideal* price point may vary in different contexts.

Moreover, the authors of the paper concluded the *ideal* price points based on the collected data. Hence, the price points were identified using empirical data rather than theoretical grounding.

6.4   Legal and Ethical Issues

Offering a feature that had actually not been implemented can be compared to selling something in a store catalogue which is actually not in stock. This might be seen as not correct ethically and there might also be legal issues attached to it. On top of that, the approach might interfere with smartphone operating system manufacturers' guidelines although neither Apple's[6], nor Google's[7], nor Microsoft's[8] guidelines cover the topic.

---

[6] https://developer.apple.com/appstore/resources/approval/guidelines.html#purchasing-currencies

[7] https://play.google.com/about/developer-content-policy.html

[8] http://msdn.microsoft.com/en-us/library/windowsphone/develop/hh184843(v=vs.105).aspx

7   Conclusion and Future Work

This paper introduces an approach that allows finding out about the real revenue of features which had actually not yet been implemented. Moreover, it provides insights and decision support on setting an adequate price for a feature. The approach was implemented in a smartphone application on two operating systems. Almost ten thousand users participated in the study.

The results are promising as they show that the approach indeed allow us to gain insights about feature revenue and pricing. However, it comes at the cost of customer dissatisfaction so that we recommend using it only for important feature implementation decisions (e.g., selecting features with significant differences in implementation cost). This serves as a motivation for future work on the approach. One way to address the customer dissatisfaction could be to provide mock-purchasers with a benefit e.g. a price reduction. On top of that, dissatisfied users could be treated in a special way, e.g., by excluding them from further studies.

The execution of the study unveiled that there is a non-negligible effort to conduct the study. First of all, the approach required sound judgments about what data has to be collected throughout the study. Second, the implementation was time-intense as the data collection needed to be implemented but also the smartphone operating systems' organic IAP processes needed to be emulated. As an example, the feature price needed to be converted and adapted to the operating systems' usual pricing thresholds. On top of that, a mechanism to both remotely start and stop the study was needed. Lastly, a mean of collecting the feedback and providing feedback forms was required. As a result, creating a boilerplate for other software developers in order to efficiently make use of the approach serves as motivation for future work.

References

1. Bakalova, Z., Daneva, M., Herrmann, A., Wieringa, R.: Agile requirements prioritization: What happens in practice and what is described in literature. In: Berry, D., Franch, X. (eds.) REFSQ 2011. LNCS, vol. 6606, pp. 181–195. Springer, Heidelberg (2011)
2. Bakalova, Z., Daneva, M., Herrmann, A., Wieringa, R.: Agile requirements prioritization: What happens in practice and what is described in literature. In: Berry, D., Franch, X. (eds.) REFSQ 2011. LNCS, vol. 6606, pp. 181–195. Springer, Heidelberg (2011)
3. Halkjelsvik, T., Jørgensen, M.: From origami to software development: A review of studies on judgment-based predictions of performance time. Psychological Bulletin 138(2), 238–271 (2012)
4. Lacey, M.: Prioritization. Website (January 2012), http://msdn.microsoft.com/en-us/library/hh765981.aspx (visited on April 17, 2013)
5. Buhl, H.U., Kundisch, D., Schackmann, N., Renz, A.: Spezifizierung des kanomodells zur messung von kundenzufriedenheit (2006), http://www.wi-if.de/paperliste/paper/wi-142.pdf (visited on May 7, 2013)

6. Galvis Carreño, L.V., Winbladh, K.: Analysis of user comments: an approach for software requirements evolution. In: Proceedings of the 2013 International Conference on Software Engineering, ICSE 2013, pp. 582–591. IEEE Press, Piscataway (2013)
7. Wiegers, K.E.: First things first: Prioritizing requirements. Website (1999), http://www.processimpact.com/articles/prioritizing.html   (visited   on September 9, 2013)
8. Runeson, P., Höst, M., Rainer, A., Regnell, B.: Case Study Research in Software Engineering: Guidelines and Examples. John Wiley & Sons (2012)

Fuzzy Cognitive Maps as Decision Support Tools for Investigating Critical Agile Adoption Factors

Efi Papatheocharous[1], Jaana Nyfjord[1], and Elpiniki Papageorgiou[2]

[1] SICS Swedish ICT AB, Kista, Sweden
{efi.papatheocharous,jaana}@sics.se
[2] Department of Computer Engineering, Technological Educational Institute
of Central Greece, TK 35100, Lamia, Greece
epapageorgiou@teilam.gr

Abstract. A lot of discussion on how to efficiently develop software by using agile methods in enterprises and what kind of implications enterprises face on their path towards enterprise agility exists in nowadays. This paper describes how Fuzzy Cognitive Maps (FCM) can be used as Computational Intelligence (CI) tools for Decision Support (DS) in reducing the risks of the implications in this adaptation or transformation process. Particularly, FCM are used in understanding the effect of a set of critical Agile Adoption Factors (AAF) proposed in literature in the success of adopting agile. A set of preliminary experiments have been conducted to show that AAF can be evaluated with the use of FCM and their effect on adoption success is validated in three specific contexts. The scenarios investigated show that a critical implication is corporate bureaucracy. Also, results indicate that some enablers are the project teams' personal traits, such as collaborative attitude and readiness to change, as well as, the customers' level of commitment. The proposed FCM model provides an insight on the usefulness of the method for assessing agile transformation success.

Keywords: Agile, Computational Intelligence, Decision Support, Fuzzy Cognitive Maps, Software Projects.

1 Introduction

Agile methods have become the main practice in contemporary software development. As agile delivery and execution practices are woven into the main processes of organisations, they pose changes to the core organisational structure. As a result, a number of new, perhaps greater, challenges present themselves, limiting the capacity for the broader organisational success that agile seeks to deliver [1]. Some of the challenges mentioned relate for example with efficient decision-making, communication, coordination, and collaboration.

In recent agile conferences a lot of discussion is related to topics on how to scale agile in enterprises. Also, many research papers report the critical success factors towards enterprise agility. However, a large number of the original material that research is based on is reported as experiential and anecdotal [18]. Chan and Thong

B. Fitzgerald et al. (Eds.): LESS 2013, LNBIP 167, pp. 180–193, 2013.

[8] report that agile methodologies adoption is typically resisted by the IT personnel. Recent surveys [22] report the same and add upper management to the resistance forefront. Industry surveys [3] indicate that the level of acceptance of agile methodologies in organisations is still at an infant stage. Most research has focused on the early stages of agile adoption and use, and there is little evidence that agile has been effectively used beyond the adoption stage [27]. In addition, technology support in assessing and criticising the success of this transformation in enterprises is limited and fairly analysed in research.

However, the use of tools and technologies in the context of evaluating the success levels of agile adoption for an organisation is a promising concept, which can result for example to significant increase of Decision Support (DS) and project success rates. Success in adopting agile within an organisation is important because agile is believed to improve productivity and efficiency of the development process, minimise time-to-market and enable the engineering team to respond efficiently to changes of priorities and/or requirements [1]. Agility also offers opportunities for improved products in terms of quality and in satisfying customer needs and priorities.

In agile environments, software development teams and project managers need to be equipped with strong decision making, communication, coordination, negotiation, conflict resolution, leadership and interpersonal skills [10]. Typically, in self-adaptive agile teams the decision and coordination processes are in their hands, defined around the core of the agile method(s) followed (e.g. SCRUM, Kanban and XP).

Related work has identified that there is lack of understanding the critical factors that influence the success of projects in adopting agile methods [8] [18] [27]. As agile development emphasizes the "people factor" [10] we have decided to evaluate a set of Agile Adoption Factors (AAF), proposed as a framework by [18] that relate mostly to people and their organisations, because we believe that there is lack of accumulated knowledge and understanding of these factors. Especially if considering the cause-and-effect relations of these factors in the complex situations of large organisations, managing all of these factors is particularly challenging.

Computational Intelligence (CI) techniques such as Fuzzy Cognitive Maps (FCM) are popular in various domains (e.g., engineering, social and political sciences, business, information technology, medicine and environment) [21]. The main advantage of FCM lies in them being capable of modelling complex dynamic phenomena based on the experts' perceptions in a way that corresponds closely to the way humans perceive the cause-and-effect phenomena [7]. The overall purpose of the use of an FCM in our work is to increase our understanding the set of empirical critical AAF identified in [18] and evaluate their usefulness in assessing agile adoption success.

The rest of this paper is organised as follows: Section 2 discusses recent work on agile success factors. Section 3 describes the theory of the Fuzzy Cognitive Maps (FCM). Section 4 presents the experimental process and the main results obtained. Finally, Section 5 summarises the conclusions and future research steps.

2   Related Work

Only a few recent studies have systematically investigated the issue of critical adoption success factors of agile. We refer to them briefly in this section.

Karlstroem and Runeson [14] report the results of a study on the feasibility of using agile methods in traditional stage-gate project management environments. Their findings show that despite of some initial management resistance, it is possible to use agile methods in such environments. Salo and Abrahamsson [26] report the use and usefulness of XP and Scrum in complex embedded software development organisations. They found out that these organisations were able to successfully use the above agile methods.

Related work has also identified lack of understanding the critical factors influencing the success of adopting agile methods [8] [18] [27] however a few studies contribute by analyzing them [8][18][22].

The Critical Success Factors (CSF) in adopting agile practices in [18] are the following: Customer Satisfaction, Customer Collaboration, Customer Commitment, Decision Time, Corporate Culture, Control, Personal Characteristics, Societal Culture, and finally, Training and Learning. The authors primarily focused on organisational and people factors, and the factors considered were taken from literature and were validated through data collected from surveys.

Papatheocharous and Andreou [22] suggested a number of critical factors affecting software process and the adoption of agile methods found through a survey conducted. The critical factors mainly concerned difficulty in changing their ways of working and that management of the organisation was opposed to change.

The potential factors identified in [8] are categorised as: ability-related factors, motivation-related factors and opportunity-related factors. In [27] Critical Factors (CF) are the following: Management Support, Attitude, Motivation, Team Composition, Training, Agile Mindset, Technical Competence and Expertise, Agile Engineering Practices, and Methodology Champion. The authors in [27] state that the right balance and combination between the factors and an emphasis on continuous improvement are crucial for achieving agile sustainability. Agile methodology-related characteristics serve to complement successful agile acceptance.

In this work, we have decided to use of an FCM to increase our understanding of the set of empirical critical Agile Adoption Factors (AAF) identified in [18] and evaluate their usefulness in assessing success in agile adoption. The motivation behind our work is to increase our understanding of the particular People and Organisational factors that are considered highly significant to the successful adoption of agile. In addition, the comprehension of their cause-and-effect relations in the complex situations of large organisational structures is vital to ensure agile sustainability.

3   FCM Main Aspects

Fuzzy Cognitive Maps (FCM) constitute cognitive models in the form of fuzzy directed graphs consisting of two basic elements: the nodes, which basically correspond to *"concepts"* bearing different states of activation depending on the knowledge they represent, and the *"edges"* denoting the causal effects that each source node exercises on the receiving concept expressed through weights [15].

The importance of FCM has grown significantly during the last ten years as indicated in recent studies [21]. Different FCM structures have been proposed in the relevant literature, while numerous studies report their use in many contexts with highly successful modeling results. The main advantages of FCM include the possibility of dynamic modelling based on the experience, intuition and knowledge of domain experts, simplicity in terms of definition, operation and evaluation, flexibility in terms of design, scalability and adaptability to any domain or scenario. The aforementioned advantages exploit the utilisation of FCM in a number of applications in different areas in modeling and simulating complex systems [20].

In the software engineering domain, FCM have been previously used indicating promising modeling capabilities. More specifically, Stach et al. [29] proposed two FCM models that consisted of three and five concepts respectively to aid in better software project management. The simulations indicated several observations regarding the influence of factors, such as the effect of communication on the pace of software development. Further optimisations were proposed in [28], with a parallel FCM architecture coordinated by a module for performing tasks such as triggering, checking, changing the parameters and stopping the FCM. The FCM were used to simulate the scheduling of software projects and examine the effect of various conditions on schedules. Three FCM were developed for different software tasks and the results obtained indicated how specific tasks influence the length of schedules.

A novel FCM was developed and used in [23] to assess qualitatively the underlying relationships among various software cost factors affecting productivity. Another novel model using FCM for predicting new product developments was introduced in [12]. The relationships between the main factors affecting the agile process in these developments were modelled with focus the Iranian manufacturing enterprises. The usability of common software quality character system was analysed in [30] through FCM. Software development risk analysis was also supported in [5] by FCM. The authors in [25] proposed a methodology through the use of FCM to model and map critical success factors in IT projects. Risk management was investigated in [17] for ERP maintenance projects through FCM that enable developing forecasting exercises through simulations. A software testing decision support framework proposed in [19] assisted testing managers to evaluate and handle risks. Improved negotiations and conflict resolutions were supported with the use of FCM in [24] that facilitated decision-makers to predict future negotiations behavior and, consequently, improve the chances of an agreement.

3.1   FCM Model

FCM can be provided through useful modelling tools and can simulate any dynamic system. A FCM consists of nodes and directed edges representing the effect that each node has on every other node. Nodes are typically called concepts and they represent an entity, state, variable or characteristic within a system [11]. There are two types of effects between two nodes, positive and negative. The strength of the effect is represented with fuzzy terms, such as, "high", "average" and "low".

FCM due to their simplicity and visual advantage, they can be considered easily to be understood by project managers. In addition to their simple structure and operation, they can model as many complex relationships needed. The analysis of FCM is based on simulations, considering different FCM designs and/or different starting conditions. Finally, as many or as complicated or as simple simulations can be performed depending on the decision question posed.

The main benefit from using FCM in this work is that they are considered possible to empower project managers to efficiently adjust success enablers of agile adoption and extension in organisations. The goal is to show the necessity of scaling up the necessary adjustments of these factors and changing organizational structures. The practicality of this eventually will be to support the production of qualitative software products, efficiently coordinating processes and activities in software development, reducing lead time by increasing productivity of the individual teams and the organisation and finally, moving towards agility at an enterprise level.

3.2   FCM Inference Process

After an FCM is constructed, it can receive data from its input concepts, perform reasoning and infer decisions as values of its output concepts. The FCM can then be run as a discrete simulation and produce results [16].

The steps of the FCM inference process can be found in [21] and we briefly present them here. As a first step, the initial state of the concepts is given either from experts and/or stakeholders. During reasoning the FCM iteratively calculates its state until convergence. The state is represented by a *state vector* A^k which consists of real node values $A_i^{(k)} \in [0,1]$, $i=1, 2, \ldots, N$ at an iteration k. The value of each node is calculated by the following equation:

$$A_i^{(k+1)} = f(A_i^{(k)} + \sum_{\substack{j \neq i \\ j=1}}^{N} A_j^{(k)} \cdot W_{ji}) \tag{1}$$

where f is a sigmoid threshold (activation) function $f(x) = 1/(1 + e^{-m(x)})$ and m is a constant parameter [8]. The parameter m determines how quickly the $f(x)$ approaches the limiting values of 0 and 1.

The reasoning mechanism calculates the successive states of vector **A** by iteratively making use of eq. (1). A concept is turned on or activated by making its vector element 0 or 1. Eq. (1) includes the previous value of each concept, so the FCM possesses memory capabilities and there is a smooth change after each simulation step.

3.3   FCM for Agile Adoption Factors Success Assessment

Due to the advantageous characteristics and promising modelling capabilities of FCM, we decided to use them in assessing the factors proposed in [18], with a specific focus on Organisational and People only factors, which are considered highly complex. FCM can then contribute to a better understanding of these factors in agile adoption.

The FCM constructed (Fig. 1) consists of 9 Cognitive Concept Nodes (CCN) representing the Agile Adoption Factors (AAF) and 1 additional node representing Success. The terms CCN and AAF are used interchangeably in this paper.

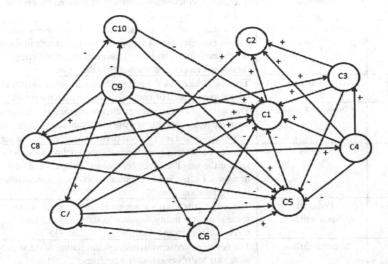

Fig. 1. Agile Adoption Factors FCM with 10 concepts

The nodes are listed and described in Table 1 and their influences (weights) are listed in Table 2. The values were obtained using cumulative knowledge and opinions of three experts in the field of carrying out software development projects for an average of 10 years. The process that was followed to reach to the FCM is as follows: Each expert involved in the experiments was given the task to read the definitions of the concepts discussed in [18]. Second, the researchers discussed the definitions with the purpose of reaching a common understanding. Third, each expert drew the map and specified the influence values of each concept to all others, if a relationship was believed to exist. Each expert was then asked to support the drawing and values specified. The values used in the experiments consisted of the averages of these values. The values are summarised in Table 2.

Table 1. Cognitive Concept Nodes (CCN) based on definitions by [18]

Code	AAF Name	AAF Description
C1	Success	The level of success achieved according the five criteria of agile project success: (1) Reduced delivery schedules, (2) Increased ROI, (3) Increased ability to meet with the current customer requirements, (4) Increased flexibility to meet with changing customer requirements, (5) Improved business processes.
C2	Customer Satisfaction	The level of customer satisfaction resulting from the team's ability to respond to change and delivering early and continuously valuable software.
C3	Customer Collaboration	The level of collaboration that exists between the customer and the development team.
C4	Customer Commitment	The degree to which customers are available on-site with the software development team, participating actively in the development process, being motivated and considering themselves responsible elements in the project.
C5	Decision Time	The time it takes for the team to make decisions (which is related to the speed of communication within the team).
C6	Corporate Culture	The degree of bureaucracy in the organisation in which the team exists, as opposed to dynamic organisations supporting collaboration and interactions between individuals and teams.
C7	Control	The degree of team empowerment and control given to the team in the way they operate, measure progress and take decisions, i.e. the level of centralisation vs. decentralisation in the organisation.
C8	Personal Characteristics	The level of the team's aggregated characteristic in terms of sense of responsibility, honesty, collaborative attitude, readiness to learn and flexibility.
C9	Societal Culture	The degree of conservativeness in the culture of the society in which the team's organisation operates.
C10	Training and Learning	The amount of training and learning required depending on previous skills and experience in the team.

Table 2. Influence values (weights) between the Cognitive Concept Nodes

	C1	C2	C3	C4	C5	C6	C7	C8	C9	C10
C1		0	0.4	0.8	-0.7	-0.9	0.7	0.85	0.6	-0.3
C2	0.7		0.8	0.3	0	0	0.4	0	0	0
C3	0	0		0.6	0	0	0	0.65	0	0
C4	0	0	0		0	0	0	0.8	0	0
C5	0	0	-0.7	-0.5		0.4	-0.5	-0.75	-0.3	0.2
C6	0	0	0	0	0		0	0	-0.6	0
C7	0	0	0	0	0	-0.6		0	0.7	0
C8	0	0	0	0	0	0	0		0.8	0
C9	0	0	0	0	0	0	0	0		0
C10	0	0	0	0	0	0	0	-0.5	-0.4	

4   Experiments and Results

4.1   Scenarios Description

In this section the scenarios are described. FCM simulations allow for analysis of several aspects of FCM, such as concepts activation levels at the final state and changes/trends in the activation levels throughout a simulation concerning either all concepts or a subset of concepts of interest to a decision maker [15]. Simulation boils down to calculating system equilibrium points over successive iterations. The simulation stops when a limit vector is reached, i.e., when $A^k = A^{k-1}$ or when $A^k - A^{k-1} \leq e$; where e is a residual, whose value depends on the application type (and in most applications is equal to 0.001).

Simulations were generated using inference equation, eq. (1), by implementing the FCM policy making approach [21]. At first, the steady state condition was determined before decision making options were considered. This was done in order to be able to see the perceived dynamic tendency of the proposed system based on the collective cognitive map and test for internal coherence. To accomplish this, we executed the FCM model with 100 different random initial states for all variables between -1, and +1 drawn from a uniform distribution. In all of these no-decision-making-simulations, the system reached a steady state after 30-50 iterations.

Next, the experiments conducted and presented were based on two hypothetical scenarios and one real case scenario. The scope of the first two scenarios was to reach to equilibrium when the two extreme scenarios are deployed and in the final scenario a real scenario was examined. In the first scenario, the Best-Case (BC) was examined, where the CCN were initialised as positive as possible. In the second scenario, the Worst-Case (WC) was examined, where the CNN were initialised to negative conditions. The third scenario, the Real-Case (RC) scenario examined a case of real project conditions. The linguistic terms of the CNN are summarised in Table 3 and also their corresponding linguistic values are shown in Table 4.

Table 3. Linguistic values of the Cognitive Concept Nodes (CCN) per scenario

Code	Best Case (BC) Scenario	Worse Case (WC) Scenario	Real Case (RC) Scenario
C1	Estimated to be Low	Estimated to be High	Estimated to be High
C2	High	Low	High
C3	Very High	Very Small	Very High
C4	High	Low	High
C5	Short	Long	Long
C6	Dynamic	Bureaucratic	Bureaucratic
C7	Centralised	Decentralised	Decentralised
C8	Adaptive	Non adaptive	Moderate
C9	Progressive	Conservative	Progressive
C10	Low	High	Medium

Table 4. Linguistic terms of the Cognitive Concept Nodes (CCN)

Code	Linguistic Terms and Values				
C1	Low ([-1,-0.33])	Medium ([-0.34,0.33])	High ([0.34,1])		
C2	Low ([-1,-0.33])	Medium ([-0.34,0.33])	High ([0.34,1])	High	Very High
C3	Very Small ([-1,0.61])	Small ([-0.6,-0.21])	Medium ([-0.2,0.2])	([0.21,0.6])	([0.61, 1])
C4	Low ([-1,-0.33])	Medium ([-0.34,0.33])	High ([0.34,1])		
C5	Short ([-1,-0.33])	Average ([-0.34,0.33])	Long ([0.34,1])		
C6	Dynamic ([-1,-0.33])	In Between ([-0.34,0.33])	Bureaucratic ([0.34,1])		
C7	Centralised ([-1,-0.33])	In Between ([-0.34,0.33])	Decentralised ([0.34,1])		
C8	Non adaptive ([-1,-0.33])	Moderate ([-0.34,0.33])	Adaptive ([0.34,1])		
C9	Conservative ([-1,0])	Progressive ((0,1])			
C10	Low ([-1,-0.33])	Medium ([-0.34,0.33])	High ([0.34,1])		

The Real-Case (RC) scenario was executed to evaluate the success of adopting agile approaches by a team of junior developers that had no previous practical experience of agile and it is described next.

The team consisted of 7 individuals coming from different countries and having different cultural backgrounds. The product they developed was a music player using streaming technologies. During the development of the product which took 6 weeks, the team studied for the first time and applied agile methods. For instance, the team used XP and Scrum as ways of working and also tools like whiteboards, post-its, automated version control and testing, and Eclipse IDE, while the development language was Java. Each week the team produced a deliverable and the customer was available over e-mail and phone at all times. The customer also met with the team at least once per week. The team adopted agile in relatively high success, the customer was highly committed and responded to the team's requests almost daily. The customer collaboration and communication with the team was quite good and the team was empowered to make decisions. The corporate culture was quite bureaucratic, as it required the team to adhere to general organisational policies and standards, such as documentation and reporting. Also, decision time was quite long due to this. Some team members were not that flexible in adapting agile due to their personal characteristics, and for example refused to follow some principles and this had an effect on the collaboration within the team. Overall, the customer satisfaction was quite high.

4.2   Results

The corresponding initial numerical values for the linguistic states of the FCM CCN are listed in Table 5. After the FCM is executed for 50 iterations the final values stabilised at equilibrium and are summarised on the same table.

The values of the results for the CCN Success are within [0, 1] due to the use of the sigmoid transformation function, which transfers them in this range using eq. (1).

The results show that the FCM converges at a final state for the three examined scenarios producing meaningful results.

Table 5. Initial and final states of the CCN per scenario

State/Scenario	C1	C2	C3	C4	C5	C6	C7	C8	C9	C10
Initial / BC	-0.90	0.90	0.90	0.80	-0.70	-0.80	-0.70	0.80	0.90	-0.80
Final / BC	0.76	0.90	0.88	0.92	0.36	0.21	0.84	0.94	0.94	0.32
Initial / WC	0.90	-0.90	-0.90	-0.90	0.90	0.80	0.80	-0.70	-0.70	0.80
Final / WC	0.04	0.00	0.01	0.01	0.73	0.87	0.03	0.03	0.03	0.77
Initial / RC	0.40	0.60	0.90	0.90	0.60	0.75	0.50	0.20	0.90	0.00
Final / RC	0.58	0.60	0.65	0.72	0.46	0.38	0.63	0.79	0.82	0.44

The results show, in the BC scenario, that the success of adopting agile was underestimated and the resulting value of the FCM for success is close to very high levels (0.76). However, the time reaching to a decision in such a scenario is considerably increased, meaning that even self-adaptive teams require spending some effort in decision making. The FCM shows that for succeeding in adopting agile, the corporate culture can be somewhere in between dynamic and bureaucratic, some effort requires to be spent for training and learning, depending on the skills of the team and finally, a decentralised structure for the team is required.

In the WC scenario, as expected, the success of adopting agile is considerably low (0.04). In such a case, the customers' collaboration, satisfaction and commitment are significantly lowered. The control is an insignificant factor in succeeding in this case, and thus it can be balanced, i.e., anything between centralised and decentralised. The teams' characteristics also are average and societal culture, either conservative or progressive does not seem to really affect the success of agile.

In the RC scenario, adoption success was underestimated a little, the customers' collaboration and commitment levels were a bit overrated and thus the FCM re-adjusted their values. The state of the rest of the concepts was maintained at similar levels, reflecting the real values of the real scenario as described in the previous section, except in the case of the corporate culture, showing a need to lower the bureaucracy degree within the company, so that agile success level would be possibly increased. The team also seems to require a more collaborative attitude and readiness to change, as well as, some additional effort in training and learning in the future.

Our results show that the factors assessed seem to have a reasonable and significant impact on the success of a team's adoption of agile. The concept model reacted successfully and recognised the dynamics of both an optimistic and a pessimistic scenario, as well as in a real case scenario utilised, and provided estimates of adoption success in each case respectively in a quantitative nature.

4.3   Discussion

The goal of this paper was to quantitatively assess a selection of Agile Adoption Factors (AAF) proposed in [18] by conducting some preliminary experiments using FCM. The simulation results are presented and validated through two hypothetical scenarios and a real one drawn from real project conditions. However, in our attempt to understand the AAF proposed in [18] we add the following discussion.

Even though the justification of evaluating the particular selection of AAF is somehow rational, we have faced the following difficulties with assessing them due to the definitions provided by the authors of the study, their scoping and mapping, as we explain below.

Definition. We encountered some problems in understanding the definition of success in the specific context of agile adoption. In the authors' paper [18], the definition of success is based on Project Management Institute's (PMI)[1] definition, i.e. they use PMI's three key components: Time, Cost and Quality as the basis for deriving their criteria of agile project success. In our point of view, the authors lack to some degree in this definition because it describes an outcome expected to be delivered from projects that are already using agile methods. The definition in our perspective spans into more factors than the specific factors contributing or impeding the adoption of new ways of working in a team. Consequently, in future work, we plan to re-evaluate and re-define the success as defined by the authors in [18] and based on other additional success criteria, re-construct the map. Our endeavour is to expand the practitioners' and researchers' understanding of agile adoption success by not focusing only on the context of adopting agile methods in a team or within a project or within an organisation. This investigation will further strengthen the relationships we believe to exist between successful adoption of agile methods and eventual software project success. Such investigations could also support our suggestion for future work to directly evaluate a project's success according to the five criteria suggested in [18] and also to other factors that we would propose.

Scoping. In terms of agile adoption success factors, we have found various studies identifying additional (or different) factors that the ones proposed in [18]. Some examples include the industrial survey conducted by Ambler and Gorans [4], where the following factors associated with the success and failure of agile teams were identified: (1) people are assigned to a single team, (2) teams have easy access to business expertise, (3) teams are organised for agile delivery, (4) organisation has an agile community of excellence, (5) organization is explicitly addressing barriers, (6) executive sponsorship, (7) teams are measured on value creation, (8) organization's IT governance strategy includes an agile path. The aforementioned study is supported by many others, presenting similar concepts, for instance the studies of Holler and Culling [13]. In this work we intentionally focused explicitly on the factors that covered factors related to people and organisational aspects, the AAF that evaluated in our experiments need further re-definition, investigation and validation in the future. Thus, in future work, we will re-consider the factors selected and their definitions as provided in [18] to ensure that our results and conclusions are better validated and confirm their usefulness to practitioners and perhaps experts from particular industries.

Mapping. It is also worth noting that the FCM technology requires that the concepts used in the model are represented as an entity, state, variable or characteristic within a system and their relationships are specified as effects between two nodes, i.e., positive and negative. To be able to simulate the influence of the AAF

---

[1] http://www.pmi.org

used in this study, we had to translate their current definitions according to the FCM principles (see Table 1). Hence, we had to slightly change in concept some of their original definitions to be able to model them as nodes, specify relationships, weights and linguistic values and simulate their effects on each other to execute the experiments and assess the underlying relationships among the various AAF affecting success. For these changes some further validation activities need to be performed and some practitioners' feedback might be useful in mapping the concepts to real factors that are found in everyday practice.

5   Conclusions

This work investigated the use of Fuzzy Cognitive Maps (FCM) in evaluating a set of critical Agile Adoption Factors (AAF) proposed in literature. However, these factors have not been quantitatively assessed in any prior work and this is the main contribution of our work. In this paper, we propose the use of an FCM to execute experiments for validation purposes of a set of selected AAF proposed by [18].

Two different hypothetical scenarios were executed and a real one. The FCM produced indications that in the first case the success was underestimated in the initial conditions and in the second case, where the results showed that success rates with regards to the agile adoption should be in lower levels than originally estimated. The hypothetical examples aimed at validating the model at the two extremes while more real case examples, other than the one presented are required. The real case scenario is interesting as an example case study as it shows the applicability of the method and the usefulness even in real project conditions.

Since this was our first attempt to experiment and model the levels of agile adoption through the FCM technology in real cases more experimentation on real projects of the industry is required. The results so far show that the use of such factors and FCM can improve the understanding of adoption success levels in projects and organisations and thus, the application can be considered overly successful in relation to the targets set.

The results, although at a preliminary stage, and even though some further validation is required, they may be considered quite encouraging and permit further experimentation with the model which will be our future research direction. Additional future work will be to improve the proposed FCM environment of experimentation in order to make the creation process more efficient. This will also include investigating the possibility of reaching to optimised weight matrices by obtaining informed opinions of agile practitioners or by employing other Computational Intelligence techniques for this optimisation, e.g. Genetic Algorithms.

Acknowledgements. This work was partially supported and carried out during the tenure of an ERCIM "Alain Bensoussan" Fellowship Programme. The research leading to these results has received funding from the *European Union* Seventh Framework Programme (*FP7/2007-2013*) under *grant agreement* n° 246016.

References

1. Agile Alliance Web site, http://www.agilealliance.org
2. Alizadeh, S., Ghazanfari, M., Fathian, M.: Using Data Mining for Learning and Clustering FCM. International Journal of Computational Intelligence 4(2), 118–125 (2008)
3. Ambler, S.: Agile Adoption Rate Survey, http://www.ambysoft.com/surveys/agileMarch2006.html (accessed July 2013)
4. Ambler, S., Gorans, P.: Agile Adoption Success Factors (March 2012), https://www.ibm.com/developerworks/community/blogs/ambler/entry/agile_adoption_success_factors30?lang=en (accessed July 2013)
5. Anand, S., Chopra, V.: Decision Support System for Software Risk Analysis During Software Development. International Journal for Science and Emerging Technologies with Latest Trends 2(1), 29–35 (2012)
6. Arell, R., Coldewey, J., Gatt, I., Hesselberg, J.: Characteristics of Agile Organizations. Agile Alliance, http://www.agilealliance.org/files/3713/4213/5176/Characteristics%20of%20Agile%20Organizations.pdf (accessed July 2013)
7. Axelrod, R.: Structure of Decision: The Cognitive Maps of Political Elites. Princeton University Press, Princeton (1976)
8. Bueno, S., Salmeron, J.L.: Benchmarking Main Activation Functions in Fuzzy Cognitive Maps. Expert Systems with Applications 36(3), 5221–5229 (2009)
9. Chan, F., Thong, J.: Acceptance of Agile Methodologies: A Critical Review and Conceptual Framework. Decision Support Systems 46(4), 803–814 (2009)
10. Cockburn, A., Highsmith, J.: Agile software development: the people factor. IEEE Computer 34(11), 131–133 (2001)
11. Dickerson, A., Kosko, B.: Virtual Worlds as Fuzzy Cognitive Maps. Presence 3(2), 173–189 (1994)
12. Fekri, R., Aliahmadi, A., Fathian, M.: Predicting a Model for Agile NPD Process with Fuzzy Cognitive Map: The Case of Iranian Manufacturing Enterprises. The International Journal of Advanced Manufacturing Technology 41(11-12), 1240–1260 (2009)
13. Holler, R., Culling, I.: Five Success Factors for Scaling Agile, http://www.versionone.com/White_Papers/Five_Success_Factors_for_Scaling_Agile/ (accessed July 2013)
14. Karlstroem, D., Runeson, P.: Combining agile methods with stage-gate project management. IEEE Software 22(3), 43–49 (2005)
15. Kosko, B.: Fuzzy Cognitive Maps. International Journal of Man-Machine Studies 24, 65–75 (1986)
16. Kosko, B.: Fuzzy Thinking, the New Science of Fuzzy Logic, 2nd edn. Harper Collins, London (1995)
17. Lopez, C., Salmeron, J.L.: Dynamic Risks Modelling in ERP Maintenance Projects with FCM. Information Sciences (2012)
18. Misra, S.C., Kumar, V., Kumar, U.: Identifying Some Important Success Factors in Adopting Agile Software Development Practices. Journal of Systems and Software 82(11), 1869–1890 (2009)
19. Mohammadian, M., Balachandran, B.M., Larkman, D.: Temporal Perspective for the Software Testing Decision Support Framework. Springer (2012)
20. Papageorgiou, E.I., Salmeron, J.L.: A Review of Fuzzy Cognitive Map Research during the last decade. IEEE Transactions on Fuzzy Systems 99, 1–14 (2013)

21. Papageorgiou, E.I.: A new methodology for Decisions in Medical Informatics using Fuzzy Cognitive Maps based on Fuzzy Rule-Extraction techniques. Applied Soft Computing 11, 500–513 (2011)
22. Papatheocharous, E., Andreou, A.S.: Evidence of Agile Adoption in Software Organizations: An Empirical Survey. In: McCaffery, F., O'Connor, R.V., Messnarz, R. (eds.) EuroSPI 2013. CCIS, vol. 364, pp. 237–246. Springer, Heidelberg (2013)
23. Papatheocharous, E., Rossides, G., Andreou, A.S.: Qualitative Software Cost Estimation Using Fuzzy Cognitive Maps. In: 18th European Conference on Artificial Intelligence, Patras, Greece (2008)
24. Rodrigues, A.S., Papatheocharous, E., Andreou, S.A., Moreira de Souza, J.: Evaluating Risks in Software Negotiations through Fuzzy Cognitive Maps. In: 11th International Conference on Enterprise Information Systems, pp. 380–383 (2009)
25. Rodriguez-Repiso, L., Setchi, R., Salmeron, J.L.: Modelling IT Projects Success with Fuzzy Cognitive Maps. Expert Systems with Applications 32(2), 543–559 (2007)
26. Salo, O., Abrahamsson, P.: Agile methods in European embedded Development Organizations: a survey study of Extreme Programming and Scrum. IET Software 2(1), 58–64 (2008)
27. Senapathi, M., Srinivasan, A.: Sustained Agile Usage: a Systematic Literature Review. In: 17th Conference on Evaluation and Assessment in Software Engineering (2013)
28. Stach, W., Kurgan, L., Pedrycz, W., Reformat, M.: Parallel fuzzy cognitive maps as a tool for modeling software development project. In: North American Fuzzy Information Processing Society Conference, pp. 28–33 (2004)
29. Stach, W., Kurgan, L.: Modeling software development project using fuzzy cognitive maps. In: 4th Workshop on Quantitative and Soft Software Engineering (2004)
30. Xiangwei, L., Zhou, Y., Zhang, W.: Software Usability Improvement: Modeling, Training and Relativity Analysis. In: 2nd International Symposium on Information Science and Engineering (ISISE), pp. 472–475 (2009)

Agile Project – An Oxymoron?
Proposing an Unproject Leadership Model
for Complex Space

Juha Rikkilä, Xiaofeng Wang, and Pekka Abrahamsson

Faculty of Computer Science
Free University of Bozen-Bolzano
piazza Domenicani, 3
Bolzano, Italy
{juha.rikkila,xiaofeng.wang,pekka.abrahamsson}@unibz.it

Abstract. Without doubt much of the success in developing software solutions are due to proper project management, supported by many prominent and dedicated organizations and professionals. During the recent years the volatility and uncertainty in software development have, however, undermined the success. The agile and lean software development approaches have also brought up a profound difference between dealing with ordinary problems and wicked problems, but have failed to provide the management with solid theoretical background helping them to take proper decisions. Generally, the complexity theory is often referred to, but only at a superficial level. This paper attempts to explore what it means to build a leadership approach for software development that is based actually on complexity theory. We propose a novel approach called the unproject leadership model. The proposed model translates and maps the specific complexity concepts to the software development domain, consolidating them with the contributions already achieved by the lean and agile literature. As a result, the proposed model reverses many of the core project management practices. There are severe ramifications to large parts of contemporary organization management: converting leadership into interaction between people, flattening hierarchies and removing formal structures, abandoning top-down rules and plans. An initial validation of the proposed model is presented as well as the future directions are outlined.

Keywords: Software development, complexity, project management, leadership, emergence, unproject.

1 Introduction

Projects are everywhere. As the means of organizing work without organization limits the project model has become the standard operational practice in many organizations [1]. For several decades, the academic and professional institutions, consultants and other companies have provided an ample amount of literature and guidance. It is evident that much of success and valuable results can be attributed to the successful application of the project model in practice.

B. Fitzgerald et al. (Eds.): LESS 2013, LNBIP 167, pp. 194–209, 2013.

Therefore, it seems a bit disconcerting that a commonly accepted definition of what project management is does not exist [1, 2]. Recently, Garel [2] argued that the project management model should be distinguished from the project management practices, and that often the research on projects and the development of the management of projects place more focus on practices than on the generic model holistically. Further, Winter et al. [1] suggest that the current management practices are actually evolving further away from the development of theoretically sound common models. In software development field this separation has also become visible. The recent introduction of agile methods has challenged the traditional leadership and management practices.

The purpose of the project management is to ensure predictable outcome on predictable performance level [e.g., 5]. A simplified model for project management has three main areas of activity: problem definition, solution definition and solution implementation [3-4]. The underlying logic can be characterized as reductionistic, causal and linear. Reductionism means that a property of the whole can be divided into smaller elements that explain the whole completely. For example, the user need (i.e., epic) in agile development can be further subdivided into features, user stories and tasks. Careful implementation of these elements should, in theory, lead to realization of the expressed user need. Causality and linearity means that the elements can be ordered based on some rational reason. In software development this means in practice that for example tasks that are required to implement a feature can be ordered into a series of development, integration, testing and acceptance tasks that produce the desired features as expected.

The reductionist view in the project management literature generally and in software development specifically has been dominant for many years. The most influential sources are the project management body of knowledge (PM-BOK) [5], the CMMI model [6] and the software engineering body of knowledge (SWEBOK) [3]. The vast supply of support, education, consultancy, and certification services has further enforced the practice.

However, the theory and the practice have become often severely challenged. Koskela and Howell [7] challenge the scientific basis for current project management and consider it flawed. Whelton et al. [8] claim that also the understanding of the project outcome is considered defective. Further, Winter et al. [1] suggest that the hard basis of the project management is evading and softer elements are becoming dominant. Several studies have pointed out growing complexity of the development efforts [e.g., 9-13, 47] and analyzed its nature and characteristics, but have avoided building on the complexity theory, the characteristics of which deviate significantly from the concept of complexity in layman's terms. The complexity theory gives a very different direction to the practices dealing with the complexity itself and these practices are profoundly different from the traditional project management practices.

Also agile (and later lean) software development community has challenged project management in several ways, and the outcome has been a large variety of proposals ranging from agile and lean project management models [14-17] to hybrid models [18, 19] and people management models [20, 21]. In the recent years, some practitioners have proposed more radical views such as abandoning all models

altogether. A well-known agile method Scrum, for example, does not have an explicit role for a project manager at all. It is evident that the guidance offered to the management is contradictory and confusing, and often not well reasoned.

This paper proposes a novel model for leadership – "unproject leadership" model, which has solid theoretical groundings in the complexity literature, and can accommodate well the agile and lean approaches. The 'concept' unproject emphasizes the radical shift in thinking about project management in complex context.

The remainder of the paper is structured as follows: Section 2 presents the related work on project management. Since the space is limited, the focus is mainly on the works of previous decade. Section 3 introduces the concept of complexity in relation with the software domain. Section 4 defines the key concepts of complexity science bearing relevance to software project management. This is followed by the construction of the new model and its theoretical basis is shown. The initial validation of the model is presented in Section 5. The paper is concluded with a discussion where also the limitations are identified. Finally, the contributions to research and practice are shown and the future research directions outlined.

2   Related Work

The history of the software project management practice begins in 1950's where software development was commonly seen as a part of a large product development project. Department of Defense (DoD) in the US was one of the main organizations driving the software and project management practice. [2] In the coming years, the size of the software grew and its role became more independent laying foundation for the battle between incremental and iterative and the waterfall methods [22]. The principal question was if any content could emerge during the project, or should it be all defined in the beginning. During the 1990's the process development culture became dominant and placed the project management in the central focus [23]. It culminated in the process maturity models like CMM/CMMI [6] and ISO15504 [25] that are still continuously and extensively used. Their main goals are to remove uncertainty and ambiguity and enable the company to produce predictable results. Project management is the very first focus area for process improvement before anything else. The process thinking forces an organization to define, standardize and control the process to achieve predictability and high performance.

As a counter reaction to strict process culture, the outbreak of agile development methods took place in the late 1990's and early 2000 [22, 24]. Agile software development approaches have had a critical attitude towards the project management 'cult' and have proposed several strategies altering or even totally removing the traditional project management practices. Several interpretations, and consequently implementations have taken place. Indeed, variations in agile organizations vary from tightly disciplined and CMMI compliant [26] projects to a very free development style or even completely informalized organizations. The debate of the 'right way' of leading agile development have been vivid on Internet, as can be confirmed for example with search using keyword "micromanagement", which in September 2013 produced 1.3M hits.

The project management community has not remained still either. Söderlund [27] shows that the project research and failure studies have placed focus on the following key aspects: optimization, factors, contingency, behavior, governance, relationship and decision making. The Project Management Institute (PMI) has continuously developed the PM-BOK and recently also added an agile project management in their certification program. The project management journals continuously report on advancement of the project knowledge. Much of it, however, continues to build on the traditional project management model.

From 2003 to 2006 a research was conducted in UK [1], which called for transition in project research focus. Winter et al. [1] summarized their main results in the form of future research directions shown in Table 1. Sauer and Reich [28] proposed the work to be expanded suggesting broader conceptualization of the project concept. It consists of 5 processes: action process, social process, emotional process, knowledge process, and economic process, surrounded by complexity.

Table 1. Directions for future research [1]

From	Towards
The lifecycle model of projects and project management	Theories of the complexity of projects and project management
Projects as instrumental processes	Projects as social processes
Product creation as the prime focus	Value creation as the prime focus
Narrow conceptualization of projects	Broader conceptualization of projects
Practitioners as trained technicians	Practitioners as reflective practitioners

Pollack [29] calls for a change of the project management paradigm, emphasizing projects' soft characteristics. Atkinson et al. [30] proposed 7 characteristics helping to understand uncertainty and ambiguity better. These characteristics are goal clarity, goal tangibility, success measures, project permeability, number of solution options, participation and practitioner role, and stakeholder expectations.

The "wicked problems" are problems that cannot be accurately defined and therefore their solutions cannot be defined either. The term was coined by Rittel and Webber [31] and these problems were further refined by Buchanan [4] and later by Whelton and Ballard [9]. Wicked problems are located at the very 'soft' end of the scale. Such problems are dependent on other problems and continuously varying, which makes finding a solution difficult since each problem is unique and thus the solution must be unique as well.

Wicked problems are impossible to deal with traditional project practices because an analysis will not lead to the expected result. Even when using highly sophisticated analysis means such as system dynamics models on project management [32] it is not possible to understand and control the many different variables in projects that are seeking solutions to wicked problems. Yet these situations are not uncommon since for example start-up companies are continuously seeking solutions for wicked problems.

The central concept here is 'complexity'. The Oxford online dictionary defines complexity as "the state or quality of being intricate or complicated". In the project literature there are several context dependent refinements [e.g., 9-13, 47]. Some authors in the project literature as well as in software engineering literature have tied the concept with the complexity theory. Then the focus may be in the complexity of the software and computer system [51, 52]. Or the focus may be wider having both the information system as well as the development effort as parts of the complexity [48, 49] attempting to demonstrate how this whole evolves as a complex system. There is also literature where the main focus is the management of complexity [50, 53]. Some researchers [33-35] have attempted to map the complexity theory to agile development. Cook-Davis et al. [36] offer an in-depth discussion about the key complexity concepts and how they can be seen from the project management perspective. All of these authors point out the relevance of the complexity science for software development and its management.

The literature presented above attempts to contain the 'complexity', i.e., to have control over it and to act on it in a planned manner. This, however, assumes that the number of issues can be kept limited so that it becomes humanly possible to analyze all the relations and to plan the actions accordingly. When the limits are exceeded, the containment strategy becomes impossible to apply and a resilience strategy is needed. This strategy requires building the capability to maneuver in ambiguity, uncertainty and unpredictability. This paper attempts to demonstrate how such a strategy can be developed. The next section identifies the theoretical basis for it.

3   Theoretical Basis

The theoretical basis of the proposed 'unproject leadership' model lies in the complexity science and in particular the subset, which applies to the principles on management. The main theoretical sources are the Cynefin sensemaking framework [37] defining complex state and its relation to other states, leadership of emergence explaining the means to influence complex development situations [38], and complexity leadership describing management in complex organizations [39]. Further more general complexity literature is used to explain the key characteristics related to unproject leadership model. Particularly emergence and the related concepts [38, 40, 41] are in focus.

3.1   Cynefin

The Cynefin framework [37] is a generic model for making sense out of various management contexts in which decisions must be made. In this paper we interpret it in the context of managing software organizations and projects.

The Cynefin framework is divided into two major parts: ordered and unordered. The ordered view means reliance on reductionism, causality and predictability. This means that problems can be analyzed, solutions can be defined, gap between the current state and the future state and steps to fill the gap can be specified, and a work plan can be made. In practice planning and control become the main drivers for the management.

The unordered view on the other hand takes the opposite viewpoint. According to Snowden and Boone [37] future is ambiguous and unpredictable, and reveals itself only when penetrating into it, i.e., solution cannot be specified, but needs to be found out step by step. When applied in software development, this means short development steps and experiments revealing the needs of the user, capabilities of people and limits of the technologies in use. Decisions can be made about the next steps and experiments, and a solution emerges rather than being imposed apriori. The solution is not final but an exploitable result of a given moment.

On the ordered side there is simple order and complicated order. Simple is fully defined order that is typical especially in organizations with very authoritarian management. Complicated order is based on rules and rational following of those rules. They are, however, so complicated that it takes an effort to fully understand, decide and follow along those rules. On the unordered side there are complex and chaotic domains where the difference is the amount of coherence. In chaotic domain all actors behave independently according to their own individual interests. In complex domain there is also coherence of agents' behavior, which means that agents give up some of their independence in order to pursue for some common goal. Yet they keep their identity and diversity, which together with active interaction is basis of emergence, appearance of new ways of working together, and new forms of end results.

The fifth domain in the middle is disorder, the characteristic of which is indecisiveness, not knowing what domain to be in and what approach to take. Communication is random.

The Cynefin framework offers the key concepts to describe the different management contexts. When applied on projects, the five domains can be characterized as:

— Simple: stakeholders have an agreement on the end results and steps to get there, and they act on it. (sense-categorize-respond)
— Complicated: through and possibly continuous analysis and planning stakeholders where agree on the solution and steps to get there, and they act accordingly. (sense-analyze-respond)
— Complex: through experimentation stakeholders agree on the evolving problem and an evolving solution to it and continue until a valuable solution is reached. (probe-sense-respond)
— Chaotic: stakeholders have no shared interest, but act individually in the same domain according to own interests. (act-sense-respond)
— Disorder: stakeholders have no agreement of the situation or the problem, or don't share common interest of acting on it; they become inactive.

3.2   Emergence

The emergence [38, 40, 41] is one of the key properties of complex systems, and it is used as the starting point for unproject leadership model. If a problem cannot be analyzed to the roots and solution defined in the beginning, finding the solution in an emergent manner becomes an option.

Emergence arises in systems that consist of diverse agents that interact vividly and share some common interest that makes them interdependent on each other. Several variables influence emergence either slowing or amplifying it. This enables new structures, new behaviors, and new solutions to appear that are unpredictable by nature. The outcome may be positive but negative as well from the perspective of the interests of the system. The emergence and related concepts are shown in Figure 1.

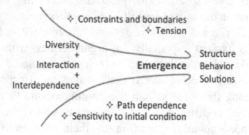

Fig. 1. Model of emergence

The system with emergent properties is not controllable from outside. However, environment has influence on the different variables influencing the emergence. While emergence of structures and behavior relates to self-organization, emergence of results is related to innovation and creativity.

Identity and diversity of agents and their interdependence are the basis for emergence. Tension within and with the environment gives energy to it. The influencing key variables are boundaries and constraints, tension, sensitivity to initial condition, and path-dependence. Boundaries and constraints can be set, and tension can be created, but influencing to sensitivity and path-dependence can be done only indirectly by influencing the underlying mechanisms.

The literature in the complexity science defines many more characteristics and attributes. This initial selection was made based on relevance to Cynefin and leadership of emergence, the two other cornerstones of this model. The second reason was their feasibility to apply influence on, as the purpose of this research is to find the ways to influence in complex system in order to get positive results. The correctness of the selection will be one of the main topics in verification.

When applying emergence in software project context, agents include many kinds of people (customers, developers, technical and team work experts, business stakeholders and such), having their own identity. Diversity and interaction are essential for emergence. In addition to people the elements both in solution and development environment have also a role in this interaction.

3.3   Leadership of Emergence

According to Lichtenstein and Plowman [38] there are four "conditions for emergence" defined as: 1) dis-equilibrium state, 2) amplifying actions, 3) recombination/self-organization, and 4) stabilizing feedback. The dis-equilibrium state means being capable of and under continuous pressure to adapt to changes in the environment. The dis-equilibrium state means lack of order, lack of certainty, and lack of predictability but also capability to initiate action and respond. It includes diversity of actors, and conflict and controversy that creates tension, and consequently need to emerge behavior patterns and results towards the purpose of the system. Amplifying actions are intended to maintain and enhance the state of dis-equilibrium, so that system remains sensitive to any influence, which may lead to unanticipated and significant changes and outcomes. While a traditional, ordered system absorbs or diminishes the change, the system in dis-equilibrium state amplifies it. Significant outcome may be produced, but also negative results or falling off to chaos or disorder is possible. Stabilizing feedback is intended to enforce some pattern that is considered to produce desired results and behavior. In general patterns are not directly manipulatable, but emerge from basic mechanisms, which can be influenced on. Stabilizing feedback is also the means to transition the team from complex state to complicate state, in order to fully exploit the results of innovation.

The dis-equilibrium state is the result of continuous self-organization, which cannot be enforced. In particular, an external force cannot directly and intentionally alter the state, but either behave as an environmental factor creating tension, or be in the system as one more interacting agent. Contrary to the traditional management practice where leadership is often pointed to a person, or considered as what a person does, leadership in complex domain is something what happens in the interaction between the agents of the system. Self-organization is continuously forming new structures and patterns, simultaneously taking place on many levels.

3.4 Complexity Leadership

The complexity leadership [39] provides a view to organization and leadership accommodating both properties of complexity and also "normal" functions. It consists of the concepts of adaptive, administrative and enabling leadership, where adaptive responds to complexity, administrative respond to ordered needs and enabling is the mediator between the two. It points out the change needed in organization management in order to accommodate development efforts that behave in the manner typical to complex domain. Here it is brought up to point out of its necessity, but left out of the scope of this paper.

4 Unproject Leadership Model

Our research consists of theory development and its initial validation. As van Maanen et al. [55] show there are drawbacks in either having theory first or looking for cases and evidence first. We rely on research done in complexity in management, but our mapping to software development context may introduce flaws in the approach we are developing. Further, in complex domain the traditional research relying on scientific method and particularly straightforward causality cannot deal with so many interrelated topics, as we have reasoned in [54]. Thus evolving the approach and its evaluation with different means continue parallel. This section describes the theory building and the next section 5 the validation of the unproject leadership model.

Initially this work started with agile and lean approaches in order to develop a relevant leadership model [46]. That, however, had weak theoretical bases, though from the practical viewpoint it had many of the elements presented here. This paper goes far beyond, offers the theoretical underpinning as well as provides a model that can be empirically validated. The foundation is in complexity theory and the requirements and constraints come from project related literature discussed above. The agile and lean approaches underpin the operational model of software development.

4.1   Unproject Model, Characteristics, and Practices

The unproject leadership model implements resilience strategy for developing complex software in complex situation. That is, it builds capability to live with the complexity, on the contrary to containment strategy that traditional project management applies in order to confine and control the complexity. Resilience strategy maps to the complex domain in Cynefin, and includes the transitions to and from the ordered domain as well. Dealing with chaos and avoiding the disorder are also essential. The overall goal can be formulated as targeting to "ensure implementation within innovation" as contradictory to traditional way of "enabling innovation within implementation". Next the unproject leadership model, its characteristics and main practices are described.

4.1.1   The Unproject Leadership Model

The unproject leadership model is encapsulated into three emerging focus areas and integrating leadership over them (Fig. 2). The three focus areas proceed in parallel and the timeframe of decisions is the current moment. The overall scope of the problem is wide, larger than what solution will cover, and the tasks to do in each focus area are small, of safe-to-fail size. The large scope is needed in order to properly assess the value for the whole, and be able to focus on the most valuable elements in it. The size of the tasks must be small, because many of them will fail technically or give useless result but are needed to get the knowledge for the future decision-making.

The emergent behavior is needed in three main areas, in finding the real value, in obtaining the needed knowledge and creating the environment for delivering the value, and in developing the desired content. Finding the value means continuously assessing the emerging solution with the value it provides for the problem owners, observing that the problem is simultaneously evolving with the solution. Wicked problems are prone to permute, so the value consideration needs to evolve correspondingly. There is need of maintaining a wider scope in order to find feasible boarders for the problem, and see its environment and possible adaptations to it.

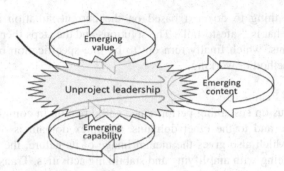

Fig. 2. Unproject leadership model in practice: Iteration of value, capability and content

The second focus area is the emerging capability to produce the content and value. As the problem is not completely understood, especially in the beginning, there is no full understanding of the competencies and technologies needed for solving it either. And the permutation of the problem increases uncertainty. Thus competence and technology options need to evolve with solution evolvement, which leads to continuous competence development, involvement of experts, and technology scanning during the efforts. The team is not stable and the knowledge needed in the team is continuously evolving. Learning becomes a continuous must, covering both learning of the problem and the solution, but including learning of the technology as well.

The emerging content complies closely with the ideal agile that is discussed in agile community, which is different to currently more common process oriented implementations of agile approach. This is further described in discussion section 6 below.

4.1.2   Dominant Characteristics

The dominant characteristics of unproject leadership are parallel, emergent and meshed. Parallel means simultaneous and interactive progressing in all areas of activity, particularly progressing with the three iterations. Emergence springs from diversity, interaction, and interdependence, gets its energy from tensions with the environment and within the team, and navigates within boarders and constraints applied on it. Outcome is new structures and patterns for behavior, and innovations related to the problem and its solution. Meshed means continuously evolving and adapting network-like structures both in problem and its solutions, as well as in the network of people and their tools and technologies.

Several variables influence this emergent behavior. Some of them are natural and hard to affect, like sensitivity and path dependence, some of them can be worked on like boarders and constraints, and tensions. Typically those properties that can be worked on are smaller, mechanism like behaviors or technologies, which then produce consequences that can be observed as patterns. The outcome of influencing can be positive or negative as compared to the desired.

There is very limited visibility to the future. The problem and solution as well as the ways to get to the solution are ambiguous and uncertain. Decisions focus on what is most valuable thing to do next based on the current situation and the current knowledge, and what is "safe-to-fail". The solutions and the steps there emerge within growing constraints, which finally turn out to be like specification of the system or architecture, or method of working.

4.1.3   Focus of Practices

The practices focus on sustaining performance and direction in complex domain, and transitioning from and to the other domains. Complex domain is often called "the edge of chaos", which also gives the mental image of its nature, the need to stay on the edge by balancing with amplifying and stabilizing activities. Transitions are either intentionally moving between the complex and desired other domains or unintentional falling off from complex and consequent rescuing from undesired domain. Amplification practices vitalize emergence or help moving from ordered to complex, and stabilizing feedback slows down emergence and help moving to ordered domain. Further practices are needed to prevent or avoid disorder, or rescue from disorder.

Sustaining performance and direction in complex domain calls for leadership that is based on self-organization and takes place in interaction. Tension creates performance and transparency enables decision making. Yet neither cannot be taken for granted, but require continuous care in leadership.

5   Validation of the Unproject Model

The validation of this model has so far been based on "in vitro" unprojects in Software Factory [42, 43, 56], and one of the author's own experiences in a large software organization. Additional evidence is to be found in mapping existing principles and practices "in vivo" with this model by interviewing managers in different organizations, which is our next step of the validation process.

5.1   Tests "in vitro"

The first rounds of testing the unproject concept have been conducted in software factory network [42, 43] "in vitro", that is Empirical Study with Students (ESWS) [44]. It is a viable option, *"when piloting experimental methodologies"* and *"obtaining preliminary evidence in favor of or against a research hypothesis"*. Software factory forms teams where there is an entrepreneur with an idea of a product, and students with different skills to develop the software. Often there is also special expertise in the team like usability and design experts, architects and so on. The main constraint of doing is demonstration of results every week, from week two onwards. The product idea evolves in the team, constraints increase over time when knowledge increases, and towards the end work focuses more and more on implementation of the identified functionality.

The results in software factory are encouraging, both as results and as ways of working. Prototypes with innovative features and the use of latest of software and hardware technology have been demonstrated in most unprojects. As a method of learning high level of motivation and energy have been created.

The results confirm also the high risk of falling into disorder and then difficulty of leaving that state. The other significant risk is to start planning unplannable. The third risk is to start implementing too large and still fuzzy ideas, moving to complicated domain without proper dealing with the complexity and then falling into traditional problems in projects. The effort will be spent but that does not progress the goal.

There is also a deep-rooted belief and trust of having a leader that would solve problems for everyone and keep the work proceeding. This goes with reluctance of taking such a role even when situation and persons own capabilities would allow it. Formal pointing or naming of a leader is often expected.

5.2   Author's Experiences

The impact of one of the author's own experiences in this model and its validation can best be described as reflection-in and on-action [45]. The first phase of several years in a large and multinational product organization developing software intensive products consisted of assessing process, auditing quality management and supporting agile and lean transformations, and pointing out successes and problems in project management and supporting processes. The second phase produced the paper [46] where this experience was reflected though agile and lean approaches, apriori. It partially challenged the traditional approach of managing product development in programs and projects. The third phase is now this paper and related work with it, where the previous experience, added with the experience in several validation unprojects in software factory network, is reflected with complexity theory, producing the first draft of the unproject leadership model.

6   Discussion

In lean and agile communities there has been plenty of discussion of "the right way" of using these approaches. This paper adds to that discussion by introducing the ordered and complex implementations and clarifying the management requirements for complex. We argue that management context and organization culture have decisive impact in which way agile and lean approaches come up in an organization. Yet, we don't put them in any order of preference or define one better than the other, but point out the profound difference between them. Though they are in the same continuum, they have profound difference by nature.

The ordered environments and implementations refer to process tools like CMM, process improvement, and aim at predictability and containment of complexity. Typical to it is predefined team, defined sets of practices and tools, given release times, product scope and quality definitions and a controlled backlog. The complex implementation of agile and lean accommodates emergence, focus on continuous growth of knowledge and realignment of teamwork, and living in the presence. Typical to it is variable team, emergent process and tools, releasing on opportunity and "sudden death" delivery, emergent, value driven product scope and backlog. Clearly the unproject leadership model is for the latter.

So is the agile project an oxymoron? The answer is yes, when the implementation is one and the expectations are as if the other. Most often this means ordered implementation but with expectation of creative and self-organizing behavior. The answer is no, when the expectations and the implementation are congruent. That, however, requires that implementation of "ideal agile" or "lean software development method and thinking" is accompanied with unproject approach.

The use of the complexity theory as basis is expanding in many areas of science, including management science from what this paper draws most of its theoretical background. Yet the extensive proof of results is still missing. It is hard if not impossible to find software organizations that would have applied these principles in conscious and comprehensive manner. We have worked around this in two ways. On one hand we have used Software Factory as the platform that provides near business like environment for running student projects. The real entrepreneur from outside university, the real aim to produce business class prototype, and continuous demonstration of results give strong impression of start-up company, which has been our hypothetical main target for the unproject leadership model.

The second source of evidence is from existing organizations having partially similar elements of leadership. Complexity in itself is not new in software development, so efforts of dealing with it are not new either. Though many of these attempts have been done containment in mind, clearly efforts are made to become resilient with it as well. That means utilizing emergence and creativity, which are the typical characteristics of complexity, for the benefit of the project. Collecting that evidence is our next step in validating the unproject leadership concept.

7   Conclusions

In this paper we have presented a complexity theory based alternative for the current managing of software development, particularly having agile and lean approaches of software development in mind. Though several agile proponents have referred to complexity theory as background of agile, very little has been done to realize it in practice. Our paper describes what it means to have complexity leadership in place for software development. Typically the effort is to contain the complexity, we have suggested ways to become resilient with it.

We have also translated the complexity of the complexity science into practical terms. Obviously other translations can be made, and we are still to indicate the usefulness of our version, though some early results indicate positive outcome. One limitation of our definition and implementation of the unproject leadership model is that it is pragmatic and leaves out a vast amount of concepts relevant to the complexity. This has made the model simpler to understand but carries the risk of omitting something vital for everyday use. Our research continues to explore the topic and we will complement the model accordingly.

We want to emphasize that the unproject leadership model presented in this paper is not a replacement of the current project management approach, but complements it. Often these two approaches need to live parallel and capability to move between the two is essential. That does not happen without adjustments to the current management models and without significant growth of understanding the complexity theory in practice.

References

1. Winter, M., Smith, C., Morris, P., Cicmil, S.: Directions for future research in project management: The main findings of a UK government-funded research network. International Journal of Project Management 24, 638–649 (2006)
2. Garel, G.: A history of project management models: From pre-models to the standard models. International Journal of Project Management (2013), http://dx.doi.org/10.1016/j.ijproman.2012.12.001
3. IEEE computer society, Guide to the Software Engineering Body of Knowledge, SWEBOK (2013), http://www.computer.org
4. Buchanan, R.: Wicked Problems in Design Thinking. Design Issues 8(2), 5–21 (1992)
5. Project Management Institute, A Guide to the Project Management Body of Knowledge (PMBOK(R) Guide), 4th edn. Project Management Institute, Newton Square (2008)
6. Software Engineering Institute, CMMI for Development, Version 1.3. Carnegie Mellon University, Pittsburgh, Pennsylvania, Technical Report CMU/SEI-2010-TR-033 (2010)
7. Koskela, L., Howell, G.: The Underlying Theory of Project Management is Obsolete. Project management Institute (2002)
8. Shenhar, A.: Strategic Project Leaderships Toward a strategic approach to project management. R&D Management 34, 5 (2004)
9. Whelton, M., Ballard, G.: Wicked problems in project definition. In: Proceedings of the 10th Annual Conference of the International Group for Lean Construction, Brazil (August 2002)
10. Ditillo, A.: Dealing with uncertainty in knowledge-intensive firms: the role of management control systems as knowledge integration mechanisms. Accounting, Organizations and Society 29, 401–421 (2004)
11. Remington, K., Pollack, J.: Tools for Complex Projects. Gower Publishing Ltd. (2007)
12. Geraldi, J.G.: The balance between order and chaos in multi-project firms: A conceptual model. International Journal of Project Management 26, 348–356 (2008)
13. Maylor, H., Vigden, R., Carver, S.: Managerial Complexity in Project-Based Operations: A Grounded Model and Its Implications for Practice. Project Management Journal 39 (2008)
14. Highsmith, J.: Agile Project Management, Creating Innovative Products. Pearson Education Inc. (2004)
15. Schwaber, K.: Agile Project Management with Scrum. Microsoft Press (2004)
16. Thomsett, R.: Radical Project Management. Prentice Hall PTR (2002)
17. Holcombe, M.: Running an Agile Software Development Project. Wiley-Blackwell (2008)
18. Boehm, B., Turner, R.: Balancing Agility and Discipline, A guide for the Perplexed. Pearson Education Inc. (2004)
19. Vinekar, V., Slinkman, C.W., Nerur, S.: Can Agile and Traditional Systems Development Approaches Coexist? An Ambidextrous View. Information Systems Management (2006)
20. Appelo, J.: Management 3.0, Leading Agile Developers, Developing Agile Leaders. Pearson Education, Inc. (2011)
21. Denning, S.: The Leader's Guide to Radical Management: Reinventing the Workplace for the 21st Century, 1st edn. Jossey-Bass (2010)

22. Larman, C., Basili, V.R.: Iterative and Incremental Development: A Brief history. Computer (June 2003)
23. Paulk, M.C., Curtis, B., Chrissis, M.B., Weber, C.: Capability Maturity Model for Software, Version 1.1, Software Engineering Institute, CMU/SEI-93-TR-24 (1993)
24. Rikkila, J.: Agile, Lean and Service-Oriented Development, Continuum Or Chasm. In: Wang, X., Ali, N., Ramos, I., Vigden, R. (eds.) Agile and Lean Service-Oriented Development, Foundations, Theory, and Practice. Information Science Reference, IGI Global (2013)
25. ISO/IEC 15504-2. Information Technology – Process Assessment – Part 2: Performing an Assessment. International Standards Organization (2003)
26. Jakobsen, C.R., Sutherland, J.: Scrum and CMMI Going from Good to Great. In: Agile 2009 Conference, pp. 333–337 (2009)
27. Söderlund, J.: Pluralism in Project Management: Navigating the Crossroads of Specialization and Fragmentation. International Journal of Management Reviews 13, 153–176 (2011)
28. Sauer, C., Reich, B.H., Rethinking, I.T.: project management: Evidence of a new mindset and its implications. International Journal of Project Management 27, 182–193 (2009)
29. Pollack, J.: The changing paradigms of project management. International Journal of Project Management 25, 266–274 (2007)
30. Atkinson, R., Crawford, L., Ward, S.: Fundamental uncertainties in projects and the scope of project management. International Journal of Project Management 24, 687–698 (2006)
31. Rittel, H.W.J., Webber, M.M.: Dilemmas in a General Theory of Planning. Policy Sciences 4, 155–169 (1973)
32. Lyneis, J.M., Cooper, K.G., Els, S.A.: Strategic management of complex projects: a case study using system dynamics. System Dynamics Review 17(3), 237–260 (2001)
33. Augustine, S., Paune, B., Sencindiver, F., Woodcock, S.: Agile project management: Steering from the edges. Communications of the ACM 48(12) (December 2005)
34. Meso, P., Jain, R.: Agile Software Development: Adaptive Systems Principles and Best Practices. Information Systems Management (2006)
35. Vidgen, R., Wang, X.: Coevolving Systems and the Organization of Agile Software Development. Information Systems Research 20(3) (2009)
36. Cooke-Davis, T., Cicmil, S., Crawford, L., Richardson, K.: We're not in Kansas anymore, Toto: Mapping the strange landscape of complexity theory, and its relationship to project management. Project Management Journal (2007)
37. Snowden, D.J., Boone, M.E.: A Leader's Framework for Decision Making. Harvard Business Review (November 2007)
38. Lichtenstein, B.B., Plowman, D.A.: The leadership of emergence: A complex systems leadership theory of emergence at successive organizational levels. The Leadership Quarterly 20, 617–630 (2009)
39. Uhl-Bien, M., Marion, R., McKelvey, B.: Complexity Leadership Theory, Shifting Leadership from the industrial age to the knowledge era. The Leadership Quarterly 18, 298–318 (2007)
40. Marion, R.: Complexity theory for organizations and organizational leadership. In: Uhl-Bien, M., Marion, R. (eds.) Complexity Leadership, Part I: Conceptual Foundations, pp. 1–16. IAP-Information Age Publishing, Inc. (2008)
41. Heylighen, F.: Complexity and Self-organization. In: Bates, M.J., Niles Maack, M. (eds.) Encyclopedia of Library and Information Sciences. Taylor & Francis (2008)

42. Ikonen, M., Kettunen, P., Oza, N., Abrahamsson, P.: Exploring the Sources of Waste in Kanban Software Development Projects. In: Proceedings of 36th EUROMICRO Conference on Software Engineering and Advanced Applications, SEAA (2010)

43. Fagerholm, F., Oza, N., Münch, J.: A Platform for Teaching Applied Distributed Software Development. In: CTGDSD 2013, San Francisco, CA, USA (2013)

44. Carver, J.C., Jaccheri, L., Morasca, S., Shull, F.: A checklist for integrating student empirical studies with research and teaching goals. Empirical Software Engineering 15, 35–59 (2010)

45. Schön, D.: The Reflective Practitioner. Temple Smith, London (1983)

46. Rikkilä, J.: New Approach for Managing Lean-Agile Development: Overturning the Project Paradigm. In: Abrahamsson, P., Oza, N. (eds.) LESS 2010. LNBIP, vol. 65, pp. 139–150. Springer, Heidelberg (2010)

47. Geraldi, J., Maylor, H., Williams, T.: Now, let's make it really complex (complicated), a systematic review of the complexities of projects. International Journal of Operations & Production Management 31(9) (2011)

48. Benbya, H., McKelvey, B.: Toward a complexity theory of information systems development. Information Technology and People 19(1), 12–34 (2006)

49. Benbya, H., McKelvey, B.: Using coevolutionary and complexity theories to improve IS alignment: a multi-level approach. Journal of Information Technology 21(4), 284–298 (2006)

50. Lee, G., Xia, W.: The ability of information systems development project teams to respond to business and technology changes: a study of flexibility measures. European Journal of Information Systems 14(1), 75–92 (2005)

51. Schneberger, S.L.: Distributed Computing Environments: Effects on Software Maintenance Difficulty. Journal of Systems and Software 37(2), 101–116 (1997)

52. Schneberger, S.L., McLean, E.R.: The Complexity Cross - Implications for Practice. Communications of the ACM 46(9), 216–225 (2003)

53. Xia, W., Lee, G.: Complexity of Information Systems Development Projects: Conceptualization and Measurement Development. Journal of Management Information Systems 22(1), 45–83 (2005)

54. Rikkila, J., Abrahamsson, P., Wang, X.: The Implications of a Complexity Perspective for Software Engineering Practice and Research. J. Computer Engineering & Information Technology 1, 1 (2012)

55. Van Maanen, J., Sørensen, J.B., Mitchell, T.R.: The Interplay between Theory and Method. Academy of Management Review 32(4), 1145–1154 (2007)

56. Abrahamsson, P., Kettunen, P., Fagerholm, F.: The Set-Up of a Valuable Software Engineering Research Infrastructure of the 2010s. In: VASOP 2010 Workshop, Limerick, Ireland (2010)

Exploring the Tensions between Software Project Portfolio Management and Agile Methods: A Research in Progress Paper

Roger Sweetman and Kieran Conboy

Discipline of Business Information Systems
National University of Ireland, Galway
{r.sweetman1,kieran.conboy}@nuigalway.ie

Abstract. Agile practices and Software Project Portfolio Management (SPPM) have both been individually investigated, but the relationship between them remains poorly understood. The different emphases of SPPM and agile can lead to tensions between the portfolio and the project. This research-in-progress identifies those tensions and sets out a plan to examine the financial and project portfolio literature for potential solutions that can be adapted to Information Systems Development to mediate between SPPM and agile.

Keywords: software project portfolio management, agile, real options analysis, financial theory.

1 Introduction

A significant number of software development teams have embraced agile principles [1, 2]. They have done this to overcome the serious problem of information systems development (ISD) project failure [3, 4]. In Agile, the client takes responsibility for the outcome of the project [5]. Agile is a bottom up, flexible philosophy that embraces change even late in development [5]. These changing requirements can result in projects losing alignment with the strategic goals of the organization.

Business organizations must align their IT software projects to their business strategy [6] through a process known as Software Project Portfolio Management (SPPM). SPPM's focus on the alignment of projects with strategic intent makes it a top down approach.

The conflicting emphases of SPPM and Agile can lead to tensions between the project and the portfolio. This research in progress paper identifies the potential tensions between SPPM and agile from their individual bodies of literature and proposes an approach to adapt a technique from the more mature discipline of financial portfolio theory to mediate these tensions. The article is laid out as follows: the next section lists the tensions between agile and SPPM, the third section compares financial and software project portfolios, the fourth section discusses financial techniques in SPPM, the fifth section presents the research question and the final section summarizes the work.

B. Fitzgerald et al. (Eds.): LESS 2013, LNBIP 167, pp. 210–217, 2013.

2   Tensions between SPPM and Agile

In response to questions about the scalability of agile methods across the organization [7, 8], some research has been carried out to establish an "agile portfolio" e.g. [9], however more research is required into the relationship between the two. Agile adoption may no longer be a bottom up voluntary decision, but can be imposed through formal requirements [10] and an agile approach can be taken to SPPM. However the different emphases of SPPM and agile can still lead to different results. The potential tensions between SPPM and agile are listed below.

2.1   Portfolio Success versus Project Success

ISD research has, in general, focused on the project and not the portfolio as the decision unit [11]. This approach can lead to project interdependencies and significant risks being ignored [12]. Portfolio success is about doing the right projects. Project success is about doing projects right [13]. High project failure rates have focused attention on the "software crisis" [14]. This crisis forces project managers to address the possibility of project failure in advance. Individual project managers fight for resources for the benefit of their own projects at the expense of the portfolio [15]. However a successful portfolio requires projects to be stopped or de-prioritized when in the interest of the business [6]. The reprioritization of software projects leads to the regular movement of people between projects. This can cause morale issues [16] and undermines the agile principle of self prioritization.

2.2   Strategic Alignment versus Operational Responsiveness

The nature of agile teams is to prioritize the customer and embrace change [17]. Their customer focused approach can cause projects to diverge from original plans. Rapidly changing customer requirements can result in projects losing alignment with the overall strategic intent of the portfolio. The intended strategy of most organizations changes slowly [18]. This change is generally only as an adaptive response to a major stimulus [19]. Minzberg's use of the term "strategy formation in an adhocracy" [20] has been deemed particularly appropriate to the process of software development in complex development environments [21]. For example a team might deliver a deluxe version of a product to a customer when the strategic intent of the organization was to deliver a low cost service.

2.3   One Way Communications versus Two Way Conversations

Agile promotes the idea of face to face communication in self organizing teams. This is not compatible with the traditional method of articulating strategy where leaders cascade goals down through the organization [17]. Many people now accept that strategy is best articulated as a conversation [22]. However the traditional model of a top down strategy is still widely used. In contrast an agile organization relies on everyone being involved in strategy development. Indeed "an organization is only as flexible as its people" [23]. Unfortunately technical people can often stop communicating in order to avoid conflict. This makes it impossible for them to resolve serious problems [24].

2.4   Satisfying Divergent Clients versus Single Client Priorities

Different clients prioritize different features. This makes it difficult to maintain the synergies and strategic alignment in a portfolio that serves many clients. Individual teams regularly revise and reprioritize their backlog on the basis of demands from a single client. One of the characteristics of projects in an ISD portfolio is the existence of strong interdependencies [25]. These interdependencies can have a major influence on how projects are prioritized and the order in which they are carried out. Changes to the prioritization of features on one project can impact all the projects in the portfolio when they share code.

2.5   Command and Control Versus Self Organizing Team

It is long held principle that structure follows strategy [26]. However some organizations have agile imposed on them. These organizations may not be structured appropriately for it. This is particularly a problem if SPPM is imposed in a top down manner. It will cause major issues if the priorities chosen by agile development teams in conjunction with the customer are different from those set by portfolio managers. Agile believes that people work best in self organizing teams. Yet, many organizations have a hierarchical structure that is not conducive to this.

2.6   Shareholder versus Customer Interests

A potential conflict can arise between self-organizing agile teams and strategic managers. Self organizing teams are focused on client priorities. Strategic managers act as agents for the shareholder [27]. Legislation such as Sarbanes Oxley places a fiduciary duty on company directors to act in the interest of the corporation [28]. Agile's highest priority is to "satisfy the customer" [5]. Amazon CEO Jeff Bezos argues that only in the long term customer and shareholder interests are aligned [29]. However in the short term directors must satisfy the earnings requirements of shareholders while agile teams must deliver what the customer wants. Implementing an expensive feature with a long payback period could result in a dip in short term profits. Research has shown that legal destruction of shareholder value by firms trying to meet short term earnings targets is pervasive [30]. Conversely a commonly cited criticism of agile is where complex architectural design is de-prioritized in favor of short term cosmetically appealing functionality [2].

The potential effect of these tensions on the strategic alignment of a portfolio of projects is illustrated in fig. 1. The projects are affected by a combination of portfolio (e.g Sarbanes Oxley or a development platform change) and agile (e.g. customers requesting or rejecting additional features) forces.

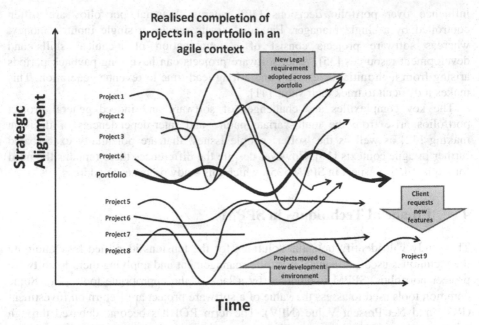

Fig. 1. Projects under conflicting strains from agile and PPM

3   Financial and Project Portfolios

SPPM can trace its roots back to Modern Portfolio Theory (MPT) [31] and IT Portfolio Management [32] and the broader field of financial theory. This makes financial theory a logical place to look for solutions to the tensions outlined above. MPT presents the selection of a portfolio of financial assets as a problem where investors try to maximize their return for an acceptable level of risk. ISD portfolios, like financial portfolios, must be evaluated on their overall performance, not on the performance of individual projects [12]. However, software development is a multi-objective problem where the requirements of cost, quality and development time must be balanced.

The similarities between SPPM and financial portfolio theory have been acknowledged [33]. But there are also significant differences between software and financial portfolios. Software investments tend to be irreversible [34], while stocks are generally liquid. Mission critical ISD projects cannot be cancelled overnight, whereas underperforming stocks can be sold [35]. Software project selection is influenced by the relationship between business and ISD [36], whereas stocks are selected on the basis of expected returns. Project outcomes tend to be highly correlated [37], often a result of the interdependencies between projects [25], while financial portfolios exploit diversification by selecting assets with moderate negative correlations [38]. Software projects can have asymmetric outcomes, with projects either succeeding or failing [39] whereas the gains or losses from a financial asset can vary continuously. ISD projects can have multiple stakeholders that can exert influence over portfolio decisions [40] wheras financial portfolios are offten controlled by a single manager. Financial assets require a single input – money, whereas software projects consist of a combination of technical skills and development resources [35]. Also, software projects can have long payback periods arising from high initial investment and a long lead time to revenue generation. This makes it difficult to track their value [41].

The key complexities and challenges of software and indeed general project portfolios arise from the multi-variate nature and inter-dependencies of decision making [42] as well as the 'softer' people issues, that are potentially exacerbated further in agile contexts [10]. However despite the differences there remains the need for a quantitative aspect in SPPM [35], which this study proposes to address.

4   Financial Techniques in SPPM

This study will identify potential solutions for the tensions identified by examining the techniques used in financial portfolio management and applying them to software project portfolios. SPPM is hindered by a lack of the appropriate tools [43]. Some common tools used to assess the value of a software project are Return on Investment (ROI) and Net Present Value (NPV). The term ROI has become debased through misuse and over use, however robust economic analysis is necessary for software projects [44]. Instead it has been argued that the software community has focused on cost benefit analysis and while neglecting business strategy and valuation [44]. These are two key aspects of SPPM. Value based SPPM has started to address this deficit, It does this by considering risk and return [12]. Risk is dealt with by using NPV to value software projects with a "weighted average cost of ISD" [35]. This calculation ignores interdependencies between projects [12]. A more recent approach has seen the use of modern portfolio theory to aggregate projects into portfolios, with intratemporal dependencies (e.g. where projects require the same resources) modeled by correlations [45]. Intertemporal dependencies (e.g. where projects serve as the basis for follow up projects) have been modeled as real options with an expanded NPV used to value the project plus the options associated with it [41].

Financial flexibility is an important property of agility [46], making traditional methods of discounted cash-flows inappropriate as functionality can rapidly change. According to some, *"real options underlie agile practices"* [47]. Options are central to both agile project management and project portfolio management. Viewing decisions as options can help decision makers compare alternatives and make the best fit between business goals and current alternatives [48]. Real Options theory suggests that the value of the delay and the importance of the flexibility can be incorporated into the decision analysis [34]. This is particularly appropriate for projects with high levels of uncertainty [49]. However, option pricing models can be complex and have been rejected by some as being unsuitable for use in project management [47] [50]. They can also ignore certain interdependencies [12]. While there is some research on real options in software project management e.g. [41, 51, 52], little research has focused on real options and in agile or SPPM.

5   Research Question

Significant tensions can arise between agile and SPPM. This research will investigate for the presence of these (and other) tensions in the portfolios of a number of organizations. It will then select a specific tension. We will review the project management and financial literature for potential solutions which can be adapted and tested in a number of organizations. This will be done to address the following research question: *"How can financial techniques effectively be used to mediate tensions between Software Project Portfolio Management and Agile methods?"*

6   Conclusion

Agile and PPM have both been studied individually but despite the issues that arise between them, there has been insufficient investigation into the relationship between them. This research will make a contribution by identifying the key tensions between agile and SPPM (portfolio v. project success, strategic alignment v. responsiveness, communications v. conversations, shareholder v. client priorities, organizational structural issues, and customer v. shareholder interests) and determining a solution to resolve some of these tensions. The next step is to review the financial portfolio literature for analogous problems in financial portfolios and identify potential solutions which will be adapted for use in software development and tested within a number of organizations.

Acknowledgements. This work was supported, in part, by Science Foundation Ireland grant 10/CE/I1855 to Lero - the Irish Software Engineering Research Centre (www.lero.ie). The authors would also like to acknowledge the contribution of Dr. Orla O'Dwyer for her advice and support, and all the "Wednesday Group" for their feedback. We would particularly like to thank the two anonymous reviewers for their helpful suggestions.

References

1. Abrahamsson, P., Conboy, K., Wang, X.: 'Lots done, more to do': the current state of agile systems development research. European Journal of Information Systems 18(4), 281–284 (2009)
2. Dybå, T., Dingsøyr, T.: Empirical studies of agile software development: A systematic review. Information and Software Technology 50(9-10), 833–859 (2008)
3. Conboy, K.: Project failure en masse: a study of loose budgetary control in ISD projects. European Journal of Information Systems 19(3), 273–287 (2010)
4. T. Standish Group, CHAOS Manifesto The Laws of CHAOS and the CHAOS 100 Best PM Practices (2010)
5. Fowler, M., Highsmith, J.: The Agile Manifesto. Software Development, 28–32 (August 2001)
6. De Reyck, B., et al.: The impact of project portfolio management on information technology projects. International Journal of Project Management 23(7), 524–537 (2005)

7. Smits, H.: The impact of scaling on planning activities in an agile software development center. In: Proceedings of the 40th Hawaii International Conference on System Sciences (HICSS 2007), Waikoloa (2007)
8. Orr, K.: CMM versus Agile Development: Religious Wars and Software Development. Agile Project Management Executive Report, Arlington, MA (2002)
9. Thomas, J.C., Baker, S.W.: Establishing an agile portfolio to align IT investments with business needs. In: Proceedings of Agile 2008, Toronto (2008)
10. Conboy, K., Coyle, S., Xiaofeng, W., Pikkarainen, M.: People over Process: Key Challenges in Agile Development. IEEE Software 28(4), 48–57 (2011)
11. Urli, B., Terrien, F.: Project portfolio selection model, a realistic approach. International Transactions in Operational Research 17(6), 809–826 (2010)
12. Diepold, D., Ullrich, C., Wehrmann, A., Zimmermann, S.: A real options approach for valuating intertemporal interdependencies within a value based it portfolio management – a risk-return perspective (2009)
13. Petit, Y.: Project portfolios in dynamic environments: Organizing for uncertainty. International Journal of Project Management 30(5), 539–553 (2012)
14. Agerfalk, P.J., Deverell, A., Fitzgerald, B., Morgan, L.: Assessing the Role of Open Source Software in the European Secondary Software Sector: A Voice fi-om Industry. In: Scotto, M., Succi, G. (eds.) Proceedings of the 1st International Conference on Open Source Systems, Genoa, Italy, pp. 82–87 (2005)
15. Elonen, S., Artto, K.A.: Problems in managing internal development projects in multi-project environments. International Journal of Project Management 21(6), 395 (2003)
16. Blichfeldt, B.S., Eskerod, P.: Project portfolio management – There's more to it than what management enacts. International Journal of Project Management 26(4), 357–365 (2008)
17. Fowler, A.: Performance management: the MBO of the 90s. Personnel Management 22(7), 47–51 (1990)
18. Rumelt, R.: Choosing the right strategy. Director (00123242) 64(11), 28 (2011)
19. Mintzberg, H., Waters, J.A.: Of strategies, deliberate and emergent. Strategic Management Journal 6(3), 257–272 (1985)
20. Mintzberg, H., McHugh, A.: Strategy Formation in an Adhocracy. Administrative Science Quarterly 30(2), 160–197 (1985)
21. Harris, M.L., Collins, R.W., Hevner, A.R.: Control of Flexible Software Development Under Uncertainty. Information Systems Research 20(3), 400–419 (2009)
22. Groysberg, B., Slind, M.: Leadership Is a Conversation. Harvard Business Review 90(6), 76–84 (2012)
23. Correa, H.L.: The Flexibility of Technological and Human Resources in Automotive Manufacturing. Integrated Manufacturing Systems 5(1), 33–40 (1994)
24. Humphrey, W.S.: Managing Technical People. Addison-Wesley Longman, Reading (1997)
25. Kundisch, D., Meier, C.: A new perspective on resource interactions in it/is project portfolio selection. In: ECIS 2011 Proceedings (2011)
26. Chandler, A.D.: Strategy and structure: chapters in the history of the industrial enterprise. M.I.T. Press, Cambridge (1962)
27. Limmack, R.J.: Corporate Mergers and Shareholder Wealth Effects: 1977-1986. Accounting & Business Research 21(83), 239–251 (1991)
28. Fairfax, L.M.: Spare the Rod, Spoil the Director? Revitalizing Directors' Fiduciary Duty Through Legal Liability. Houston Law Review 42, 393–457 (2005)
29. Ignatius, A.: The World's Top CEO. Harvard Business Review 91(1-2), 10 (2013)
30. Graham, J.R., Harvey, C.R., Rajgopal, S.: Value Destruction and Financial Reporting Decisions. Financial Analysts Journal 62(6), 27–39 (2006)

31. Markowitz, H.: Portfolio Selection. The Journal of Finance 7(1), 77–91 (1952)
32. McFarlan, F.W.: Portfolio approach to information systems. Harvard Business Review 59(5), 142–150 (1981)
33. Frey, T., Buxmann, P.: IT project portfolio management - a structured literature review. In: ECIS 2012 (2012)
34. Weeds, H.: Strategic Delay in a Real Options Model of R&D Competition. Review of Economic Studies 69(240), 729–747 (2002)
35. Verhoef, C.: Quantifying the value of IT-investments. Science of Computer Programming 56(3), 315–342 (2005)
36. Thomas, G., Seddon, P.B., Fernandez, W.: IT Project Evaluation: Is more formal evaluation necessarily better? In: Pacific Asia Conference on Information Systems, Auckland, New Zealand, pp. 78–98 (2007)
37. Burke, J.C., Shaw, M.J.: IT Portfolio Management: A Case Study. In: AMCIS 2008 Proceedings (2008)
38. Hight, G.N.: Diversification Effect: Isolating the Effect of Correlation on Portfolio Risk. Journal of Financial Planning 23(5), 54–61 (2010)
39. Fichman, R.G.: Real options and IT platform adoption: Implications for theory and practice. Information Systems Research 15(2), 132–154 (2004)
40. Meskendahl, S.: The influence of business strategy on project portfolio management and its success — A conceptual framework. International Journal of Project Management 28(8), 807–817 (2010)
41. Bardhan, I., Bagchi, S., Sougstad, R.: Prioritizing a Portfolio of Information Technology Investment Projects. Journal of Management Information Systems 21(2), 33–60 (2004)
42. Drury, M., Conboy, K., Power, K.: Obstacles to decision making in Agile software development teams. Journal of Systems & Software 85(6), 1239–1254 (2012)
43. Kendall, G.I., Rollins, S.C.: Advanced project portfolio management and the PMO: multiplying ROI at warp speed. J. Ross Publishing (2003)
44. Erdogmus, H., Favaro, J., Strigel, W.: Return on investment. IEEE Software 21(3), 18–22 (2004)
45. Santhanam, R., Kyparisis, G.J.: A decision model for interdependent information system project selection. European Journal of Operational Research 89(2), 380–399 (1996)
46. Steindl, C.: From agile software development to agile businesses. In: 31st EUROMICRO Conference on Software Engineering and Advanced Applications (2005)
47. Matts, C., Maassen, O.: 'Real Options' Underlie Agile Practices (2007), http://www.infoq.com/articles/real-options-enhance-agility (cited February 18, 2013)
48. Racheva, Z., Daneva, M.: Using Measurements to Support Real-Option Thinking in Agile Software Development. In: Proc. 2008 Int'l Workshop Scrutinizing Agile Practices or Shoot-Out at the Agile Corral (2008)
49. Erdogmus, H.: The economic impact of learning and flexibility on process decisions. IEEE Software 22(6), 76 (2005)
50. Mathews, S., Datar, V., Johnson, B.: A Practical Method for Valuing Real Options: The Boeing Approach. Journal of Applied Corporate Finance 19(2), 95–104 (2007)
51. Angelou, G.N., Economides, A.A.: A Decision Analysis Framework for Prioritizing a Portfolio of ICT Infrastructure Projects. IEEE Transactions on Engineering Management 55(3), 479–495 (2008)
52. Benaroch, M., Lichtenstein, Y., Robinson, K.: Real options in information technology risk management: An empirical validation of risk-option relationships. Mis Quarterly 30(4), 827–864 (2006)

Author Index